Praise for *Israeli Salvage Poetics*

"Through meticulous research and elegant readings, Jelen offers a fresh look at canonical writers, recovers lesser-known works of these writers, and introduces almost-forgotten writers, bringing them together in a compelling narrative. A major contribution of the book is the way it clearly defines the term 'salvage poetics': as the intersection between past and present, ethnography and aesthetics; as a way to understand, preserve, and substitute for the vanished world."

—Nancy E. Berg, professor of Hebrew and comparative literature, Washington University in St. Louis

"This fascinating book weaves together literary and ethnographic discourses to explore how Israeli writers have engaged with Yiddish and Yiddish literature as a way of salvaging the world of eastern European Jewry. Through the lens of salvage poetics, Sheila Jelen provides innovative and perceptive analysis of both canonical and overlooked Hebrew texts and how they return, again and again, to a past that was supposed to have been forgotten."

—Naomi Brenner, The Ohio State University

"The study extends the notion of salvage poetics so successfully and impactfully explored in Jelen's prior book on American Jewish salvage poetics to the Israeli literary scene. The book makes a significant contribution to the field of Jewish literary and ethnographic studies and post-Holocaust recuperation."

—Wendy Zierler, Sigmund Falk Professor of Modern Jewish Literature and Feminist Studies, HUC-JIR

ISRAELI SALVAGE POETICS

ISRAELI SALVAGE POETICS

SHEILA E. JELEN

Wayne State University Press
Detroit

© 2023 by Wayne State University Press, Detroit, Michigan, 48201. All rights reserved. No part of this book may be reproduced without formal permission.

ISBN 9780814348963 (paperback)
ISBN 9780814348970 (hardcover)
ISBN 9780814348987 (e-book)

Library of Congress Control Number: 2022951627

On cover: Women picking oranges at Ein HaHoresh kibbutz, ca. 1940. Ein HaHoresh Archive, from PikiWiki. Cover design by Michel Vrana.

Publication of this book was made possible through the generosity of the Bertha M. and Hyman Herman Endowed Memorial Fund. Wayne State University Press gratefully acknowledges the Zantker Foundation for supporting the publication of this book.

Wayne State University Press rests on Waawiyaataanong, also referred to as Detroit, the ancestral and contemporary homeland of the Three Fires Confederacy. These sovereign lands were granted by the Ojibwe, Odawa, Potawatomi, and Wyandot Nations, in 1807, through the Treaty of Detroit. Wayne State University Press affirms Indigenous sovereignty and honors all tribes with a connection to Detroit. With our Native neighbors, the press works to advance educational equity and promote a better future for the earth and all people.

Wayne State University Press
Leonard N. Simons Building
4809 Woodward Avenue
Detroit, Michigan 48201-1309

Visit us online at wsupress.wayne.edu.

To my children:
Malka Aliza (b. 1998), Nava Tehila (b. 2001),
Akiva Menahem Isaac (b. 2006), and Meirav Sarit (b. 2010)

For keeping me honest and loving—
two skills that are immeasurably helpful both in life and in scholarship

Contents

Acknowledgments — ix

Introduction: Israeli Salvage Poetics — 1

I. RECALLING EASTERN EUROPE

1 "An Homage to Yiddish": The Struggle for Salvage Poetics — 21
2 "Things as They Were": Ethnopoetics and Salvage Poetics — 43
3 "The Ravages of My Happiness": A Mother of Sons Salvages What Remains — 65
4 "A Third Voice": What Must Not Be Forgotten — 89

II. RECONSIDERING THE NEGATION OF THE DIASPORA

5 "Houses of Study": Salvaging the Texts of Jewish Tradition — 113
6 "Suddenly There Is Singing": Musical Worlds and Salvage Memory — 131
7 "Stories Full of Blackberries": Literary Genealogies and Acts of Salvage — 149

Postscript: A Yiddish Postvernacular in Israeli Literature — 173

Notes — 185
Selected Bibliography — 205
Index — 215

Acknowledgments

I acknowledge, with gratitude, my colleagues at the University of Maryland and at the University of Kentucky who have provided me with a community of like-minded scholars during the long period that has elapsed in the course of my writing this book. Thank you to Avner Holtzman for permission to print Leah Svirsky Holtzman's birthday party photograph (chapter 4), and to the YIVO Institute for Jewish Research for permission to publish the photograph of Ita Kalish (chapter 2). Thank you to University of Pennsylvania Press for permission to publish an altered version of chapter 2 ("Things as They Were," originally published as "Ethnopoetics in the Works of Malkah Shapiro and Ita Kalish: Gender, Popular Ethnography, and the Literary Face of Jewish East Europe"), to *Prooftexts* and Indiana University Press for permission to publish an altered version of the postscript ("A Yiddish Postvernacular in Israeli Literature," originally published as "Salvage Poetics in *See Under: Love*: Momik, Mottel, and a Yiddish Postvernacular in Israeli Literature"), and to *Journal of Jewish Identities* and Johns Hopkins University Press for permission to print a revised version of chapter 5 ("Houses of Study," originally published as "Salvage Poetics: S. Y. Agnon's *A Guest for the Night*"). An earlier version of chapter 7, "Stories Full of Blackberries" was previously published as "Oz's Literary Genealogies," in *Amos Oz: The Legacy of a Writer in Israel and Beyond*, ed. Ranen Omer-Sherman (SUNY Press, 2023) and has been significantly revised here. I am grateful to the Office of the Vice President at the University of Kentucky for funding to support the writing of this book. Thank you to Madison Cissell for her assistance with research and logistics and to Michele Alperin for her expert editing. Annie Martin at Wayne State University Press encouraged me to write this book and Sandra Korn graciously took over the editing of this book with Annie Martin's departure from the press. My deepest gratitude to both. As always, I acknowledge with love and appreciation my husband, Seth Himelhoch, for his support throughout the process of writing this book, even in spite of the obstacles presented by my personal health and a global pandemic. Finally, I am grateful to my children, Malka, Nava, Akiva, and Meirav, who have traveled back and forth to Israel with me many times as I have reconciled myself to raising them in the United States and who have made all the journeys I have taken in my life since their births worthwhile.

INTRODUCTION

Israeli Salvage Poetics

Israeli Salvage Poetics explores Hebrew texts written between 1939 and the early twenty-first century, a period when writers in Mandate Palestine and Israel grappled with their eastern European legacy. There, despite the fact that the founding generation of the Jewish state was to a large degree from eastern Europe, the Yiddish language and anything that evoked the millennium spent in eastern Europe were considered a liability to the nationalist political ambitions of the modern Zionist project. One would have expected this to change with the Holocaust. However, if anything, in Palestine and subsequently in Israel, the Holocaust intensified the negative image of eastern European Jewish experience and culture. The extermination of the Jews was presented as the natural culmination of statelessness and minority identity. Those who had survived were under suspicion of somehow manipulating their way to survival at the expense of those who had succumbed, and those who had succumbed were viewed as having been led "like sheep to the slaughter." Only those who engaged in armed resistance and lived to tell the tale were embraced and valorized. I am, therefore, not the first to assert that the Israeli treatment of its eastern European legacy after the Holocaust nearly completed the work of the Nazis. However, eastern European Jewish culture has remained present in Israel in myriad ways, which can only attest to its staying power in the individual and collective memories of a nation born out of its ashes.

Salvage poetics are stylistic mechanisms through which texts, be they verbal or visual, acknowledge the destruction of a culture and reframe artifacts of that culture for popular consumption, across an abyss of time and place. By "artifacts," I mean literary texts, documentary photographs, and other media that are constructed by popular audiences to metonymically represent crucial aspects of the culture in question. The concept of salvage poetics describes a relationship between artist and audience, between past and present, wherein ethnography (descriptive writings about a culture) and aesthetic works (such as fiction or photography) are wedded to one another, creating a hybrid between cultural observation and artistic invention. Within modern Jewish culture since the turn of the twentieth century,[1] salvage poetics have articulated both desire and imperative: the desire to understand a world that is disappearing and the perceived imperative to find ways to represent that world to those who desire to understand it. Salvage poetics take on different forms in different environments. My previously published work on salvage poetics focused on the phenomenon in the United States. As a way of introducing the concept within an Israeli framework, I will briefly recap some of the discussions out of which my understanding of the American variation grew. In so doing, I hope to lay a foundation for salvage poetics in Israel, pointing out not only their continuities with those I identified in the United States but also their differences.

With the destruction of eastern European Jewry in the Holocaust, writers and scholars in America sought ways to reconstruct that world. They translated, framed, adapted, and mediated artifacts of that world for Americans. Such was the case with *The World of Sholem Aleichem* (1943), in which Maurice Samuel glossed for American audiences the stories of *Tevye the Milkman* under the pretense that Tevye could provide Americans with a multilayered, complex, and accurate understanding of eastern European Jewish life.[2] Such was the case as well with Abraham Joshua Heschel's *The Earth Is the Lord's*, originally delivered in 1945 as an oral eulogy at the YIVO Institute for Jewish Research but subsequently turned into an essay on eastern European Jewish life.[3] Just as Samuel in *The World of Sholem Aleichem* drew on the Tevye stories as his artifacts for adaptation to an American audience, in *The Earth Is the Lord's* Heschel's artifacts comprised Hasidic stories that he translated, retold, and framed as a means of gaining insight into a philosophical and spiritual portrait of a people murdered. For Americans, these methods worked to build bridges between the "old" world and the "new" one.

Salvage poetics can be found, in an American context, in texts conceived as forms of "folk ethnography," or ethnography by the people for the people.[4] Alongside Samuel and Heschel's works, Mark Zborowski and

Elizabeth Herzog's *Life Is with People: The Culture of the Shtetl* (1952) was another such text.[5] Barbara Kirshenblatt-Gimblett argues that *Life Is with People* "established American Jewish ethnography as a popular art in its own right,"[6] and I embellish her remark in my own study of American Jewish salvage poetics by noting that her "observation comes out of several decades during which American Jews had grown accustomed to reading ethnography in places where ethnographers did not place their work."[7] "Suddenly it became possible," I continue, "for non-anthropologists to be writing ethnographies of the lost culture because formal ethnographies themselves, like *Life Is with People*, had been authored by non-anthropologists and were viewed among popular audiences as culturally definitive."[8]

Indeed, Zborowski and Herzog were not anthropologists. Their work, however, was supervised by Margaret Mead under the auspices of Columbia University's 1946 Research in Contemporary Culture Project. *Life Is with People* exemplified a new method of approaching inaccessible cultures, either those that had been extinguished, like Jewish life in eastern Europe or those that were located behind the iron curtain. "Culture at a distance" challenged the orthodoxies of anthropological fieldwork in situ and presented the possibility of expanding the study of cultures to those cultures that were no longer in a position to host visiting researchers. The study of culture at a distance while posited within the academic field of anthropology, paved the way for a looser engagement with the cultures under discussion, an engagement that often veered off into the realm of "native" informants who were basing their information on literary encounters as opposed to experiential encounters with the culture they represented. In *Life Is with People*, for example, informants referred not to their childhoods or their own lives in Europe, but to the literature of Mendele Mocher Sforim (Sholem Yankev Abramovitsh [1836–1917]) or Sholem Aleichem (Sholem Rabinovitch [1859–1916]) when describing the culture of the shtetl.[9]

This sense of Yiddish literature as equivalent to in situ anthropological fieldwork was my starting point for coining the concept of salvage poetics. I asked the question of how literature came to stand in for the world of eastern European Jewry. The notion of folk ethnography, an ethnography created by nonanthropologists, enabled me to better understand the organic way in which laypeople selected and valorized aesthetic artifacts as testaments to a culture. Cultural anthropologist Jack Kugelmass writes that "folk ethnography is different from the purely intellectual pursuits and speculation of academic ethnography. It exists not to advance human knowledge but to focus group understanding of the self and thereby reinforce the cohesiveness of the population that sponsors it and consumes it."[10] In my study of the American Jewish context for salvage poetics, I express gratitude to Kugelmass for providing me with a term that captures the reflexivity of the concept of salvage poetics, which is "focused on the work of constructing a sense of self, community, and history for the Jewish population of eastern European provenance in post-Holocaust America."[11] By identifying folk ethnography as the force underlying the creation of salvage poetic texts, I was able to differentiate my interest from the work of professional ethnographers and to explore, from my unique vantage point as a scholar of literature, how some texts came to be understood by popular audiences as comprehensively descriptive of a culture, while others did not.

In this study of Israeli salvage poetics, my interest in folk ethnography remains the same, but the vantage point I am investigating differs. While within an American context, I was investigating how and why American Jewish writers gravitated toward the works of Sholem Aleichem, Mendele Mocher Sforim, and Abraham Joshua Heschel as artifacts of eastern European culture, in this book I consider the way that Hebrew writers in Israel of eastern European descent work pre-Holocaust eastern European culture into their own sense of Israeliness. While historians of the post-Holocaust period have debated the nature and the timing of American Jewish responses to the destruction of eastern European Jewry, it is probably accurate to assert that the sense of culpability was minimal and the degree of horror maximal. American Jewry, following the experience of other immigrants as they assimilated to American life, had moved with each generation beyond immigration away from their historical origins linguistically and culturally. Consequently, American Jews rendered eastern European Jewish experience historical and obsolete, but they did not demonize it as did Israeli Jews, whose experience of the eastern European Jewish past has been notably different from the American one. American Jewish writers such as Samuel and Heschel in their salvage poetic hybrid works may have been addressing American Jews who had lost their Jewish linguistic and textual literacy, but Israeli writers such as Amos Oz and S. Yizhar (Yizhar Smolenski [1916–2006]) grapple in their work with their own lack of Jewish literacy. In just one generation, these Israeli children of eastern European immigrants, had been "reprogrammed" or disabused of the culture and language of their own parents.

The formation in 1924 of the Gdud Megine ha-Safah, or the "Brigade for the Protection of the Language," within Mandate Palestine illustrates the vehemence with which Hebrew language "purity," and with it a demonization of Yiddish and its eastern European origins, were pursued. Naomi Brenner, in her study of Yiddish literary culture alongside Hebrew literary culture both in Europe and in Palestine in the decades prior to the establishment of the state, tells us that

> the Brigade had advocated, at times violently, for the Hebrew language and against all other languages within the Jewish community in prestate Palestine. Its predominantly young members protested against signs written in languages other than Hebrew, pressured publishing companies not to print in Yiddish, and warned theaters not to allow non-Hebrew performances and lectures. The Brigade also intimidated people who did not speak Hebrew in the streets, distributing pamphlets with their beliefs and slogans such as . . . "Hebrew, speak Hebrew."[12]

While the oft-told history and escapades of the brigade make it seem like a far more dominant movement than it actually was, nevertheless the vehemence with which it mandated Hebrew speech on the streets of Palestine tells a significant story about the importance given the Hebrew language, at the expense of the Yiddish language, in the early years of the Jewish state. Opposition to Yiddish specifically was articulated by the Hebrew literary critic Joseph Klausner (Amos Oz's great-uncle) when he stated, "That *zhargon* is more dangerous to us than any other foreign language precisely because it is not so foreign to us."[13] Indeed, special ire was reserved for the Yiddish language. As Klausner said, because so many people on the Yishuv spoke it natively it was perceived as a special threat to the establishment of a Hebrew-speaking state. Rachel Rojanski explains that before the Holocaust "certain Jewish ideological circles thought it appropriate that Yiddish should be the national language of the Jewish people. Thus Yiddish might have posed a threat to Hebrew, primarily by hindering the spread of Hebrew in Israel."[14]

The story of Israel's silencing of Yiddish, of its treatment of the Jews who survived the war and immigrated to Palestine, of the ridicule and the resentment directed at those from eastern Europe that went hand in hand with the denial of a millennium of culture, text, and traditions, is at the center of the definition of salvage poetics within an Israeli context. Israeli salvage poetics represent the recuperation of a culture, through artifacts, for an audience that feels to a large extent responsible for the silencing and extinction of that culture. Those Israelis who are interested in their eastern European legacy live with an awareness of their own culture's role in the repression of that legacy. In interviews and discussions, they assert repeatedly their desire to right the wrongs of the past by engaging with the Yiddish language and Yiddish theater, by traveling to eastern Europe, by reading books about the world of eastern European Jewry, and in the case of the texts we will explore in this study, writing about their own relationship with that cultural legacy.

Since the very birth of modern Hebrew and Yiddish literature, critics have been identifying an "ethnographic" idiom in the early writings of each of those literatures. What, I asked myself at the beginning of my work on salvage poetics, do literary critics such as David Frischmann, from the turn of the twentieth century, and Dan Miron, from the turn of the twenty-first century, mean when they say that a fiction writer writes "ethnographically"?[15] Lending the work of Mendele Mocher Sforim a profoundly ethnographic valence, Frischmann writes:

> Let's imagine, for example, that some terrible flood came and erased every bit of that world from the earth, along with the memory of that world, until there was not one single sign of that life left, and by chance all we were left with was *The Book of Beggars*, *The Vale of Tears*, *The Travels of Benjamin the Third*, and *Of Bygone Days*, along with his small sketches and stories; then there is no doubt that on the basis of these sketches the critic could re-create the street life of the Jews in the Russian shtetl totally accurately.[16]

Miron, in his study of the place of folklore in modern Hebrew and Yiddish literature, puts it this way:

> Yiddish writers, particularly writers, particularly writers of prose fiction, used "folkloristic" materials as a matter of course as part of their presentation of contemporary Jewish individuals as well as contemporary Jewish society. However, they also often stopped to observe these materials and describe them without direct reference to plot and character. With a typically anatomical intent they set about analyzing and recording various facets of the vast panorama of traditional Jewish cultural behavior: Jewish dress, Jewish superstition, rites of passage, holiday rituals, domestic life, patterns of sexual behavior, cultural characteristics of various professions, jokes, proverbs, curses, dialectic idiosyncrasies and so on. They did this with gusto and with a sense of mission, and they

managed to cover such broad areas of the traditional Jewish milieu and to endow their works with such a potently suggestive sense of descriptive plenitude that it became a commonplace that with all its ideological bias, nineteenth-century Yiddish literature contained a complete and faithful replica of the social, economic, and cultural scene of the time. This notion was asserted by successive generations of historians, ethnographers, folklorists, and literary critics who based their historical reconstructions and literary evaluations and interpretations on it.[17]

As he describes it, Miron discerns a trend in the Yiddish fiction of the turn of the twentieth century toward "folkloristic" descriptions for their own sake and not for the sake of plot or authenticity. Indeed, these texts by Mendele (as described above by Frischmann), and others, were self-consciously written as a form of ethnography and embraced as such, according to Miron, by generations of critics.

What, in other words, does ethnography mean to a literary critic, and particularly to a literary critic of modern Hebrew and Yiddish literature? I could not find an answer to those questions in the critical discourse of literary or anthropological studies. After years of research on the crossover between literature and ethnography, I finally realized that the discourse I was seeking did not exist; I was looking for discussions of literary works by literary critics in ethnographic terms, not for discussions about the literary properties of ethnographic texts. The latter discussion was easily identified in the writings of Clifford Geertz and James Clifford, dating from the 1970s, when ethnographers began to be aware of their work as formally constructed, not just a "transparent" representation of a culture. The former discussion, however, the assignation of ethnographic valence to literary texts, was something I had really found only in the criticism of Jewish literature produced at the turn of the twentieth century. The critics who aired these observations did so in an uncritical way—they saw it as self-evident that the Hebrew and Yiddish writings during this time would be "ethnographic," and they did not question their own use of the term or the concept. Why would a generation of critics be on the lookout for fiction that told the story of a culture? Why were some writings more prone to those kinds of readings than others at that moment? What might a readership be looking for in this new modern fiction that suited their own sense of departures and arrivals?

The story of the modern Jewish experience is one that has been told in many places. It is for Jews a story of new political opportunities and a new cultural and intellectual openness, tempered by non-Jewish entrenchment in old patterns of discrimination and violence against the Jews, even those who had become "enlightened." Zionism was born out of the impulse to leave behind the status of a minority nation among unpredictable majority cultures. Although Jews had been the beneficiaries of tolerance and accommodation at particular times and places, again and again they were reminded of the general unwillingness to allow them to function as an integral part of the societies they had worked so hard to join once given the freedom to do so. Zionism sought to remedy this situation by leaving behind the impulse toward assimilation and conciliation and to create opportunities for Jews to become a nation among other nations on its own terms. This necessitated, to some degree, a kind of isolationism and dogmatic chauvinism that pushed against the legacies that Jews from a wide variety of backgrounds brought with them from different cultures to the New Yishuv. The literature that was written, particularly in Hebrew, during the period in which Zionism was becoming a more popular and ever more viable movement by the start of the twentieth century, was to a large extent a literature with its feet in two worlds—the world of the past and the world of the future. To some, Hebrew literature provided a venue for the projection of an imagined world of autonomous governance, freedom, and safety. To others, Hebrew literature provided a repository for images of the world soon to be left behind. Just by writing in modern Hebrew, and in the process inventing a modern Hebrew literary idiom, modern Hebrew writers participated in the creation of a blueprint for the future.

I began my exploration of what was to become salvage poetics many years ago with an essay about Malkah Shapiro and Ita Kalish, two Israeli women born in eastern Europe to important Hasidic families who wrote about their families of origin, the first in a novel and the second in a highly literary memoir, but whose work was received in a strictly ethnographic vein by their English translators. At that juncture, I called what I was looking at "ethnopoetics," in keeping with S. Ansky's (Solomon Rappoport's [1863–1920]) notion of ethnopoetry.[18] Ansky, the architect of a famous ethnographic expedition through the Pale of Settlement from 1912 to 1914, defined "ethnopoetics" as the deployment of traditional Jewish content in modern aesthetic form. Preservation and innovation thus went hand in hand for modern Jewish arts and artists. The future of Jewry, he posited, depended not on abandoning Jewish traditions but on bringing them up to date. I realized, however, that the term "ethnopoetry" did not quite capture the complexity of what I was observing in the critical reception of Jewish literature around the start of the twentieth century. What I sought was not simply to answer the question of how Jewish artists preserved tradition in modern form. Rather, I was asking how modern Jewish artists and critics negotiated their own role in the destruction of traditional Jewish culture even while trying, to the best of their abilities, to preserve it. Therefore, early in my work I realized that what I was looking at was also informed by the notion of salvage ethnography.

Salvage ethnography, developed by Franz Boas and his students at Columbia University, presupposes the disappearance of a culture as part of its justification for studying it. Critics have suggested that part of the reason the cultures studied are in decline is because they are, in fact, being studied. Thus, the forces of preservation are also the forces of destruction; this was particularly the case in the American academic study of Native American communities. In my formulation of salvage poetics, I felt that the use of "salvage" would simultaneously invoke an anthropological movement and a sense of responsibility for the destruction of a culture as intrinsic to its preservation. Those very figures who chose to depict "the Jewish street" at the turn of the twentieth century were participating in the very modernization (creating a secular Hebrew vernacular, for example) that was destroying the traditional Jewish backbone of those communities.

In my refinement of the concept of Israeli salvage poetics, I have written many different kinds of essays in different genres (volume chapters, conference papers, book reviews, and literature reviews) that aimed to answer the question of how ethnography and literature in modern Jewish experience worked hand in hand, particularly at the turn of the twentieth century. I began, as already mentioned, with Shapiro and Kalish and moved on to literary critics who sought to understand their mothers through an exploration of eastern Europe through the works of canonic Hebrew writers of the modern Hebrew renaissance. This took me to the work of S. Y. Agnon, the Hebrew author par excellence who wrote about eastern Europe. Next, I found myself writing about authors from *dor hamedina*, the first generation of native- or near-native-born Hebrew writers in Palestine whose fiction became emblematic of the "Israeli" style. Did S. Yizhar and Amos Oz engage with eastern Europe at all? At what point in their careers did they do so, and what was it they were trying to accomplish? I then turned to the work of David Grossman on post-Holocaust culture in Israel and contemplated how Israeli children of Holocaust survivors negotiated the demonization of eastern European Jewish culture and sought means of understanding what had been destroyed "over there."

Finally, and most recently, in the writing of Rivka Guber, a Ukrainian immigrant to Palestine between the two world wars who came to be known as "the Mother of Sons" after the death of her only two sons fighting in the War of Independence, I found an eastern European voice in Hebrew that did not demonize its origins, but valorized them, despite Guber's status as an Israeli national icon.

One important difference between the American trajectory of salvage poetics that I traced in my last book and the Israeli trajectory traced here is that the Israeli dynamic is about sixty years behind the American one. Israel today, I argue in this book, strives in some instances toward a fully formed salvage poetic, a fully fleshed out commitment to representing eastern European Jewish pre-Holocaust culture in the post-Holocaust era through a reframing of its artifacts for edification of a committed audience. In other instances, what we see in Israeli literature, I reiterate throughout this study, is more of a "postvernacular" inclination, the construction of a "general sense" of eastern European Jewry. I draw, in my invocation of a postvernacular from Jeffrey Shandler's discussion of Yiddish in America in the years since the Holocaust. His notion of postvernacular Yiddish culture describes "the symbolic value invested in the language apart from the semantic value of any given utterance in it." Further, he writes:

> Yiddish culture now has a sizable constituency independent of a vernacular speech community. There are many who profess a profound, genuine attachment to Yiddish who also admit that they don't really know the language; furthermore, they don't see their lack of fluency as interfering with their devotion. While this disparity between enthusiasm and mastery can prove confounding, even distressing, for some champions of the language who are fluent speakers, it needs to be considered as a distinctive cultural phenomenon in its own right. Having an affective or ideological relationship with Yiddish without having command of the language epitomizes a larger trend in Yiddish culture in the post-Holocaust era. . . . This privileging of the secondary level of signification of Yiddish over its primary level constitutes a distinctive mode of engagement with the language that I term "postvernacular Yiddish."[19]

The "secondary level of signification" that Shandler identifies in a postvernacular Yiddish world points to a fascination with Yiddish that exceeds its linguistic identity and extends to encompass a whole constellation of cultural formations. Yiddish in America is no longer the language of the

Jewish streets. It is, rather, a feeling state, a culinary orientation, a political stance.

How does a postvernacular relationship to eastern European culture in Israel distinguish itself from a salvage poetic one? This is reflected in the way that Israelis seem to have a harder time choosing, framing, translating and contextualizing artifacts from eastern Europe that they feel they can access and mediate for their audiences; while, for example, they choose literary artifacts just like Americans do, they seem unable, in many cases, to find good strategies for building a bridge between those artifacts and their Israeli audience. The difference, therefore, lies more in a failure of adaptive imagination than in the recognition of the artifacts themselves. Thus, it seems to me that in Israel, salvage poetics are still more aspirational than actual, with postvernacularism dominating—an approximation as opposed to a realization of eastern European Jewish imaginary reconstructions.

Israeli Salvage Poetics is divided into two parts. The first, "Recalling Eastern Europe," focuses on the works of noncanonic Israeli women writers. Zionist ideology has long been marked as masculine, with its formulation of the "New Jew" as a muscular, militarized, male farmer. While women played a significant role in the ideology of Zionism as "mothers of sons" (like Rivka Guber), femininity was generally viewed as the antithesis of Israeliness. Indeed, eastern Europe, as the foil to Palestine and Israel in the Zionist imagination, was figured as feminine within the negative constellation with which femininity has traditionally been associated—as passive and weak, as a cipher, not an agent. It was therefore presumably easier, one could argue, to maintain a grip on memories of eastern Europe or to even reject the idea of the "negation of the diaspora" from a female perspective, because embedded in Israeli femininity was an inherent connection to that diaspora. Looking at Yaniv Iczkovits's rendition of a fictional woman named Motel, alongside Ita Kalish, Malkah Shapiro, Dora Weinberg Gertz, Leah Svirsky Holtzman, and Rivka Guber in the first half of this study, what we see is a working out of how to write about the diaspora, and specifically the eastern European diaspora, unapologetically, in an Israeli environment. It is the formalized, literary, rendition of "recalling eastern Europe," as executed by these authors.

The second part of this study, "Reconsidering the Negation of the Diaspora," takes us into the realm of übercanonic Hebrew writers, representatives of the generation of the modern Hebrew renaissance, the generation of the State, and of contemporary Israel. S. Y. Agnon, S. Yizhar, Amos Oz, and David Grossman are all male, and all have been celebrated and valorized within Israeli literary historical taxonomies as the embodiment of alternatives to Jewish literatures of the diaspora. All these writers, in one way or another, as we will explore, find ways to reconsider the compulsory "negation of the diaspora" implicit in the work of canonic Israeli writers, particularly male ones, either early on in their careers (Grossman) or belatedly (Yizhar and Oz). Even Agnon, who was considered a "diasporic" writer by many critics in the early Israeli literary establishment (such as by Oz's own great-uncle, Joseph Klausner), in the novel under discussion here acknowledges his own departure from eastern Europe and laments his own role in the demise of traditional Jewish eastern European literatures and cultural formations.

One might ask why all the authors explored in this study are of eastern European origins, either first- or second-generation Israelis. Indeed, it is possible for others in Israel to write about the strangely Ashkenazi-centric legacy of a Jewish country located in the Middle East. To explain my choice of featuring only those authors from an eastern European background, we must return for a moment to my conceptualization of the mechanisms of salvage poetics. Within an American context, I posited as essential to salvage poetics the desire of authors to build a bridge between the world of the past and the world of the present through their own supposed embodiment, real or imagined, in that past. In my discussion of Roman Vishniac's documentary photographs, for example, I suggested that he engaged in the creation of "auto-ethnographic salvage." In a comparison between his framing of *Polish Jews* (1947) and *A Vanished World* (1983) over a forty-year period, I note an exponential increase in verbal storytelling that posits his own personal engagement with the subjects of his photographs. There I argue that

> [t]racing the development of the captions across the two publications and focusing specifically on the captions in *A Vanished World* from a literary perspective provides a fascinating insight into the ways in which Vishniac sought to construct a particular kind of narrative in America in the decades after the Holocaust. His increased emphasis on verbal storytelling to supplement the photographs and the personal nature of many of these stories reveal Vishniac's consciousness of the importance of telling the story of a lost culture through the story of a living self, bringing together a salvage impulse with an autobiographical one, or what I have called here "an auto-ethnographic impulse."[20]

This notion pertains as well within an Israeli context. As mentioned above, beginning in Part II, we focus on canonic Hebrew writers who incorporate their connection to eastern Europe, real or imagined, into their present identity as Israeli writers. Even Agnon, whose link to eastern Europe where he was born and raised is self-evident, must imagine himself becoming reintegrated into his Galician hometown years after having left it for Palestine. Yizhar, Oz, and Grossman, all children of eastern European immigrants to Palestine write works that grapple with variations on inserting the self into the repressed past; the Israeli writer raised to negate the diaspora tentatively reapproaches that world not simply as a revenant but as a living, breathing piece of the present. Because one of the key elements of salvage poetics is the situating of the self within the framework of the represented culture, I have chosen to look at works by those whose familial origins in an eastern European past facilitate their "reconsideration" of the negation of the diaspora, as articulated eponymously in the title of Part II. While it might be possible to consider the ways in which eastern, or Mizrahi, immigrants to Israel and their descendants represent the dominant culture of eastern European immigrants in Israel, that is not within the purview of this study. That would entail a discussion of cultural dynamics surrounding minoritarian and majoritarian ethnic discourses in Israel—an excellent topic for another project.

The first chapter in this volume situates Yaniv Iczkovits's *Tikun 'aḥar ḥatsot* or *The Slaughterman's Daughter* (2015) in its relationship to "An Homage to Yiddish," a day of praise given to Yiddish at the Israeli Knesset in 1993 to commemorate the seventy-fifth anniversary of the death of the Yiddish writer Sholem Aleichem (1859–1916). In this chapter I consider the unique parameters of salvage poetics within their Israeli environment and how salvage poetics and a postvernacular Yiddish exist on a continuum there. *The Slaughterman's Daughter* is a contemporary Israeli novel written in the style of Mendele and the voice of Agnon, and features an unusual character, Motel—a religious Jewish woman who sets out on a journey to track down her brother-in-law who has abandoned her sister. In her youth, Motel had wanted to be a ritual slaughterer, like her father, but couldn't become one because she was a woman. Yet she kept her father's gift to her before his death—his slaughterer's knife—tucked under her dress and used it for very un-lady-like purposes (like self-defense and murder) during her travels across the Pale of Settlement in search of her errant brother-in-law. What we see in Iczkovits's novel is a repositioning of the relationship between eastern Europe and femininity, with historical eastern European

Jewry being populated by knife-wielding, self-defending, aggressive, and justice-seeking women. The artifacts identifiable in this particular variation on salvage poetics are not so far distant from what we see in the American *Life Is with People*: Iczkovits draws on the literary texts of classic Hebrew and Yiddish writers to create a contemporary text, accessible to Israelis today, that not only thematizes eastern Europe as a Jewish place but also models itself on classic Jewish literature written in and about Jewish eastern Europe as a vibrant and essential part of Israeli literary history.

Turning next to the work of European-born women who immigrated to Palestine during the interwar period (Shapiro in 1925 and Kalish in 1933), in chapter 2 I posit the necessity of identifying "a new style" in works such as those produced by Ita Kalish and Malkah Shapiro, daughters of Hasidic dynasties (Kozniecze and Warka, respectively), within an Israeli context. What, I ask, is the unique blend of ethnographic consciousness and literary artistry that populates these texts, and how can this style best be classified and understood? Focusing, in part, on the gender of these authors, I explore the possibility that Israeli eastern European–born women writers saw themselves as the natural conservators of the memory of life in eastern Europe. Gesturing to the history of eastern European Hebrew literature and Shapiro's and Kalish's stylistic allegiances to many of its norms, I look at the ethnographic readings largely imposed on these texts by their English translators. In so doing, I identify "cross-disciplinary translation"—when the process of framing and adapting a text for an audience that desires to better understand a lost culture changes the genre of that work and puts it into an ethnographic camp, as opposed to an aesthetic one—as the basis for salvage poetics.

Picking up on the role of female writers in early Israel as the voices of eastern Europe, the third chapter in this volume considers the literary corpus of Rivka Guber (1902–81), a pioneer during the Fourth Aliyah from Ukraine who became known in Israel, after the deaths of her two sons in the 1948 War of Independence, as the Mother of Sons. In this chapter I reflect on how Guber, an icon of maternal Zionism, one that required mothers to sacrifice their sons for the greater nationalist purpose, managed from the platform of her personal bereavement to preserve her dignity as an eastern European Jew and the dignity of other eastern European Jews, particularly after the Holocaust. Rather than "forgetting" the world she came from, she writes about it in glowing terms; rather than espousing Israel's focus on fissure and reinvention, she espouses continuity and pride in the eastern European Jewish diaspora experience.

Continuing the discussion of the image of the mother within early Zionist ideology, chapter 4 differs somewhat from the other chapters in its focus not on literary or autobiographical writings but on biographical writings. Here I explore the work of two Israeli literary critics, Avner Holtzman and Nurit Gertz, writing about their mothers' histories in Europe and in the nascent State of Israel. I place this chapter at the heart of the book because, as mentioned earlier, my original conception of salvage poetics grew out of an observation I made many years ago about how Hebrew literary critics, both at the beginning and the end of the twentieth century, had adopted the concept of ethnography as a way to explain Hebrew literature set in eastern Europe; the only way some of these critics could make sense of Hebrew writers writing about eastern Europe in Hebrew, which was meant to be used for "nationalist" purposes and to describe hopes for a Zionist future, was to argue that this literature was written as a kind of cultural description, or an ethnographic set piece. In using Holtzman's and Gertz's writings about their mothers as a lens through which to view the eastern Europe they left behind, I have found that moving into the twenty-first century we have arrived back at a place where critics seek to reclaim eastern Europe, but in a different way than they did a hundred years earlier. Whereas Frischmann, in his reading of Mendele, claimed to have found a repository of images and descriptions of the eastern European Jewish shtetl, what we find in the work of Holtzman and Gertz is a turn toward personal history and family as that repository.

Both Holtzman and Gertz know very little about the worlds their mothers inhabited before emigrating. To learn more, they turn to particular artifacts that they must salvage, with the help of their mothers, to create what Barbara Myerhoff, the preeminent ethnographer of American Jewish life, has called a "third voice."[21] By third voice, Myerhoff means a voice that emerges from a text created out of a dialogue between two people who are working together to describe a culture; one is the native informant and one is the ethnographer or interviewer. This third voice, I argue in this chapter, is created by Gertz and Holtzman as they work with cultural artifacts provided by their mothers—for Gertz it is her mother's memory, and for Holtzman it is a photograph of his aunt Hanale's birthday party. How, I ask in this chapter, does the third voice created by each writer—a voice independent of their own and their mothers' but one that is created by the meeting of the two—succeed in creating a cultural portrait not only of eastern European Jewish pre-Holocaust culture but also of the many obstacles to accessing that world in contemporary Israeli experience?

Alongside the development of a third voice in Holtzman's and Gertz's treatments of their mothers' pasts in eastern Europe, I also return at this point in the discussion to Israel's national politics of forgetting. Yael Chaver in *What Must Be Forgotten*, a study of Yiddish literary production on the Yishuv, stages an imagined discussion between Ernest Renan in 1882 and Homi K. Bhabha in 1994. "The essence of a nation is that all individuals have many things in common, and also that they have forgotten many things," says Renan, and Bhabha rejoins, "It is through this syntax of forgetting—or being obliged to forget—that the problematic identification of a national people becomes visible."[22] What, Chaver asks, "are the things that the members of the nation have forgotten and that, if remembered, might endanger the nation's essence?"[23] Here, in my discussion of Holtzman's and Gertz's respective accounts of their mothers' pasts, we trace their perspectives on what must not be forgotten as a revision of what was so aggressively "forgotten" in earlier generations.

Chapter 5 examines S. Y. Agnon's *Oreaḥ natah la-lun* or *A Guest for the Night* (1939), a novel published on the eve of World War II, for its salvage poetic resonances. As one of the original essays I wrote about salvage poetics, it marks the beginning, in this volume, of my examination of canonized literary works of modern Hebrew literature. I argue here for a reading of this text as a kind of hybrid of the two world wars. Whereas "hybrid" in the discourse of salvage poetics usually refers to the hybrid created out of texts that exist on the border between the ethnographic and the fictional, in this instance I allude to *A Guest for the Night* as hybrid in an earlier version of that formation—as a splicing together of times and places. And indeed, what are salvage poetics if not a splicing together of times and places in the perceived need to use fiction about the past as a representation in the present of a lost culture?

Chapter 6 is organized around the question of how S. Yizhar, a central figure of *dor ha-medina*, negotiated his role as one of the first native-born representatives of an autonomous political identity in a Jewish national homeland, alongside his consciousness of cultural forces that exceeded a territorial nationalism. For Israelis, reconciling their national present with their eastern European past is made so much easier when the figures of the *dor ha-medina* exhibit a stake in that past. Thus, Yizhar's fashioning of an autoethnography for himself of that past, out of his relationship to the music of his eastern European–born parents, becomes an essential part of the process of beginning to understand it.

Next focusing on Oz's autobiographical novel, I consider the parameters of his particular return to Europe in *Sipur 'al 'ahavah ve-ḥoshekh* or *A Tale of Love and Darkness* (2002). Chapter 7 brings together many of the different threads introduced in the earlier essays, ranging from an allegiance to Agnon as the one canonic eastern European Hebrew writer that Israelis draw from to represent eastern Europe to the idea that Israelis have entered a period of a "back to the roots" movement wherein contemporary Israelis are seeking an access point to their eastern European legacy through literature. Finally, taking us back to the second, third, and fourth chapters in this book, the ones that discuss the writings of European-born Israeli women Malkah Shapiro, Ita Kalish, Rivka Guber, and the mothers of Avner Holtzman and Nurit Gertz, I focus in this chapter on Oz's literary debt to his eastern European–born mother and the legacy of European folktales she passed on to him. The constellation of Europe, gender, and literature comes together here to create a portrait of salvage poetics at the height of their powers. In this book, Oz manages to salvage his memory of his mother, the memory of her European background, and the memory of Oz's most powerful literary influences.

In a postscript, I turn to David Grossman's post-Holocaust Israeli novel *'Ayen 'erekh 'ahavah* or *See Under: Love* (1986) and argue that he approximates Yiddish in this novel by making intertextual references to earlier Hebrew writing that resonates with Yiddish for the first generation of native-born Israelis due to that earlier Hebrew's archaisms. In doing so, Grossman mostly sidesteps Yiddish as an actual language within his novel by approximating it as an eastern European–inflected Hebrew. The protagonist of the novel, a child of Holocaust survivors, grows up in an Israeli milieu that silences discussions of the world "over there," so he seeks out that world on his own. Hebrew literature of the modern Hebrew renaissance and Yiddish literature in translation become his artifacts of "over there," and he makes his way to Yiddishland with their assistance. While the Hebrew used here is archaic enough to be temporally parallel to Yiddish, and metonymically representative of it, because it is Hebrew, it is comprehensible.

In my analysis of David Grossman's *See Under: Love*, I return to the notion of a postvernacular Yiddish in Israel, which is the point with which the volume began. A postvernacular, I argue in chapter 1, is a steppingstone to salvage poetics. It expresses a desire to affiliate with eastern European Jewry and with the Yiddish language, but it is satisfied with sound bites and with metonymic associations; it is an "affective" and "ideological" relationship with a culture, not a fully realized commitment. In contrast, salvage poetics, as earlier discussed, indicate a deeper commitment to understanding a lost culture. They reflect an author's need to move beyond sound bites and into a description of a culture, based on artifacts that are, themselves, suited to building bridges between a world destroyed and the present. The fact that this book begins with a discussion of *The Slaughterman's Daughter* as an example of a text that successfully crosses the border from a Yiddish postvernacular and salvage poetics, and ends with Grossman's *See Under: Love* as an example of a book that stops just at the border between the two, indicates the state of Israeli society vis-à-vis eastern European Jewry today. Israelis are ready to go deeper, but they are just not there yet. Salvage poetics are a work in progress for them. This exposition, spanning several decades of my thinking about the topic in an Israeli context, does not come to a tidy conclusion for that reason. It travels through the many different manifestations of Israeli willingness and unwillingness to consider its own role in repressing its history, and its own stake in reclaiming it.

I

RECALLING EASTERN EUROPE

1

"AN HOMAGE TO YIDDISH"

The Struggle for Salvage Poetics

On January 4, 1993, in commemoration of the seventy-fifth anniversary of the death of the Yiddish (and Hebrew) writer Sholem Aleichem, the Israeli Knesset called a special session "dedicated to the Yiddish language and Yiddish culture," which they called "An Homage to Yiddish."[1] Five Knesset members, including its speaker, Shevah Weiss, a Polish Holocaust survivor, and its deputy speaker, Ovadiah Eli, a native of Iraq, spoke in praise of Yiddish. They were joined by Mordechai Tsanin,[2] chair of the Association of Yiddish Writers and Journalists in Israel, who shared the following remarks:

> This initiative is opening wide the gates of the ghetto into which Yiddish writers were thrown, first in Palestine and then in the State of Israel. It is difficult to summarize the damage caused to the culture of our people by the driving of Yiddish writers into this ghetto. . . . There is no doubt that this admirable act of the Knesset is the result of the pressure of the young generation in Israel and in the diaspora, the generation free from the complexes to which the Zionist ideologists were subjected in the period from the First World War and up to the first decade or even first two decades after the establishment of the state.[3]

As described by Tsanin above, and as discussed in the introduction to this volume, during the prestate decades and in the early years of the State of Israel, Yiddish was viewed by many (though not all) as a national liability, being, as it was, the language of a thousand years of Jewish diaspora. Zionist ideologues, most notably David Ben-Gurion, Israel's first prime minister, wanted the new state to represent a historical leap, one that "was not a continuation of Jewish life in East Europe, but a new beginning that fit well into the past of Joshua, David, Uzziah and the early Hasmoneans."[4] As such, Yiddish, the language of the European Jewish diaspora, was considered by many to be not only irrelevant but an actual threat to Hebrew, the ancient textual language that had been selected by Zionist ideologues as a central aspect of Jewish self-determination within the nascent nationalist culture of the Jewish state.

The suppression of Yiddish was only a part of the broader movement to expunge Europe from the Israeli consciousness and lifestyle despite the fact that the vast majority of Jews who arrived in Palestine from the period of the First Aliyah in 1882 through the Second Aliyah (which concluded with the establishment of the state in 1948) came from western and eastern Europe. For example, twenty-five thousand Jews immigrated to Palestine from Europe between 1882 and 1891, joining an extant Jewish population (the Old Yishuv) of just twenty-four thousand. By 1950 the number of Jews coming primarily from Europe to the Yishuv had increased the Jewish population to 1,203,000 in the aftermath of the Holocaust.[5] The enormous rhetorical and political effort invested in turning an entire culture against its own origins is a story that has been told in many different historical and cultural studies. The ways in which Hebrew literature has grappled with that legacy, however, has not been examined in depth.

The 1993 "Homage to Yiddish" in the Knesset provides a brilliant illustration of the possibility of salvage poetics and also their limits in Israeli representations of eastern European Jewry. Salvage poetics are the mechanisms by which aesthetic works, such as fiction and photographs, are deployed in the aftermath of a cataclysmic event to represent the culture that was destroyed. How can a short story or a documentary photograph become a stand-in for a culture? A bridge must be built, through exposition, translation, and contextual framing, for that one work to metonymically represent the whole culture. The "artifact," or original work, must be carefully selected to provide a strong foundation for the work of adaptation and presentation to an audience primed to receive it.

To mediate and alter an artifact requires consensus on what constitutes an artifact. In the 1993 "Homage" all the speeches had a common denominator: they identified Yiddish culture with Yiddish literature. Speaker after speaker, as they began, alluded to Sholem Aleichem, which is understandable because the event was scheduled to coincide with the anniversary of his death. But once on the topic of Sholem Aleichem, each of the speakers elaborated in ways that are highly relevant to our understanding of salvage poetics. Avraham Burg, the chairman of the education committee of the Knesset, put it this way:

> In the cultural attic of Yiddish we find classical works of the Jewish past that seem to be dead but I am not sure that they really are because their contribution to our culture is still very important and they can be called the heralds of modern Jewish culture. It is sufficient to name several of them: Sholem Aleichem, Mendele, I. L. Peretz, and many other authors from the almost endless list of those who create in Yiddish.[6]

For his part, Dov Shilansky, deputy speaker of the Knesset, heralding the death of the language and the culture, invokes characters from the works of Sholem Aleichem, alongside well-known Yiddish songs: "Oh, how precious Yiddish is for me. Shloymeleh and Moysheleh, with Menahem Mendl and Tevye der milkhiger and Motl Peysie dem ḥazens. Oh, how I miss you, Yiddish songs with 'a rozinkes mit mandeln and 'ofn Pripitshik' and 'Reizele' and 'Der Rebi Elimelekh.' With 'Margaritkeleh' and 'Hamerl klap'—songs of poverty, toil and sweat."[7] In this list of totemic classic literary characters and stereotypical folksongs, what we see here is a catalog of greatest hits, but nothing deeper. Shulamit Aloni, minister of education and culture, picks up on the theme of the literature as the culture, and the culture as, essentially, the literature:

> In those days, and I am still speaking about Sholem Aleichem, there was no television, and only wealthy people and workers of the electrical company had radio sets. For recreation father used to read to us Sholem Aleichem's stories. But he could not help his Yiddish pronunciation.... We were not the only children who used to read books together. Through those books which were at that time our television and radio we got to know Menahem Mendl, Tevye and Motl Peysie dem ḥazens and Kasrilievke.... You mentioned Mendele Mocher Sforim, I. L. Peretz, and Sholem Aleichem. You can also add Sholem Asch and Joseph Opatoshu and others. Yiddish is not just a language. It is a way of life. It is love, dreams, troubles, illusions, and castles in the air. Menahem Mendl has remained, in one way or another, the prototype of all of us, perhaps until today. Perhaps Benjamin ha-shlishi is still alive in us, a

sort of strange Don Quixote who has not lost his illusions. To say nothing of others, of the stories of Peretz, of the struggle between Litvakim and Hasidim, and all in Yiddish. This is a great part of a culture that should be preserved and cherished because it is not enough to go to Auschwitz and learn about the pain and terrible antihuman murder that took place there, without knowing what was really destroyed.[8]

Despite expanding on the brevity of Shilansky, Aloni resorts as well to the most totemic and stereotypical texts. Having been reprimanded by her colleagues just before this passage for speaking too much about Sholem Aleichem, Aloni acknowledges her inability not to speak of him, while broadening the scope of her discussion to include other writers: Mendele, Peretz, Asch, Opatoshu, and others. These writers, for Aloni, represent the "great part of a culture that should be preserved and cherished" because, she says, ultimately it was destroyed in the ovens of Auschwitz.

Evident here is an unabashed focus on Yiddish literature in lieu of more detailed expositions of the rich history and culture that preceded and framed these modern texts. The Yiddish literature written during the late 1800s and early 1900s, it seems, is all that remains—based on the attention given it by the Knesset speakers—of the culture later destroyed in the Holocaust. The only speaker who separates the Yiddish culture from Yiddish literature, Mordechai Tsanin, is not a Knesset member. He is also the only speaker to acknowledge the Israeli negative attitude toward Yiddish, and toward its writers, for the entire existence of the political state and even before it.

In Jeffrey Shandler's discussion of "Yiddishland," an imaginary "land" in which Yiddish is the metonymic representation of Jewish experience even in the absence of a "native land" or a single geographic locale, he identifies Yiddish's transformation in America, Israel, and Europe from a Jewish vernacular to a Jewish "postvernacular."[9] A postvernacular Yiddish, according to Shandler, performs Yiddish not as a spoken language but as a desire for the culture represented by that spoken language. What constitutes a Yiddish postvernacular in America, and what constitutes a Yiddish postvernacular in Israel? In America, bagels, Dr. Brown's soda, challah, kugel, *Fiddler on the Roof*, and the Tenement Museum on the Lower East Side all converge into a "sense" of Yiddish as opposed to a real engagement with it. In Israel, it is familiarity with the Sholem Aleichem novel *Motl Peysie dem ḥazens* (1907–16), klezmer festivals, and Yiddish theater. In other words, for Israelis, Yiddishland is a land of literature and culture.

For Americans, it is a world circumscribed by gastronomic preferences and by the geography of American Jewish neighborhoods within the history of immigration and Americanization.

In its "An Homage to Yiddish," the Israeli Knesset turned to modern Yiddish literature as it attempted to acknowledge the culture that Israel had actively demonized. The goal, it seems, was to use that literature—with which most Israelis were at least moderately familiar, through translations taught as part of the school curriculum—to provide an access point to an entire world. In Israel, which had demonized eastern European Jewish culture, the kind of reparative work that members of the Knesset were tasked with in 1993 left them at a significant disadvantage. What was left for them to work with? Does the fact that the Israeli government gave some speeches in 1993, during one of their sessions, about their love for Sholem Aleichem reflect any significant effort on their part to educate the masses about the world destroyed? Not really. While Yiddish literature, within a salvage poetic framework, can serve as an artifact with which to launch the reconstruction of an eastern European Jewish world, it cannot serve as its sum total. In the "Homage" it appears to represent both a starting point and an ending point because if Yiddish literature is all that is invoked, and all that is provided, nothing can be salvaged from it. Keep in mind that salvage poetics rely not just on the selection of artifacts but also on the translation, reframing, and reengagement of those artifacts. None of that happens here.

But, as Tsanin indicated in his Knesset speech, there has been a movement among young people in Israel in the last several decades to go beyond the artifact and engage in a sincere effort at salvage. This is reflected, in part, in the initiation of trips to Poland within the formal framework of public high schools throughout the country in the 1980s. In 1990 the Knesset passed the Yiddish and Ladino Heritage Law, which led to the creation of the National Authority for Yiddish Culture, and grassroots efforts followed. An organization called YUNG YiDiSH was founded in 1991 under the direction of Mendy Cahan, who, using religious language to characterize the reintegration of Yiddish into contemporary Israeli culture, has said, "Yiddish is like the lamp in the Temple that kept on burning even though there was only a small amount of oil."[10] In 2005 the Yiddishpiel theater attracted eighty thousand audience members. The reintegration of Yiddish into Israeli culture has manifested itself in literary production as well. Rutu Modan and Yirmi Pinkus, graphic novelists, have focused their work on their grandparents' generation; David Grossman, as we will explore in this book's postscript, writes in his monumental *See Under: Love* (1986) about the generation of children of survivors who grew up in the 1950s in veritable madhouses, caught between the nightmares of their parents and the chauvinism of the new state; Ilan Sheinfeld has written a novel about a fictionalized Szedlitz, a shtetl in Poland, in which he adopts the tone and style of Hasidic hagiography, but his main protagonist is not a great rabbi but rather a giant Jewish frog; and Israeli journalist and Yiddish translator Beni Mer leaves Israel altogether to write a microhistory of a street from the Jewish neighborhood of Warsaw: Smocze.

Beni Mer's approach to Smocze Street in *Smocze: The Biography of a Jewish Street in Warsaw* (2018) is worth looking at in some detail as we consider the intersecting dynamics of salvage poetics and postvernacular Yiddish within a specifically Israeli context. As indicated in the title, the book is the "biography" of a street from the Jewish quarter of Warsaw, a street characterized by deep poverty and rich Jewish culture, boasting a Yiddish theater, a Hebrew school, and a synagogue.[11] Why did he write the book? he asks himself in his introduction. "Because," he responds, "to some degree Smocze St. is the Yiddish among all the languages. It wasn't the most important, and certainly not the nicest street in Warsaw. Even so it serves as a microcosm for an entire life and for the lives of Jews in particular, between the two world wars."[12] Mer's likening of Smocze to the Yiddish language here situates his study squarely in the heart of Israeli culture. Yiddish, in Israel, is a symbol of the marginal, the repressed. The Yiddish language and a street in Warsaw become overlapping quantities for him, with the part representing the whole of a culture:

> This street had all the genetic material necessary for a historian or an author. One street, not particularly central, not well connected like Gajebovski or Twarda where the rich Jews lived, or famous like Krochmalna of Isaac Bashevis Singer and Janusz Korczak. But just like Yiddish, which is a kaleidoscope that brings together surprising and beautiful connections from a linguistic and cultural perspective, so too is Smocze: an infinity of intentions and combinations of sights, smells, sounds, of Poles and Jews of all types: Orthodox, Bundists, Zionists, Communists, and hoi polloi.[13]

Utilizing the mechanisms of a postvernacular as "secondary" approximation of a culture, Mer invokes identifiable Yiddish tropes—in the guise of people and street names—to mark eastern European culture as a whole. It

The Struggle for Salvage Poetics 27

Smocze Street during World War II. From the Collections of the E. Ringelblum Jewish Historical Institute.

is enough to say "Singer" and "Korczak" to think of Jewish Warsaw. It is enough to mention Twarda Street or Krochmalna Street to do the same. But Smocze? It is because he must flesh it out for us, because he must narrate it, that Smocze becomes an important artifactual receptacle for salvage poetics. A postvernacular operates on the basis of sound bites, with "Singer" stepping in for Yiddish literature, and "Korczak" as a shortcut to Jewish Warsaw during the war. Salvage poetics, on the other hand, operates on the basis of translation and framing, of careful selection and the construction of a microhistory.

Essential to the deployment of salvage poetics to build a bridge between worlds is a clear sense of the artifact's origin and an even clearer sense of the artifact's audience. Mer, the Israeli son and grandson of eastern European Jews, lives in a moment during which Israelis are ready to start listening to the voices of their peers who are trying to reconstruct the repressed past. At various points in his explanation of why he has chosen this particular street to inhabit fully and to introduce his audience to, Mer situates it in Israel:

> Smocze is kind of like Neve Sha'anan Street beside the Central Bus Station in Tel Aviv. This comparison, even if it is somewhat crude, explains

Portrait of the "Warsaw Magician of Smozce Street," a sixteen-year-old beggar. From the Archives of the YIVO Institute for Jewish Research, New York.

to some extent the estrangement that many Poles felt vis-à-vis the Jewish neighborhood of Warsaw. Just as Jews from other neighborhoods in Tel Aviv see in the Neve Sha'anan neighborhood a strange, frightening enclave, a kind of Africa, not just in its sights but also its sounds and its smells, so too many Poles saw in Smocze a no-man's-land. Just as I had a hard time finding mention of Smocze in the Polish archives, it will be difficult one day for the Sudanese or Eritrean researcher to find materials in the Tel Aviv city archives or the National Library in Jerusalem on the African population that lived here for so many years. The history that will be found in the Hebrew papers will be primarily about the crimes that happened in these streets. But for a child who grew up in this neighborhood, Neve Sha'anan was a world and everything contained within it, all the good and the bad that could be found there.[14]

The Struggle for Salvage Poetics 29

Women selling fruit from large baskets on Smocze Street. From the Archives of the YIVO Institute for Jewish Research, New York.

Mer chooses to build a bridge here not between Israeli Jews and Polish Jews but between Polish Christians and Israeli Jews, by illuminating their respective relationships with Jewish Warsaw and African Tel Aviv. Here Mer racializes the Jews in Poland, likening them to the black Africans in Israel. He reminds Israelis that Polish Jews were not just impoverished Poles; they were absolute "others" within the culture of Poland. Their neighborhood was not just off the beaten track; it was a foreign country. Even writing this description Mer is forced to acknowledge how far away it is from his own experience. He brings himself to the fore of the discussion, asserting that the example he has drawn from is not an example from his own intimate life experience but from an arsenal of examples that he believes will be effective in its capacity to illustrate alienation, even if it is alienating: "I don't live in Neve Sha'anan, in the same way that Sholem Aleichem didn't live in Kasrilievka, to whose little people he dedicated his great work. After I have translated his works and the works of other great Yiddish poets, Avraham Sutzkever, for example, I go home, to the people in whose midst I am comfortable."[15]

As a translator, Mer brings worlds together, and yet he acknowledges that he is rendering accessible a place to which neither he nor his readers truly belong. He is not translating into Yiddish; rather he is translating from Yiddish into Hebrew. Of course, he must have a good mastery of Yiddish, but it is only when he is translating into an idiomatic and fluid Hebrew that he is really pressed into service. Similarly, by likening Smocze to Neve Sha'anan and articulating his own alienation from the latter as the basis for his comparison of it to the former, he drives home the fact that he is only comfortable representing Smocze to Israelis because they share the implicit understanding that he is, like they are, inherently alienated from his subject matter.

When salvage poetics come into play, the mediating voices (the translators, editors, or framers) often go out of their way to rationalize their right to be building the bridge between the source culture and the audience. The audience, we must keep in mind, is at a distance from the object of inquiry; it is being exhorted to take a second look, to try to understand, to overcome its alienation. At the same time, that very process of rationalization, that very insistence on the mediator's being an insider when he or she is really an outsider, draws attention to its own contrived nature. Roman Vishniac, for example, in his 1983 narrative surrounding the images in *A Vanished World*, writes himself into the scenes he photographs, trying hard to make himself into one of his own subjects, even though he could not have been more alienated from them: he was from a wealthy Moscow family, did not know Yiddish, and was hired by the Joint Distribution Committee to take pictures of impoverished traditional Jews.[16] So why did he insist that he had spoken to his subjects directly, that they had shared their concerns with him in their moments of greatest distress, that he had slept with them in crowded cellars? Because he wanted to be a participant observer who would gain credibility by presenting their images to the Western world not simply as a hired outsider but as a member of their cohort as well.

In a postvernacular universe, being an insider means being an outsider, acknowledging that you can only get so close and priding yourself on knowing just enough to signal familiarity. In a salvage poetic universe, however, there is more at stake: a world has been destroyed and it cannot be re-created. Strong measures need to be taken to familiarize an audience, at a distance that spans time and space, with that world. Salvage poetics require a thoughtful selection of artifacts to begin to build that bridge and a self-conscious mediator who can justify his or her presence in the process.

The 1993 Knesset presentations limited themselves to engaging in a postvernacular presentation of Yiddish literature as a stand-in for the eastern European Jewish culture that had been erased from Israel. Even though several of the speakers were native Yiddish speakers who came from eastern

Europe themselves, neither they nor their peers were comfortable engaging with that culture in such a deep or intimate way that would designate them as personally committed to fostering understanding. A general view, a flirtation with the familiar, but nothing more committed or detailed, was what was called for, and that was what was delivered. Beni Mer discusses this in terms of Roman Vishniac's photographs:

> All these streets have become unified in our consciousness as one single street, a blind alley at the intersection of exile and impoverishment. The photographer Roman Vishniac, who went out in 1935 on a photographic mission to Yiddishland of East Europe, left behind him a rich testament to Jewish life in the "eleventh hour." But he . . . didn't differentiate between villagers from the Carpathian Mountains and Socialists in Lodz, between a Talmud Torah in Munkacz and a modern school in Warsaw. Yiddishland occupies a single place in our memories.[17]

Yiddishland and a postvernacular Yiddish exist on a continuum. And indeed such is the case with the Knesset remarks. All the speakers hearken back to a land that is familiar to Israelis, a land that does not exist outside of literature, and as such can easily be acknowledged and dismissed. Not so for Mer nearly thirty years later. In 2018, it seems, Israel was finally ready to put its ideological hesitations and critique to rest. Mer's microhistorical approach to a Jewish street in Warsaw reflects a commitment to reconciling worlds, to educating a public that thirsts for more.

Moving as Mer did from a postvernacular consciousness to a salvage poetic one is no small feat. It indicates the desire not simply to convey a sense of a world but also to salvage the memory of a world or to reconstruct that world in the experience and imagination of a new generation. A readiness to engage in salvage poetics, in the identification of an artifact from Jewish eastern Europe and a reframing of it for substantial engagement and education, is also evident in Yaniv Iczkovits's 2015 novel *Tikun 'aḥar ḥatsot*, or *The Slaughterman's Daughter*.

The Slaughterman's Daughter is an extraordinary novel within its original Israeli context. Although it is not my practice to summarize literary works, a summary is necessary at this juncture as the details of this novel beg discussion within the constellation of postvernacular norms and salvage poetics in Israel. *The Slaughterman's Daughter* is a picaresque novel about the pursuit of a wayward husband: Zvi-Meir Speismann has abandoned his wife, Mende, and their two children in Motal, a shtetl in Ukraine, to find his fortune in Minsk. Mende's sister, Fanny Keissman—mother of five children, faithful wife of the cheese maker Nosson-Berl, and a free spirit of sorts—has set off to track down Zvi-Meir. Because traveling alone across Ukraine in the 1850s would be dangerous for any Jew, but especially so for a Jewish woman, she is accompanied by the village idiot, Zizek Breshov (previously known as Yoshke Berkovits), who in classic Yiddish literary fashion (as in I. B. Singer's "Gimpel the Fool") is not really such an idiot after all. Zizek is a Motal native whom the Jewish community had kidnapped as a child from his impoverished family to satisfy the community's recruitment obligations to the Russian army. Through a twist of fate, Zizek is adopted in the army by a superior who teaches him to read and write in several languages, positioning him as chief adviser to another superior and thereby enabling Zizek to have a surprising amount of power over his superior's military decisions. After Zizek's skills have transformed him into a hero, he becomes a legend in the Russian army and thereafter is known by all as "The Father." But as *The Slaughterman's Daughter* begins, Zizek has been discharged from the army and has been living in his hometown of Motal for many years, alone and an outsider to the Jewish community, into late middle age.

For unclear reasons, Zizek decides to help Fanny find Zvi-Meir. As Zizek and Fanny set out for Minsk, they encounter a family of brigands who try to rob, rape, and kill them. Fanny, the daughter of a *shohet* (a kosher slaughterer) carries a slaughtering knife with her at all times, having learned her father's trade as a young girl. The knife is her father's legacy to her, and though she has had to put her trade aside because of her gender and her position in the Jewish community as a wife and mother, she keeps the knife strapped to her thigh. In their nighttime encounter with their adversaries, she kills three of the brigands—two sons and a mother—in self-defense. From that moment on, she and Zizek are on the run from the authorities. Along the way they pick up two others: Shleimel Cantor and Patrick Adamsky (formerly known as Pesach Avramson). Shleimel Cantor is a homeless Jew who sings the Adon Olam prayer all over the countryside in exchange for spare change. Patrick Adamsky, another Jewish boy kidnapped from his family by the Jewish community to fill the Russian army quota imposed on the Jews, was a childhood friend of Zizek's in the army. Whereas Zizek distinguished himself in the army as a savvy and self-sacrificing friend to his fellow soldiers because of the influence his powerful intellect afforded him over his superiors, Adamsky distinguished himself during those same years as a physically powerful and brutal soldier. Best friends at the beginning of their military journey, Adamsky and Zizek part ways, reconvening when Zizek and Fanny seek shelter at Adamsky's tavern following their nighttime encounter with the family of brigands. Through a series of high jinks run-ins with the law, this foursome—Fanny and Shleimel Cantor, Zizek and Adamsky—manages to track down Zvi-Meir and restore him to Mende, his abandoned wife. They successfully evade the death sentence and pit the army and the police against one another. Former identities are resumed, new identities are adopted, and the story of Jewish experience in Ukraine in the 1850s is represented.

Why do I call this novel extraordinary? Unlike most other contemporary Israeli novels that address an eastern European past (if at all) from an Israeli vantage point within the narrative, *The Slaughterman's Daughter* is set in eastern Europe and is framed by a narrator in eastern Europe. Contemporary Israel plays no part in this novel; rather, the literature of the modern Hebrew renaissance, originating in eastern Europe at the turn of the twentieth century, and modern Yiddish literature serve as its models. Strongly felt here is the style of Mendele Mocher Sforim, with his peripatetic characters and his strongly apostrophic narrator, not to mention the fact that one of the book's main characters is named "Mende," a female variant of Mendele.

Mendele is best known as the "grandfather" of both modern Hebrew and modern Yiddish literature, writing in both languages simultaneously. Mendele created a literary idiom in both languages that captured the feeling on the "Jewish streets." In Hebrew he was prescribing a new vernacular style that did not yet exist; in Yiddish he transformed what had been primarily used, until modernity, to translate sacred texts and to render accessible a religious tradition for those unschooled in Hebrew (as well as to provide European romance novels to the Yiddish reading masses) into a secular literature that spoke in the voices of "Jews on the street" in their own idiom. Dan Miron, in *A Traveler Disguised*, charts the development of the Mendelian narrator as the key to the birth of a modern Yiddish literature.[18] And indeed the presence of a strong interactive narrator, both for the main protagonists in modern Yiddish literature and for the readers of those texts, is a common denominator for the most famous of them. Mendele is an insider facilitating the movement of stories around among insiders.

At first glance, *The Slaughterman's Daughter*, set in eastern Europe, resembles Mendele's stories—a story told by an insider to insiders. But on closer scrutiny, there is only one homodiegetic narrator in *The Slaughterman's*

Daughter, and he appears only for a short time within a framed narrative in which the story of Zizek's transformation into a hero ("The Father") of the Russian army takes place. This story is told by an army portraitist to Fanny as he paints her portrait. Thus, with such a limited homodiegetic narration, the overall narrative of *The Slaughterman's Daughter*, while resembling classic Yiddish literature, in fact comes much closer, under scrutiny, to resembling the work of the classic modern Hebrew renaissance writer S. Y. Agnon (on whom we will focus in chapter 5). With the exception of some of his narratives of childhood ("The Kerchief") and stories of Jerusalem ("Tehilah") the classic Agnonian narrator does not take a homodiegetic role in the narrative (although he does in the novel we will discuss in chapter 5). Rather, he is personable and chats with his reader, providing signposts for his digressions, acknowledging his own authority over the text as its originator without necessarily becoming embodied. In *The Slaughterman's Daughter* we see a similar role for the narrator in passages such as the following, in which Pazhari, an important military persona, reflects on his own childhood encounter with a Jewish boy whom he mistakenly identifies as Zizek, who is now at his mercy, on the run from the law. Note that this is not a first-person narrative but rather a mediated third-person narrative, avoiding homodiegetic mechanisms:

> As Pazhari sits down before Zizek and Fanny, he feels as if his whole life has been leading up to this moment, the peak of his existence, no less. When he had first heard the Father's story, he had known at once that he had met him before, that their paths had crossed at the Komarovs'. The fugitive that he had concealed in the shed had been Yoshke Berkovits. Pazhari felt it in his bones. People who knew more about the Father's legend would have probably made a more reasonable assumption: it could not have been Yoshke Berkovits whom Pazhari had met in the shed, but it might have been Motl Avramson, Pesach's renegade brother. It had been roughly at that time and in that area that Motl had fled; many details matched, more or less. Naturally, only a kindhearted orphan like Pazhari, even once he had become a colonel and deputy camp commander, could believe that in the vast Russian expanses that stretch between the empire's preposterously long borders, such a coincidence could be possible. Once he heard about the Father, this conviction settled in his mind and would not relent, as if there had been no other thieving boys in the empire, including *zyds*, that he could have met. In fact, his belief was quite unfounded, but nonetheless,

Pazhari's fancy might still benefit the arrested pair, which is a serendipitous coincidence in and of itself.[19]

The narrator in this passage gestures to us from behind Pazhari's back, giving us access to Pazhari's mistaken identification of Zizek with the boy he sheltered as a child. The narrator acknowledges the logic of Pazhari's mistake and presents us with some alternatives to his misidentification: the boy might have been the brother of Pesach Avramson (Patrick Adamsky), who was also *khopped*, or kidnapped, for the army and escaped. Indeed, the boy could have been any thieving Jewish child. The narrator clearly identifies himself or herself as a Jew in referring to Patrick as Pesach. At the same time, this is a Jew who acknowledges the seamier side of Jewish experience in his articulation of the fact that the countryside, during Pazhari's childhood, was probably crawling with little Jewish thieves. This narrator, like Agnon's narrator, is the unmistakable central consciousness of this novel, the consciousness that mediates between the reader and the characters, shaping the text and manipulating our perceptions.

Even more explicitly in dialogue with Agnon is the tendency of Iczkovits's narrator to engage the reader throughout the novel in pseudosacred reflections that make it sound, at moments, like the text is a sermon or a piece of midrash: "The Master of the World extends his arm and overwhelms the sun with a mighty hand and an outstretched arm, and now the heat is over and the wind is blowing on the three companions."[20] Or, for instance, we read:

> When God created the Heaven and the Earth, darkness hovered over the void. There was no need to create darkness, only light. The Almighty illuminated even the miserable souls of men, lest they stagnate in their primordial form, that is, in terrible loneliness. This is why He created them male and female, in His shape and form, as though to say: "You humans are incapable of civility. You will only really be human beings once you have learned to live together in harmony."[21]

Compare this to the famous lead-in to Agnon's signature story, "Agunot" (1908):

> It is said: A thread of grace is spun and drawn out of the deeds of Israel, and the Holy One, blessed be He, Himself, in His glory, sits and

weaves—strand on strand—a prayer shawl all grace and all mercy, for the Congregation of Israel to deck herself in.[22]

Like Agnon's narrator in "Agunot," Iczkovits's narrator in *The Slaughterman's Daughter* takes on not just a directive voice but also a rabbinic one—the voice of Jewish religious authority. Agnon's great achievement as a modern Hebrew writer throughout the twentieth century was taking on that very voice while still maintaining his reputation as a writer of modern Hebrew. Even while ventriloquizing the rabbis, he was known as a modernist.

Iczkovits's intimations of Mendele but explicit allusions to Agnon through his narratological construction of *The Slaughterman's Daughter* returns us to the issue of salvage poetics and a postvernacular. Agnon was the Israeli writer of the eastern European shtetl par excellence. While other writers, such as Dvora Baron (1887–1956), continued to write about the eastern European shtetl once having immigrated to Palestine, Agnon was the only one who was still considered a "voice" of Israel and Israeliness despite his eastern European focus. This can, perhaps, be attributed to the fact that he is the only Israeli writer, to this day, ever to have won a Nobel Prize in literature and therefore would be hard for Israelis to reject. While other Hebrew writers whose works spanned the nineteenth and twentieth centuries, like Y. H. Brenner, Yaakov Steinberg, Dvora Baron, Haim Hazaz, Uri Zvi Greenberg, and Avraham Shlonsky, started off in Europe but immigrated to Palestine (as did Agnon), Agnon, with his distinctive style marked by its Judaic rhetoric, even at the height of the secularization of the Hebrew language and its literature, has become the most identifiable address for an eastern European Hebrew literary idiom. For a writer like Iczkovits, seeking out a precedent for a novel of eastern Europe in Hebrew, Agnon is probably the best model.

As we saw in the Knesset's "An Homage to Yiddish," the best way for Israelis to access Yiddishland was, for an earlier generation, through modern Yiddish literature in translation. But for Iczkovits's generation, it seems, Agnon functions in a similar vein—like Yiddish literature in a Hebrew translation. Like the American Jewish illiteracy in the postwar period that kept American Jews at arm's length from traditional Hebrew and Yiddish materials and necessitated the intervention and mediation of texts such as Maurice Samuel's English rendition of Tevye in *The World of Sholem Aleichem*, Agnon, it seems, serves as the Maurice Samuel of this generation of Israelis: Agnon, as evidenced by Iczkovits's engagement with him, provides access to an eastern European world within a uniquely Israeli idiom, albeit a somewhat archaic one.

This is not to say that Israelis find Agnon particularly accessible. Indeed, as a nonnative Hebrew speaker and scholar who studied Agnon in high school and who was trained to read him as a graduate student, I think it is easier for me to understand him than it is for some of my Israeli peers, particularly the secular ones who are not well versed in traditional Jewish literature and liturgy. However, it may be Agnon's archaic Hebrew usages, similar to those of Hebrew before it was a spoken language, that make him such a good model for a Hebrew novel written in a postvernacular Yiddish, as I argue in my reading of David Grossman's *See Under: Love* in the postscript to this book; the Hebrew of the Jewish Enlightenment and the modern Hebrew renaissance is so far removed from contemporary Hebrew that for a Hebrew reader today it resonates more with Yiddish, a Jewish vernacular written in Hebrew letters, than with modern Hebrew.

The Slaughterman's Daughter is highly conscious of its "Yiddish" identity despite its having been written in Hebrew. Like the Hebrew literature of the turn of the twentieth century, it thematizes the study of Hebrew as a foreign language (with Fanny subversively teaching her daughter Hebrew), even though the book is written in Hebrew, indicating that the implied language of the narrative as a whole is something other than Hebrew; in this case, as in those earlier texts, it would be Yiddish because of the geographic location of the drama in eastern Europe and the languages the protagonists can reasonably be expected to know. Additionally, as in most postvernacular Yiddish texts, *The Slaughterman's Daughter* peppers Yiddish throughout the tale. In a monologue by Fannie's mother-in-law, for example, we read: "Who am I to talk about Adam and Eve? *Kvatsh mit zozze*, nonsense in gravy."[23] And Fanny points to Yiddish itself as a language of isolation and unadulterated Jewishness. As she reflects at one point on giving up her slaughterer vocation, she observes: "[E]veryone in Grodno was like her mother: isolated from the world in the safety of their homes. A Jew cannot call himself a Jew unless he hides behind the walls of Yiddish and dwells in the citadel of the shtetl."[24]

The Slaughterman's Daughter resembles its Yiddish forebears in its own criticism of Yiddish itself. Before the birth of a secular Yiddish literature in the works of Mendele and Sholem Aleichem, Yiddish satire was a distinct genre. Written by critics of Hasidism, works such as *Dos poylishe yingel* (The Polish boy, 1867) were written in Yiddish, begrudgingly, by their Maskilic (Jewish Enlightenment) authors to attempt to reach the masses. Many

Yiddish writers, in fact, used pseudonyms because they were ashamed to be known as Yiddish authors in their own names. Fanny's venturing out of the shtetl as a woman in search of a treacherous man, her insistence on teaching her daughters Hebrew, and her critique of Yiddish and the shtetl, as presented above, all reflect an interesting synthesis of a modern feminist sensibility of this century and a modernizing sensibility of the previous one. The overall effect of the novel, therefore, is that it reads like a classic Yiddish novel, critical of its "little people" albeit in a loving way, unabashedly representing a Yiddish milieu for lack of a better alternative, in Yiddish. In this case, however, the Yiddish is a postvernacular one.

Like Mer, Iczkovits is clearly writing this for an Israeli audience. Just as Mer uses African Tel Aviv as his point of comparison with Jewish Warsaw, so too does Iczkovits situate most of the action of this novel in a military milieu that would be familiar to Israeli readers. As an American reading this book, I can barely distinguish among a sergeant and a colonel and a lieutenant because the army simply is not part of my lived experience. For Israelis, however, I imagine that the military descriptions and military jargon build an instant rapport. Indeed, the descriptions of army life and army personalities carry much of the book's humor.

Iczkovits shares other assumptions with his Israeli readership that make it natural for him to try to build a bridge between them and the world represented in his text through particular strategies. As we discussed earlier, it takes more than simply invoking an artifact to create salvage poetics. It takes a reframing and translation of that artifact for its new readership. Aside from its focus on military culture, one of the most striking ways that Iczkovits manages to tailor this novel to Israelis is by turning a critical eye on eastern European Jewry in the guise of an anti-Semite. Like the typical Israeli who was taught to demonize eastern European Jewry and Holocaust survivors as manifestations of the dangers of diaspora, the Polish and Russian non-Jewish characters with whom our protagonists come into contact on their journey regard them with suspicion and disdain. Just as Mer, by likening Israeli suspicion of the Neve Sha'anan neighborhood to the attitudes of non-Jewish Poles toward Smocze Street, positions Israelis vis-à-vis the streets of Jewish Warsaw as non-Jewish Poles fearing and hating the "other," so too does Iczkovits position Israelis in the position of the non-Jewish policemen and soldiers who view the little Jewish gaggle trekking across Ukraine highly critically. This positioning of the Israeli Jew as alienated from the eastern European Jew thus places him or her as an outsider or skeptical observer. This becomes especially pronounced in the novel in passages surrounding Novak, a police detective who tries to track down the "criminals" (Fanny and Zizek, Patrick Adamsky and Shleimel Cantor) on the road to Minsk. To try to apprehend them, he starts to spend time in Jewish communities and makes observations such as the one described here:

> As he wandered the busy market, Novak forced himself to stop and observe the *zyds* carefully. He eyed shabby carts piled with a disarray of kitchen utensils and work tools. He was puzzled by the queue at Levinsohn's—their famous pâtissier—and he made a note of the cattle-like etiquette as the line crammed together without complaint. He studied their gestures in conversation—an old lady yelling at a vendor selling vegetables who yelled back just as loudly, only for the pair to embrace and exchange kopecks and cucumbers the next moment. There was no space, just a human mass whose every member is compelled to quarrel and complain, as if every transaction must reach climactic dissonance before it can be resolved. Every word in their bizarre language sounds conspiratorial and sickening. Why can't they find a place of their own? Why do they insist on infiltrating a country that doesn't want them?[25]

This passage represents an interesting hybrid of classic Zionist thought and anti-Semitism. Fixating on the Jews' need for their own country while remarking that no one wants them, and observing that, for that matter, no one *should* want them, Novak channels the classic Israeli attitude toward eastern European Jews. They were deformed by their own genuflections to a culture that did not want them and where they were oppressed at every given turn. They were hateful as long as they were not in their own land.

Novak, it turns out, masquerades as a Jew, being taken in for an evening by a warm and welcoming Hasidic community. Like Eli in Philip Roth's 1959 story "Eli the Fanatic," Novak has a hard time giving up the appurtenances and outfit of the ultra-Orthodox Jew once he has finished infiltrating the community. Also, as in the classic 1913 Sholem Aleichem story "On Account of a Hat," the clothing makes the man and Novak, in effect, becomes a Jew when he dons Jewish garb. This is strongly evocative of one of the central mechanisms of salvage poetics wherein the mediator often goes to lengths to demonstrate that he or she is a member of the community he or she seeks to represent through framing of artifacts. As a "participant observer" the mediator can more easily justify his or her investment in bridging worlds. Here the figure of the non-Jewish policeman dressed as a Jew to infiltrate the world of the Jews resembles the efforts of *The Slaughterman's Daughter* to dress in the guise of a Yiddish novel of the classical modern period as a means of infiltrating that world and bringing it into Israeli consciousness. In an interview in the Israeli newspaper *Haaretz*, Iczkovits says he wrote this book because "the lie about the unequivocal suffering of Jews in diaspora for 2,000 years" hurts him "personally" and hurts his family "personally." It is as if to say, he goes on, "that his grandparents' entire history can be condensed into the story of six million deaths." He further remarks that "in Israel today there is absolutely no engagement with how the Jews used to live. There is a leap from the Bible to pogroms to the Holocaust to the establishment of the state."[26] This book is his remedy for that.

The Slaughterman's Daughter is one of many books written in Israel that grapple with the eastern European legacy of the state's founding generation. It stands out, however, because of its explicit attempt to bridge a twenty-first-century Israeli audience with the Yiddish literature of a century earlier, not by situating itself in contemporary Israel but by situating itself in the literature of S. Y. Agnon. Despite the novel's Mendelian flavor as it captures daily life on the Jewish street in Europe, its "Yiddish" is really Agnonian Hebrew here. Iczkovits goes back to Agnon, whose narrators are largely outsiders looking in, and not really to Mendele, whose narrators are fellow insiders, in his construction of this narrative.

The Yiddishland that Iczkovits constitutes in this novel is constructed from the building blocks of an all-encompassing Yiddish and the life it reveals, not sound bites. But its packaging is Hebrew because it can't be anything else, not for an Israeli audience. And that Hebrew is a hybrid of a bygone Hebrew, an Agnonian Hebrew, but also an eastern European Hebrew. Salvage poetics, by definition, present a hybrid of an artifact from the past and an audience in the present. In this instance, the artifact is the Mendelian novel. But the needs of the present are articulated in the choice of Agnon as the model for the classic Yiddish novel—a Hebrew eastern Europe, not a Yiddish one.

The commitment to salvage poetics as opposed to a postvernacular Yiddish, to a more comprehensive, in-depth understanding of eastern European Jewry than can be afforded by catch phrases and culinary delights, is evident in *The Slaughterman's Daughter* by virtue of its literary contours. What does it take to write, or to read, a full-length novel modeled after Mendele in style, Agnon in mechanics and language? It takes a desire to better understand, to ventriloquize, to question, to appreciate. It also takes a readiness to move beyond the superficial and to begin to create something evocative for a new generation deeply aware of its own responsibility for either furthering the extinction, or arresting the extinction, of a Yiddish world lost not only in the Holocaust but in the ideological machinery of Zionism as well.

2

"THINGS AS THEY WERE"

Ethnopoetics and Salvage Poetics

Moving now backward in time, although not entirely, we look at the works of two Israeli women writers who were born in eastern Europe and made their way to Palestine as adults, during the interwar period. Why do I say "not entirely"? Because just as Iczkovits, writing in 2015, hearkens stylistically back to the late nineteenth century with Mendele and the early twentieth century with Agnon, so too we begin this discussion with an allusion to the "fathers of Hebrew literature" as a jumping-off point. In "Thank God for His Daily Blessings," Amos Oz describes a walk through Geulah, the neighborhood in Jerusalem where he grew up among Labor Zionists but that has since evolved into an ultra-Orthodox enclave: "The Orthodox Eastern European Jewish world continues as though nothing had happened, but the fathers of modern Hebrew literature, Mendele and Berdyczewski, Bialik and Brenner and the others, would have banished this reality from the world around them and from within their souls. In an eruption of rebellion and loathing, they portrayed this world as a swamp, a heap of dead words and extinguished souls. They reviled it and at the same time immortalized it in their books."[1] Oz concludes by apostrophizing his reader: "However, you cannot afford to loathe this reality because between then and now it was choked and burned, exterminated by Hitler."[2] In this statement Oz eloquently articulates the notion that those seeking to understand a destroyed world will begin by looking to the literature of that world, written by its native sons and daughters, whether in a satiric or sincere light.

To continue our discussion of the subtle balance between literary and ethnographic impulses in post-Holocaust depictions of pre-Holocaust eastern European Jewish life, I will focus on two memoiristic works by two eastern European–born Israeli authors, both daughters of prestigious Hasidic rebbes: Malkah Shapiro (1894–1970) and Ita Kalish (1903–94). The term "ethnopoetics," which I draw on here and in my previous book to conceptualize salvage poetics, has been used in a number of ways in literary theory over the past century.[3] My sense of salvage poetics is conceived partly in keeping with the notion of ethnopoetry, as introduced in 1908 by author and ethnographer S. Ansky.[4] According to Ansky, ethnopoetry represents a synthesis of different levels of literary discourse: the popular and the elite, the historical and the contemporary, the secular and the sacred, taking on the valence of a new "Torah" for eastern European Jewish culture between the nineteenth and twentieth centuries.[5]

To arrest the inevitable losses entailed in the breakdown of traditional Jewish life during that period, Ansky called for the collection of folklore and its transformation into ethnopoetry by up-and-coming young Jewish artists who could redeploy it for posterity and through it could create inspiration, Jewish cultural fervor, and historical consciousness in generations to come. Thus, ethnopoetry in Ansky's view was fundamentally an act of cultural salvage. As David Roskies points out, however, before Ansky initiated his 1912–14 Jewish ethnographic expedition in eastern Europe, his primary source for folk artifacts was limited primarily to "Yiddish and Hasidic storybooks."[6] This dependence on literature for ethnographic materials by the father of modern Jewish ethnography himself anticipates the dependence for ethnographic materials on literary texts within modern Jewish culture.[7]

Just as Ansky calls on ethnographically trained literary authors to combine their skills and to inscribe traditional ethnographically valuable Jewish literary forms into modern literature, thus preserving them for posterity, the work of literary memoirists, in the cases to be analyzed here, is also viewed as a hybrid between the literary and the ethnographic. In Ansky's conception of ethnopoetry, writers used literary expression in service of ethnographic salvage; in the cases discussed below, writers' literary expressions were deployed as works of autoethnographic witness.[8] There is one major difference, however, between Ansky's notion of ethnopoetry and my sense of salvage poetics, as derived from post-Holocaust memoiristic works about pre-Holocaust eastern European life. Ansky's artists were consciously redeploying literary and other artistic artifacts in the formation of a modern style that was meant to preserve the old forms while rendering them palatable for a new generation and thus immortalizing them for posterity. Kalish and Shapiro, on the other hand, may have been conscious of the ethnographic value of their work because of the specific memoiristic quality of their writings and the fact that the worlds they were describing had, in the intervening years, been destroyed. But they were not necessarily invested, as an ethnographer-cum-artist would be, in preserving particular aesthetic forms for posterity. Rather, they self-consciously set out to describe a milieu to which they were intimate witnesses, and they employed poetics that sought to authenticate and legitimate their point of view, particularly as women within a male-dominated Hasidic milieu.

Through the lens of Shapiro's and Kalish's works, I examine the ethnographic aspirations of literary writers who are called on by history to modify or reconsider their own poetics. To what extent are these writers, who have stylized their texts with the literary trappings of ethnographic observation, responsible for the popular ethnographic reception of their work? In the last several decades, ethnography as a discipline has become conscious of and conversant with the literary aspects of its own generation of texts, and a reciprocal awareness within literary studies has developed to acknowledge the usefulness of ethnographic discourse in making sense of a literary-critical quest for broad cultural relevance.[9] In the late 1980s New Historicism, for example, drew from ethnographic terminology to lend credence to literary critics' own project of wedding the practice of close readings to historical and cultural breadth.[10] Thus, literary texts, with the help of ethnographic discourse, were deemed "artifacts" or "thick descriptions" of particular cultures.

Post-Holocaust literature focused on a pre-Holocaust Jewish eastern European milieu raises the question of whether ethnographic consciousness and literary style can be said to have formed a new kind of union. If we move beyond the usefulness of critical ethnographic discourse in the apprehension of literary relevance, as was accomplished in New Historicism, can we detect ethnographic impulses within literary texts that deal explicitly with loss, with memory, and with cultural salvage while still maintaining our focus on the literariness of the texts in question? I am suggesting here that a new style needs to be identified and analyzed in works such as those produced by Kalish and Shapiro, within an Israeli context, but also in American literary texts by Jonathan Safran Foer and Allen Hoffman, for example. What is the unique blend of ethnographic consciousness and literary artistry that populates these texts, and how can this style best be classified and understood?

Recognition of the fundamental literariness of the texts in question takes place, despite their ethnographic resonance and relevance, when these texts are analyzed in light of the literary traditions that inspired their production. Early twentieth-century Hebrew and Yiddish literary traditions that Kalish and Shapiro seem to have been emulating were overtly concerned with representing "things as they are" (*dvarim ke-hevyatam*).[11] This preference for realist mimeticism was a reaction during this period to the stylistics of pastiche (in Hebrew) and didacticism and satire (in Yiddish) that had dominated Jewish literary production during the Jewish Enlightenment of the previous century.

The notion that literature could be used not to teach the masses or to forge a new idiom but to reflect the world of the Jewish people in their daily existence was integral to the vernacularization and popularization of Jewish literary forms. In contrast to the commitment to realist mimeticism, which can be seen in Hebrew and Yiddish literary production during the late nineteenth and early twentieth centuries, what we view in the formation of a post-Holocaust salvage poetic idiom is an interest in representing things as they *were*, not things as they *are*. Producing and reading a text that purportedly represented things as they were was thus an act of cultural salvage that drew on the literary ideologies of a previous generation. It expanded those ideologies into a broader cultural engagement that did not preclude literariness and incorporated a sense of historical obligation.

The Hebrew and Yiddish literary salvage poetics that represent eastern European Jewry is the continuation of a legacy that began in Hebrew letters following not World War II but World War I. David Frischmann, as mentioned in the introduction, was among the first Hebrew critics to employ an ethnographic idiom in reference to literary representations of eastern European Jewish life.[12] Referring to the internal Jewish process of urbanization, assimilation, and emigration as well as to the shifting national boundaries and forced internal migrations that took place during and after World War I, Frischmann's "deluge" created ethnographic witnesses out of a generation of writers who had left that world behind, satirizing and critiquing it in their writing.

While both Oz and Frischmann read the literature written by male writers of the modern Hebrew renaissance ethnographically, I will examine here a phenomenon in Hebrew letters of the mid-twentieth century in which the writing of eastern European–born women in Hebrew was received, in Israel, as primarily of ethnographic, but not literary, value. In the cases of Mendele, Bialik, Berdyczewski, and Brenner, revered literary writers, their reception as "ethnographic" by literary critics, was motivated by the disappearance of the world they had depicted; the ethnographic reception of Hebrew literary works by eastern European–born women writers, I argue, is inspired by more than the destruction of a world. Indeed, classifying Hebrew writing by women as "ethnographic" has long been a way of discounting their artistry.

Responding to the same cataclysmic decline of the Orthodox eastern European world that inspired ethnographic misprisions of works in the Hebrew canon at the outset of the twentieth century, writers such as Malkah Shapiro and Ita Kalish wrote their texts in the mid-twentieth century in a moment in Israeli history when women's writing and the memory of the Holocaust were both relatively taboo; women were writing, and the Holocaust was discussed, but both were contained and controlled by an ethnographic rhetoric.[13] The depiction of eastern European locales in Israeli women's texts was associated in Israeli critical discourse in the 1960s with the perceived inability of women to write into the center of literary traditions. Rather, just as their subject matter is marginalized within critical discourse, so is their work categorized by those critics not within lines of literary influence and affiliation, but in a kind of social-historical (as in the case of regionalism) or ethnographic one (as here).[14]

In trying to understand how the rhetoric of ethnography came to be imposed on literary depictions of eastern European Jewish life by women writers of Hebrew, we find a fascinating text inspired by Frischmann in which the publication of Dvora Baron's 1939 "Trifles" is reviewed by S. Y. Pinless: "If one day the painful image presented by David Frischmann should come to pass, and a massive deluge should eradicate Eastern European Jewry, and our nation should want to preserve in a museum an artistic reproduction of that lost world, it won't be enough simply to include the works of Mendele alone. . . . Dvora Baron's trifles, the details that she depicts, are needed to complete the portrait."[15]

Indeed, the intersection of three distinct discourses is evident here: the discourse of realism within literary parlance, ethnography within broader cultural parlance, and gender within the world of modern Jewish letters. When Pinless mentions Dvora Baron's "trifles," he is referring to her collection of short stories by that same name (*Ketanot*) and also to the general notion of what constituted her poetics. For him, Baron's trifles, operating in tandem with Mendele's street life, would preserve a vanished world as if in a museum dedicated just to that purpose. He and others criticize her for writing about the inconsequential domestic aspects of daily existence, claiming that it served not as a work of art in its own right, but as a complement to the works of the male writers of her generation.[16]

At what point did appreciation for those trifles constitute a trivialization of the work of Baron and her natural literary inheritors in Israel several decades later? Eastern European–born women writers of Hebrew depicting eastern Europe were also understood to be providing a portrait of trifles that were necessary for the preservation of Jewish cultural memory after the cataclysmic destruction of European Jewry. But were they ever able to move beyond their trifles? To what extent did women writers see themselves as the natural conservators of the memory of life in eastern Europe, and how did that influence the nature and genre of the works they produced? What I hope will become clear in this exposition is the relationship between ethnographic expectations, production, and reception in literary works that depict a culture either in decline or dead. A symbiosis emerges between literature and ethnography in the Hebrew writings of eastern European–born women writers in the mid-twentieth century that is imposed from within and without—from within the writings themselves and from the community of their readership.

Malkah Shapiro and Ita Kalish wrote during the 1960s in Israel among a cohort of other female memoirists who spanned the 1940s and 1980s, including Shoshana Ushensky, Zelda Edelstein, Sheyna Korngold, Bilhah Dinur, Bella Fogelman, Rivka Guber, Zehava Berman, Malkah Heineman, and Tova Berlin Papish.[17] Shapiro and Kalish are the best known in part because their memoirs, or excerpts from them, have been translated into English. Translation narratives, indeed, are an important consideration in understanding the birth of an ethnographic discourse in the critical reception of Hebrew literary texts (and also Yiddish ones, as we will see) featuring pre-Holocaust life in eastern Europe. Most important, Shapiro and Kalish both develop a salvage poetic idiom that illuminates the particularly dynamic relationship between ethnographic obligations and literary aspirations. These salvage poetics, to a large degree, support ethnographic classification, but they also, if scrutinized closely, lay claim to the literary aspirations behind the ethnographic trappings—the artistic intentions undergirding the historical and cultural value of the texts at hand.

Shapiro's and Kalish's texts were identified primarily as witnesses to the inner workings and personalities of particular Hasidic courts near Warsaw (the court of the Kozienice Rebbe and that of the Otwock dynasty) and were translated as such. Moving from Hebrew (in Shapiro's case) to English, and from Yiddish to Hebrew and finally to English (in Kalish's case),

Ethnopoetics and Salvage Poetics 49

each of their memoirs has been framed, primarily through their translations, as ethnographically, although not particularly literarily, valuable. Translation, as used here, is not strictly a matter of rendering a text from one language to another. Rather, translation can be viewed as cultural or historical mediation. Although I focus here on how translations of Shapiro's and Kalish's memoirs into English overdetermined their ethnographic reception for an English-reading audience, it is important to keep in mind that literary criticism, such as that performed by Frischmann on Mendele or by Pinless on Baron, is also a form of translation. In their readings of these literary works featuring the shtetl, Frischmann and Pinless translated these works from literature into ethnography. I would call this dynamic process of translation from one genre to another and from one discipline to another "cross-disciplinary translation," and I would argue that minor voices (such as women's) within minor literatures (such as modern Hebrew or Yiddish) are particularly vulnerable to cross-disciplinary translation because of their palpable absence in cultural discourse.[18]

Malkah Shapiro was the fifth of seven children born to Brachah Twersky and her husband, Rabbi Yerahmiel Moshe Hapstein (1860–1909), the incumbent rebbe of Kozienice. From 1955 to 1971, she published five books of Hebrew poetry and prose in Israel, where she had settled in 1926.[19] Shapiro's 1969 publication, *Mi-din le-rahamim: Sipurim me-hatserot ha-'admorim* (*The Rebbe's Daughter*), was her most ambitious and generically most ambiguous book. *The Rebbe's Daughter* is presented by Nehemia Polen in his English introduction to the book as an astonishing insider's perspective on the Hasidic court of Kozienice, a community fifty miles southeast of Warsaw. It encompasses the eleventh and twelfth years of its young protagonist's life, as she prepares for her betrothal and marriage to her first cousin. In *The Rebbe's Daughter*, we observe the cycle of prayer, ritual observances, holiday preparations, and meditations that punctuate life in a small, wealthy Hasidic court at a watershed moment in eastern European Jewish history, on the eve of the Russian Revolution.

Polen argues, in a section of his introduction designated "Is *The Rebbe's Daughter* Autobiographical?" that the primary argument for reading the text as such is the startling change in voice during the last two chapters—from third person to first person. According to Polen, this indicates a breaking down of the fictional pretense and surrender to the autobiographical backbone of the story.[20] But the fact that Shapiro gestures belatedly to herself as the first-person narrator of a world long gone is hardly an indication that her work is exclusively autobiographical. On the contrary, this is a classic literary trope—one that is well documented in Dvora Baron's fiction but can also be found frequently in the works of Joseph Hayyim Brenner, M. J. Berdyczewski, Mendele Mocher Sforim, Sholem Aleichem, and countless other writers whose works Shapiro surely had read.

I am not arguing that there are no autobiographical elements to Shapiro's story. On the contrary, I heartily agree with Polen that *The Rebbe's Daughter* is a very valuable witness to the insular world of European Hasidism and the particular court of the Kozienice Rebbe from the perspective of what has been called elsewhere an "intimate outsider," or a young girl in a highly rarefied and highly gendered milieu. I argue, rather, for a new orientation toward the work of Malkah Shapiro, one that does not automatically situate her in the camp of Hasidic memoirs or ethnographic testimony but that instead places her in a trajectory of eastern European–born Israeli writers of Hebrew. The ethnographic elements of Shapiro's work, therefore, are to be understood in a salvage poetic frame that views her work as primarily aesthetic, framing ethnographic elements for popular consumption and positioning herself in the world that she seeks to represent as a sort of bridge between the old world and the new. While ethnographic valence has often been assigned to women's texts in Hebrew as a form of dismissal and diminution, in this case what we see is slightly different. Here Shapiro creates a work of art, or a novel, that frames the description of a culture for ready, popular access.

What formal aspects of *The Rebbe's Daughter* create a resemblance between Shapiro's work and the more canonic works of modern Hebrew literature, written by eastern European–born writers of Hebrew? Modern Hebrew and Yiddish literature produced in the late nineteenth and early twentieth centuries concerned itself with describing its own genesis in terms of explaining the relationship between its narrator and its characters, the narrator and the author, and the particular identity of the literary text (i.e., addressing whether the text is a diary, a found text, a travelogue, etc.). The best-known examples of this can be found in the figures of Mendele and Sholem Aleichem. Mendele's identity, as we know, changes throughout Sholem Yankev Abramovitsh's corpus, but in most cases, he is a book peddler whose itinerant lifestyle creates the occasion and justification for his encounter with Jews of all types throughout the Jewish Pale of Settlement. Mendele appears in Abramovitsh's corpus as a character, a narrator, an interlocutor, and a writer. He addresses his readers through sometimes lengthy introductory prefaces and simultaneously implicates himself within, and distances himself from, the world being represented through his elaborate attempts to document the genesis of the stories within which he is featured.

In a similar, though not quite as complex fashion, the figure of Sholem Aleichem is woven by Sholem Rabinovitch into his stories to contextualize the conversations and confrontations out of which his famous monologues evolve. In *Tevye der milkhiker*, for example, Sholem Aleichem provides an audience for Tevye to hold forth in monologic fashion about his children, life, culture, and beliefs. Sholem Aleichem himself has no voice in the stories and is simply apostrophized by Tevye as he speaks on and on. However, when the rhetorical device of Sholem Aleichem disappears in the stage and film adaptations of Tevye, his centrality to Rabinovitch's vision of the culture that he is representing becomes fairly obvious. Sholem Aleichem is, to Rabinovitch, the figure of the modern Jewish writer entering the swamp of the traditional Jewish shtetl, wielding his pen to give voice to the literarily voiceless. Tevye has no trouble speaking his mind; but without Sholem Aleichem, he would never have been immortalized in literature.

Of course, as has been amply discussed by Dan Miron, Benjamin Harshav, and Robert Alter, among others, the framing devices presented by Abramovitsh and Rabinovitch in the figures of Mendele Mocher Sforim and Sholem Aleichem help to create a "skaz" effect, an effect of conversational encounters with real folk in live environments.[21] The literary work framed by bathetic literary figures performing monologues or as the speaking protagonist himself, all contribute to a poetics described by Hebrew critics such as Menachem Brinker as one of *kenut* (sincerity or authenticity).[22] The concept of *kenut* is at the foundation of the modern Hebrew renaissance, which attempted to vernacularize the Hebrew language to turn it into a means of representing life as it is in the present, not as it was in the ancient past. For our purposes, this stylistic choice reflects the seeds of an ethnographic reception, insofar as the effect that these authors create is exactly commensurate with the effect sought out by those who were trying to reconstruct a lost way of life. For Abramovitsh and Rabinovitch, this framing effect was a way to yoke literary expression with vernacular voices; for critics such as Frischmann, this was an opportunity to read rhetorical effect as cultural artifact, with the homodiegetic narrator's vernacular voice serving as a transcript of Jewish speech on the streets of the shtetl. In the work of Y. H. Brenner we find a later variation on a rhetoric of sincerity, in the form of stream-of-consciousness narratives, some framed, some not, as the anxious ramblings of disturbed individuals.[23] I would argue that the primary reason for this rhetorical framing device is the desire to express the tension experienced when the enlightened author and the unenlightened literary subject confront each other on the pages of a literary text. Concern over the appearance of a shtetl within the literary corpus of an enlightened writer may have motivated the framing devices described above.

In the case of Malkah Shapiro's narrative, we find constant, complex negotiations of the position of the narrator within the narrative, as eyewitness and as author without the folksiness, humor, and persona in Mendele's works. The gap between the world being depicted and the world inhabited by the author in the present moment, far off in the future of the text at hand, in Israel, is also palpably felt through certain narrative choices made by Shapiro. Shapiro's poetics squarely situate her alongside the great writers of the modern Jewish literary tradition—if not in quality, at least in literary affiliation. Furthermore, her awkward position as a self-appointed ethnographer and, at the same time, a creative writer places her work at a crossroads in post-Holocaust modern Jewish literary consciousness. As a Hasidic woman writer, one could argue, Shapiro is well entrenched in the world that she writes of. But the Holocaust creates the same effect that World War I created in the reception of Mendele's work. Shapiro writes across a geographic distance, a temporal gap, and a cataclysmic history that forces a constant reevaluation, in her own mind and work, of the generic identity of her writing. She is both of the world she writes about, and not of that world. She positions her protagonist (and later, narrator), Bat-Zion, as both an insider and an outsider to the literary world being presented.

Keep in mind that Shapiro's text is a look into a Hasidic court from the point of view of a young girl. While Shapiro certainly spends time depicting the women's world of the Hasidic court, she also finds ways to see into the darkest recesses of the rebbe's *tisch* and the room where her brothers study Talmud—both of which are generally closed to girls.[24] Shapiro's frequent articulations of the protagonist's location within, or unusual access to the scenes depicted resonate within the tradition of "authenticity" in Hebrew and Yiddish texts. At the same time, the ability of a young female protagonist in a gender-stratified milieu to access a world to which she would not normally be permitted reflects an ethnographic sensibility. Why else would it be so important for her to demonstrate the authenticity of her narrative? Even so, the elaborate justifications of Bat-Zion's unprecedented access to the world of her brothers and her father reveal a sense that she feels that she needs to prove the authenticity of her perspective because what she is representing has to be "true." This quest for "authenticity" gestures toward ethnographic aspiration insofar as she appears to be communicating a sense of her commitment to accurate cultural description. Gender, in effect, serves as the crucible for the meeting of different systems of meaning here—the ethnographic and the "authentic" in a literary sense—and a salvage poetic idiom, a hybrid between literary form and ethnographic aspirations, results.

In considering the conventional modern Hebrew literary rhetoric of sincerity alongside salvage poetics in the work of Shapiro, the question arises as to whether the classic eastern European–born male writers of modern Hebrew and Yiddish literature themselves employed a salvage poetic idiom. It was, perhaps, that very idiom that lent itself to ethnographically overdetermined critical readings by Frischmann and Pinless. However, the rhetoric of authenticity employed by Sholem Aleichem, Mendele, and Brenner does not reveal their ethnopoetic aspirations—that synthesis of different levels of literary discourse described by Ansky—as much as their placement at the heart of a transitional point in modern Hebrew and Yiddish literary expression. Their struggle to frame their narratives and to inject into them a voice and an aura of credibility and authenticity has more to do with the challenges that they faced as realists in a nonvernacular language (Hebrew) and of stylists in what was considered a wholly vernacular language (Yiddish) than with the burden of history and gender, as is palpable in Shapiro's work. Whereas Shapiro struggles with what I would call "ethnographic exigency," demonstrating that what she is presenting is a description of a real culture, Mendele Mocher Sforim, Sholem Aleichem, and Brenner struggle more with "generic exigency" in that they must be careful to maintain a certain folksy, vernacular style to emphasize their work's linguistic authenticity.

Shapiro, on the other hand, as the daughter of a Hasidic scion in post-Holocaust Israel, is probably not concerned with the linguistic or generic identity of her text as much as she is concerned with the place of her text within the historical abyss between the world that she depicts and the world in which she writes. Because she is a woman, her access to the worlds that she feels compelled to memorialize is tenuous. She must find some kind of middle ground, and that middle ground is a literary one, in her rhetoric of authenticity, which expresses itself as a form of ethnography. The result is a salvage poetic literary idiom.

The motif of slipping into inner sanctums, of folding oneself into drapes, of falling asleep on chairs in the corners of rooms and witnessing conversations and interactions that were generally closed off to children, especially girls, is reiterated throughout the book and serves as a sign of the text's salvage poetics. In quoting her grandmother's account of having heard an important conversation as a child, we hear, in her grandmother's words:

> I was a little girl then, just five years old. I was standing in the corridor at the entrance to the wooden shed, which was lit with oil lamps. As I listened to the story, I watched Bereleh, a shriveled fellow who was sitting next to the narrator, his head resting on his knees as if he were fast asleep, not hearing a word. Just then, a door to one of the inner rooms opened in the corridor, and my holy grandfather appeared at the threshold and called out, "Bereleh." The members of the group rose hastily, respectfully moving toward the open door, stretching out their hands to greet my holy grandfather. But only Bereleh was ushered inside. I slipped in along with this fellow. . . . That simple room, with its lone armchair, its canopy bed, and its many books, its mysteries attracted me. I saw the souls of our holy ancestors hiding in that room. I hid myself behind the armchair and, trembling, listened in on the conversation. Trying not to attract attention, I didn't move from that spot, even though the tone of my grandfather's hushed voice, his face shining like an angel of God, struck terror in me.[25]

The elaborate way in which the old rebbetzin feels the need to justify having witnessed an important conversation between a rebbe and his disciple when she was just a five-year-old girl plays itself out in myriad ways throughout Shapiro's text. There is a constant jockeying for authenticity here, alongside recognition of the marginalization of girls in the culture she is documenting and witnessing. This story, from the grandmother's mouth, is witnessed by Bat-Zion herself as she hides in her mother's room: "Bat-Zion had followed the conversation with intense anxiety as she sat behind the curtain in her mother's darkened bedroom. . . . She went out the back door without anyone noticing and ran around for a long time in the dark courtyard without a coat, until her teeth chattered from the cold of the night."[26]

Like the figures of Mendele and Sholem Aleichem who present themselves as the literary vehicles for the shtetls of Kasrilevke, Boiberik, and Anatevka, so too, perhaps, does Bat-Zion take on the role of literary bridge between the world of her father's court and the world of modern Hebrew literature. Her position here as a creative writer, betraying neither world in the process of writing about it, is quite a departure from the generally ambivalent sentiments expressed in the figures of Mendele and Sholem Aleichem vis-à-vis the worlds that they represent. The ambivalence expressed here takes on a different form: the ambivalence of a female outsider to patriarchal culture being designated as the inside informant of that culture in the aftermath of the Holocaust.

Shapiro's struggle to define her position as a literary artist bridging the Hasidic world and the secular world of modern Jewish letters can be seen in a fascinating moment in the eighth chapter of *The Rebbe's Daughter*. Here Shapiro's protagonist, Bat-Zion, to perfect her handwriting, is asked by her tutor to copy, by hand, an essay on Maimonides from the modern Hebrew journal *Hame'asef*. The essay that she copies, by a scholar named Slonimsky, deals with Maimonides's formula for the intercalation of years that is necessary to fix the dates of Rosh Hodesh, or the new moon (because the Jewish calendar is lunar and not solar). The depiction of Bat-Zion's process of transcription is described:

> Enchanted figures overwhelmed Bat-Zion's imagination. She saw the crescent moon in conjunction, there by the pond in the pine forest or there, far away in Eretz Israel between the mountains where the Sanhedrin sat. She wrote diligently until she encountered numbers and calculations, which she despised. She began to feel dizzy; and as much as she attempted to be careful about her penmanship, the letters did not come out rounded as always. And, in particular, when she reached Slonimsky's commentary, she nearly twisted the words around.
>
> As Aharon the *melamed* began examining the manuscript, a dark cloud seemed to sweep over his bluish face. He pulled impatiently on his scraggly beard, speaking in bitterness, as if to himself, "This is not what I expected! I had a different opinion of you! You can't say this is bad handwriting, but when writing is of the greatest importance, you should have been more careful. You ought to understand, my pupil, that these are the words of the Great Eagle, Maimonides; and the contemporary scholar Slonimsky is also not an ignoramus. Even though he is one of the maskilim, he should not be dismissed with a stroke of the hand."
>
> Rebbetzin Leahnu approached Bat-Zion, who stood before the *melamed* like an accused in the dock, tears gathering in her eyes. Her aunt gave her cheek, already red, a light pinch. Wanting to let her off the hook, she said, in a consoling tone: "There is absolutely nothing to be ashamed of, sweetheart. The handwriting is absolutely fine."
>
> "You're right, sister," responded Rebbetzin Feigenu as she peered at the tablet. "The writing isn't bad at all. It's not as precise as Bat-Zion's hand when she wove my name and the name of my husband—your

honored uncle, long may he live—into verses accompanying her Purim gift, but this is nice, too."[27]

The dilemma of Bat-Zion's artistry, her role in this narrative as a creative force, or merely as a cipher, is laid out here. Interestingly, the text she is asked to copy out by her *melamed* is the work of a maskil, and his scholarship, in turn, focuses on Maimonides, the greatest rationalist in Jewish history. Bat-Zion, the daughter of a Hasidic rebbe, ensconced in a household with clearly delineated nonrationalistic beliefs and practices, appears to be at a particular crossroads in this passage. She negotiates here between the expectation that she transcribe a tradition that is rather alien to her own and the internal need to create her own texts. In this case the creative texts that are alluded to are poems attached to the gift of *mishloah manot* that are distributed to the rebbe's family and friends on Purim. But in a more general sense, the presentation of this conflict with her *melamed* communicates an intellectual struggle with authorship similar to the conventional literary struggles that we have come to expect in the canon of modern Hebrew literature.

Bat-Zion, it seems, is content to find her creative outlet within the closed world of her tradition and her father's household, even though it is within that household that she is introduced to Jewish Enlightenment models. In fact, in her limited critical reception, Shapiro is described as *'admorit ha-soferet* (the female Hasidic rebbe writer) and *meshoreret he-hasidut* (the Hasidic poet).[28] Because Shapiro's creative impulse is deployed within the closed world of a Hasidic milieu, it is tempting to identify her work wholly ethnographically, particularly given the dearth of historical resources on Hasidic women. It is important to recognize, in Shapiro's work, however, a creative literary penchant, evident in the concerns, discussed above, over framing and mediation, not to be downplayed for strictly ethnographic purposes but to be understood within a modern Hebrew salvage poetic tradition.

We will turn now to a second text by an Israeli woman writer, Ita Kalish, who, like Shapiro, was born into an important Hasidic court in eastern Europe and published her memoirs. In a footnote to an essay he wrote about Shapiro's text, Polen refers to a translated excerpt of Ita Kalish's Yiddish memoir, which came out in 1965, in the thirteenth volume of the *YIVO Annual of Jewish Social Science*.[29] Titled "Life in a Hasidic Court in Russian Poland toward the End of the 19th and the Early 20th Centuries," this "translation" of Kalish's Yiddish *A rebishe heim in amolikn Poyln* is a gleaning of what were apparently deemed ethnographically relevant details of the

Hasidic milieu depicted in Kalish's memoir (the expanded Hebrew version is titled *'Etmoli* [My yesterday]).[30] The lineage of her Hasidic forebears, the idiosyncratic behavior of her rebbe grandfather before his immigration to the Land of Israel, and the personalities and life tragedies of some of her closest relatives within the confines of the Hasidic court culminate in Kalish's final lament about the destruction of this world during World War II: "The site of grandfather's villa and its large synagogue, which stood for nearly eighty years in Otwock, is now a field cultivated by a Polish peasant. O earth, cover not thou their blood!"[31] This moment in the text is one of the clearest indications of the salvage poetic intentions that govern it—the sense of ethnographic obligation as the result of historical exigency. At the same time, *'Etmoli* is a cleverly drawn, broad-ranging apostasy narrative—beginning in the world of a young girl in a Hasidic enclave and encompassing forbidden reading, the abandonment of a marriage, and the kidnapping of a child.[32] Kalish, in this memoir, introduces us to important figures in twentieth-century Hebrew and Yiddish letters, including Dovid Bergelson, David Fogel, and Yehiel Yishayahu Trunk, and, in so doing, expresses a desire to number among them.

Ita Kalish, born into the Otwock dynasty in Maciejowice, Poland, wrote her memoirs about growing up within her Hasidic enclave and then breaking from it in 1919, after her marriage, the birth of a daughter, and her father's death. Moving from Warsaw to Berlin to Paris, and finally to Palestine in 1933, Kalish worked first for the Jewish Agency and then for the newly formed Israeli civil service from 1948 until her retirement in 1967. Alluded to in several recent historical publications on women in eastern Europe, Kalish's memoir, in both its Hebrew and its Yiddish versions, has mostly been considered a valuable historical and ethnographic voice about women's education within traditional Hasidism in the early part of the twentieth century.[33] The memoir, lyrically and economically written, is also a reflection on Kalish's apostasy—her break from the ways of her family and her exploration of Jewish women's options in Europe and Palestine just before World War II and in the early years of Israel.

The very title of Kalish's Hebrew book, *'Etmoli*, distinguishes it from the generic, ethnographic way in which its English title, different from both the Hebrew and the Yiddish published titles, presents it: "Life in a Hasidic Court in Russian Poland . . ." The artfulness of Kalish's book, however, is best illustrated by the way in which it transitions from the Hasidic world to the secular world of Warsaw between the two world wars. In her depiction of her own marriage and her subsequent departure for broader, more secular, climes, Kalish deliberately plays with the identification of the subject of the text:

> World War I and its terrors disrupted our way of life. The marriage of the oldest daughter of the rabbi of Otwock was delayed. Occupied Poland became German and Austrian territory, and movement from one district to another required a special license from the occupiers. The process of obtaining one was arduous and exhausting. My brother strongly believed that his oldest sister's wedding should take place as planned, and wanted to bring the bride herself before the military court to obtain a travel license for the groom and his parents. When Father heard of this plan, he stood to his fullest height and cried: "God forbid you should bring my daughter before the court of the German occupiers!" And in the end, not too long after that, Father succeeded, despite the bureaucracy caused by the military occupation, in overcoming the obstacles, and his first daughter's wedding was celebrated in Warsaw, in the sumptuous wedding hall on what used to be Moranovsky Street.
>
> Thousands of invited and uninvited guests came to witness the rabbi of Otwock's celebration, and the hall was too small. Because of all the pushing and shoving, the sequins and seed pearls on the bride's wedding dress scattered all over the floor. The food and drink remained in the storage closets because it was impossible to push through the crowds to get to them. When the headwaiter was finally able to make his way through the crowd, waving a silver tray above the guests' heads with "golden soup" for the bride and groom who had fasted the whole day, excited cries were suddenly heard: *The rebbe is coming! The rebbe is coming!* The young groom jumped out of his place, ran outside, and was pulled away in a tide of Gerer Hasidim, who threw over tables, burst through barriers, jumped from balconies, and ran to greet their rebbe.
>
> As a keepsake of the two long braids that hung to my knees and that were cut off the day after the huppah, I have a photograph taken by Alter Kacyzne, the Yiddish author and playwright from Warsaw. Kacyzne was a photographic artist who made a living in photography, into which he poured all his artistic ability. He was a simple man, prone to fantasy. When he was asked to name a price for his work, he would remove his spectacles, shrug his broad shoulders, turn his dark, well-cultivated head of hair toward his wife, murmur, "Those are Hannah's affairs," and sneak out of the room. We, his friends, saw this as a sign of overindulgence, but we didn't hold it against him.

Alter Kaczyne and his wife, Hannah, were killed by Nazi murderers during the Holocaust. Their only daughter lives in Italy and perpetuates the memory of her father by publishing his works in Israel.

Father had high hopes for his young, faithful son-in-law because he thought the young, pure man would know how to quiet his daughter's longing to sneak out of the reality surrounding her and to forge a different way of life. But his hopes were quickly dashed. It hadn't occurred to my father that his daughter had already broken out of the narrow confines of her father's house; Father had not surmised that his daughter was learning foreign languages and reading "apocryphal" books as she put her young daughter, born about that time, down to sleep. The day finally came when his last vestiges of hope disappeared: he came to visit me in the apartment that was a satellite of his own at 14 Dzelna Street—and he saw before his very eyes, to his great shock, a stack of books in Yiddish and Polish. He was affronted and offended to his very core. He ordered them burned.[34]

Although the winds of secularization have been obliquely alluded to throughout the memoir to this point, they have not been presented as being of particular personal importance to the first-person narrator—Kalish herself. Here, calling herself "the rebbe's oldest daughter" in the generic third person, Kalish brings to mind Mary Antin's singular digression from a first-person to an omniscient third-person voice in her 1912 autobiographical novel, *The Promised Land*. Antin makes the switch to third person to share her childhood rupture with Jewish tradition—by deliberately carrying a handkerchief over the threshold of her home into the public domain to see if there are any consequences to breaking the Sabbath. Dropping her first-person "I" to narrate the scene, Antin presents herself as an unnamed "young, pious child," even as she depicts her intellectual transformation into a nonbeliever.[35] In a similar fashion, Kalish obscures our vision of the young bride in the narrative as the same figure who has been narrating the story. In her details about the bride's dress being torn apart and the young groom upending tables in his haste, along with his compatriots, to see the Gerer Rebbe, she creates a nightmarish scene. But strangely, she distances herself from it, rendering it in a completely objective, omniscient manner, without any emotional valence.

Only when Kalish turns to Kacyzne, best known for the photographs of Polish Jewish life in the interwar period that he took for the Hebrew Immigrant Aid Society and the *Forverts*, does she resume her first-person narration. She says that her braids, cut off the day after the wedding, were memorialized by Kacyzne in a photograph he took of her from that time.

Her reference to his snapshot functions as an irrefutable record of the continuity between the oldest daughter of the Otwock Rebbe and the young woman who abandoned her husband, her daughter, and her father's court to become a salon hostess to the itinerant literati of the post-Hasidic crowd in Warsaw. Perhaps the photograph's narrative position as the first acknowledgment of Kalish's return to the first person marks her irreversible break from the world that she left behind. Her voice is insufficient to capture it; it must be done with a realist artifact, which can be brought out, if need be, to prove the existence of that girl with the long hair but can also be stowed away from the curious eye. This assertion of the ethnographic artifact, the photograph, alongside its immediate sublimation by the return to the first-person narrative voice encapsulates the tension between ethnographic and literary aspirations evident in this and other women's narratives about prewar eastern European Jewish life in Hebrew.

It is, to my mind, not coincidental that the shift back to the first person occurs not only in the course of a discussion about a photograph but also about a photographer killed in the Holocaust. In reflecting on Kacyzne's character, Kalish is naturally led to refer to his murder on July 7, 1941, outside the Polish city of Tarnopol in a massacre perpetrated by a mobile killing unit. The death of the photographer Kacyzne in the Holocaust appears to be essential to the process of the text's very transformation from an omniscient third-person account of a wedding to a first-person account of apostasy and betrayal. The photograph outlives its artist, which perhaps posits a new kind of art—a salvage poetic art—built on the back of the war that made ethnographers of so many artists and that created the impulse to document where before the impulse may have been strictly to create. It is as if, along with Kacyzne, the "indulged" artist who left price negotiations up to his wife and his clients, the practice of art for art's sake died in a massacre during World War II. Hence the punctuation of Kalish's text with moments such as this one, documenting Kacyzne's life and death, changes the nature of the text, turning the third person into the first person and emphasizing the intimate, personal dimension of the genesis of this text.[36]

The artfulness with which Kalish transforms her narrative from being about her upbringing within a Hasidic enclave to being about her rebellion against that enclave distinguishes her book not simply as an autoethnographic portrait from an insider's perspective but renders it classifiable within other narratives of apostasy and rebellion in the modern Jewish

Ethnopoetics and Salvage Poetics 61

RACHEL KALISH, daughter of a Polish Rabbi, eloped with her lover to Palestine. (B. Katz, Warsaw)

רחל קאַליש, די טאָכטער פֿון אטוואָצקער רב.
איז אנטלאָפֿען מיט איהר געליעבטען
קיין פּאַלעסטינא.

From the *Jewish Daily Forward*, June 10, 1923. Original caption read "Rokhl Kalish, the daughter of the Otwock Rabbi, who eloped to Palestine with her lover." The photograph of the girl with the long, luxurious hair matches Ita's description of her own photograph taken by Kacyzne on the eve of her wedding. It seems likely that the original caption was incorrect and should have referred to "Ita" and not "Rokhl." From the Archives of the YIVO Institute for Jewish Research, New York.

literary tradition. As Alan Mintz has discussed, the literature of the modern Hebrew renaissance grew out of an autobiographical tradition in which the story of individual spiritual and intellectual rupture from the sphere of traditional Judaism came to be understood over time as the story of a generation.[37] As such, autobiography evolved into fiction, and the concrete individual came to be understood as the concrete universal. As part of this evolution, the Hebrew literature of the late nineteenth and early twentieth centuries included a transitional figure from the personal to the collective, from the autobiographical to the fictional, called the *talush*. Derived from the Hebrew root *t-l-sh*, meaning to be "uprooted," the *talush* fits neither into traditional Jewish culture nor into secular European culture. His gender exclusivity as a male figure of Jewish modernity has posed an important obstacle to allowing women's Hebrew and Yiddish memoirs, like men's, to take the leap into the realm, if not of fiction, then of belles lettres. In other words, why has Ita Kalish's *'Etmoli* been preserved as an important ethnographic essay and nothing more, while Brenner's *Ba-ḥoref* (*In Winter*), to name just one text from that period, has been preserved as a novel?

The process of translating Hebrew male autobiographical voices into fictional tropes that took place in eastern Europe during this period should also have taken place in the mid-twentieth century in Palestine for eastern European–born women. The sheer number of women's memoirs being written about the eastern European worlds left behind earlier in the century marks not only a zeitgeist but the birth of a literary trend. When looking closely at works such as Shapiro's *Mi-din le-raḥamim* and Kalish's *'Etmoli*, their literary aspirations and literary value becomes apparent. Their translations into English have, interestingly, overemphasized their ethnographic identity, undermining their literary one, and failed altogether to recognize the salvage poetics that brought the two elements together.

Shapiro and Kalish trailblazed the possibility of representing eastern European Jewish life from an Israeli vantage point. Looking back at their lives in eastern Europe, they strove to communicate, in literary form, cultures and personalities that occupied a place in modern Jewish history, but from an unusual, marginal perspective—that of young girls and young women. This perspective may indeed have provided them with the justification for writing about eastern Europe at all once they had settled in Israel. In her study of Hebrew women writers during the period of the Jewish enlightenment, Iris Parush coined the term "the advantages of marginality" to describe the way in which eastern European Jewish women who were not proficient in traditional Jewish texts or liturgy often mastered Hebrew more quickly than did their male counterparts who had received a traditional Jewish education.[38] Those men who wrote in Hebrew during the enlightenment, Parush argues, were hampered by the archaisms they had learned in their formal school environment while women, who were often learning Hebrew for the first time from tutors committed to the modernization of the language, were able to learn and write in it more easily. While the number of women in this position was miniscule, nevertheless there was, in Parush's words, an "advantage to marginality" that served the modernization of the Hebrew language well.[39] In a similar vein, we observe in the case of Shapiro and Kalish that as eastern European–born women living in Israel, they were able to write about their place of origin even if it seemed to work against the dominant ideology of Hebrew letters at the time, an ideology that stipulated that those writing in Israel should be writing about life in Israel. While Shapiro's and Kalish's writings were received in an ethnographic vein because they were writing about eastern Europe in Israel and because they were women, it is important to consider to what extent this may have laid the groundwork for further writings about eastern Europe in Israel. As we continue our discussion of Israeli salvage poetics, we will attend to the "advantages of marginality" in empowering certain Israelis, or Israelis at certain stages of their careers, to write about eastern Europe. Rivka Guber, of the same generation as Kalish and Shapiro, is one such author. In the next chapter we consider the advantages that she was able to maximize, as a maternal hero of the early state, to speak on behalf of the marginal and the disadvantaged, many of whom were survivors of the Holocaust.

3

"THE RAVAGES OF MY HAPPINESS"

A Mother of Sons Salvages What Remains

Like Malkah Shapiro and Ita Kalish, Rivka Guber (1902–81) was born in eastern Europe and immigrated to Palestine during the period between the two world wars. She was not, however, the daughter of a Hasidic dynasty, raised to a life of religious and spiritual aspiration. Rather, she was the daughter of farmers, and this became her unique link to the ideals of Zionism in the years leading up to the establishment of the state and beyond. Because Rivka Guber was an Israeli national heroine, dubbed "the Mother of Sons" by David Ben-Gurion after losing both of her sons, Ephraim (1927–48) and Tzvi (1931–48), in the War of Independence, most accounts of her life are heavily weighted toward her time in Palestine and Israel. But there are other versions of Guber's life that also deserve telling: her literary legacy and the salvage poetics she established as a shrine to the memory of her eastern European past and that of Holocaust survivors among whom she lived during her final years. This chapter explores Guber's literary legacy and how her identity as an icon of bereaved motherhood after the loss of her sons morphed into a national role that served as a vehicle for her to voice and support those eastern European elements of Israeli society that were vilified, repressed, and silenced in the years just after its establishment. The story that Guber tells throughout her writings, one that bears witness to the possibility of a kinder, gentler approach to Jewish memory of the diaspora than what was afforded most Israeli icons and national figures in the state's early years, is one I share now. This version of her life story serves as the basis for understanding the layered and nuanced approach to Israeli salvage poetics that Guber presents in her writings.

In her fourth book, *'Eleh toldot kfar 'aḥim* or *Village of the Brothers* (1974), Guber compiled and edited the memoirs of Holocaust survivors living in a village of the same name that she and her husband, Mordecai, helped establish in 1949 and which was named after Ephraim and Tzvi. In a preface to this book, Yitzhak Navon, then president of Israel, depicts what Guber represented in Israel both politically and personally and what the expectations were for parents bereaved in Israel's wars and for Holocaust survivors in the state's early years:

> It is altogether fitting that this record of sorrow and rebirth should be the work of Rivka Guber. In her own life she has bravely overcome the sorrow of bereavement, her two sons having fallen in Israel's War of Independence. She has sublimated that pain and mothered countless newcomers to the State, making it possible for them to be reborn as productive and adjusted citizens. Kfar Achim is the first village set up in the south after the establishment of the State. Appropriately named for the two sons of Rivka and Mordecai Guber, it has given new life to *olim* from Hungary and Czechoslovakia who had survived the horrors of the Holocaust. Their personal stories, here recounted, bring the incredible anguish of the Holocaust directly to us. But they also bring us the sequel which only Rivka Guber can convey to us—the rebirth in the land, symbolic of Israel's total role as the State that rose to heal the wounds of the catastrophe and reknit the life and history of the Jewish people.[1]

The explicit praise that Navon showers on Guber for sublimating her grief as a mother who lost two sons in the War of Independence is echoed by his call for Holocaust survivors to sublimate their pasts to build a better national future. Most important is how he ends his statement, by adjuring Holocaust survivors not only to sublimate the trauma of their war experiences but also to "reknit" their history, to reinvent it, forgetting their pasts.

Here we will consider the ways in which Rivka Guber defies Navon, even as she serves as a symbol of Zionist ideology; in reality, rather than sublimating the past, she holds it up as a model for the present, insisting on the continuity between the two. One way she communicates this continuity is in her representation of the Holocaust by transmitting stories told by members of Kfar 'Ahim. Because she is who she is, she gets away with doing that very thing the president says should not be done: holding on to the past while communicating its memory and values. Indeed, he goes ahead and praises her for her work communicating the stories of Holocaust survivors even as he articulates the necessity to do the opposite. Guber serves as the voice of conscience, the living proof in the early years of the state that one can believe strongly in the promise of Zionism without demonizing the past or eastern Europe. As such, she embraces her history as a Russian immigrant, extolling her education in Russia, the village she grew up in, and the Jewish values she acquired there, rather than abdicating them or demonizing them.

As we continue to explore the shape of salvage poetics in Israel, we will consider both aspects of Rivka Guber's legacy: the one overdetermined by the national ideology of her time and place and the one reflective of her own particular circumstances and strength of character. Because she played the part of the bereaved mother so well, becoming the Mother of Sons, she was able to embrace her memories and her pride in eastern Europe as she expressed her compassion for Holocaust survivors, in a way that most other national icons within the culture of early Israel were not able to do. For Guber, the idea of salvage emerges from her bereavement and the word even appears in the language she uses in the period immediately following her sons' deaths: "I walked amidst the ravages of my happiness and sought that which could be salvaged from the ruins."[2] So what is she salvaging first and foremost? Officially, it is the possibility of a life lived meaningfully even after the loss of what was most precious to her, in the cause of building the nation. Embracing her sons' deaths, "sublimating" her grief, in Navon's terms, makes her the "ideal" mother by Israeli standards in the 1950s. But she takes her grief a step further, embracing her own eastern European past alongside Holocaust survivors as part of her process of bereavement. By early Israeli standards, sacrificing your sons is good, while reclaiming eastern Europe for yourself and for Holocaust survivors is not so good. Guber, however, brings the three together to represent the possibility of Israeli identity as one of continuity with the recent past, not one of rupture from it. Perhaps it was the loss of her sons that made Guber simultaneously an Israeli "loyalist" and a purveyor of salvage poetics, which, especially at this time in Israeli history, were not yet deemed a legitimate form of engaging with the recent eastern European past of so many of the state's founders and inhabitants. Once she acknowledges and embraces the tragic loss of her sons, Guber is able to talk about her own lost background, as well as the lost worlds of all those who survived the Holocaust. The nationalized personal rhetoric of loss that rewards the bereaved parents of Israel at that time becomes a useful way for her also to acknowledge the loss of her family and community of origin.

The book that grew out of Guber's bereavement and set her on the path of becoming an icon of Israeli motherhood was *Sefer ha-'ahim* (*The Book of the Brothers*, 1950). Famously, when Prime Minister Ben-Gurion read this book, which compiled the writings and correspondence of her recently deceased sons, he named her "'Em ha-Banim," or the Mother of Sons; he praised her fortitude as a Jewish mother in the modern State of Israel who had made, willingly and proudly, the ultimate sacrifice. In a letter to her, he wrote:

> From the moment I read your words in *The Book of the Brothers*, I knew that a great mother had arisen in Israel, a mother who hasn't existed for hundreds of years and whose words are memorialized in the eternal writings of human glory. Our generation doesn't entirely recognize you yet, but I can guarantee that in the coming generations the light of your motherly strength and your great and eternal words will shine out for all of the children of Israel, and maybe even not just for them. If there are mothers like you in Israel, we can meet our future with confidence.[3]

Here Ben-Gurion employs his usual grandiose rhetoric to praise Guber at the expense of all the mothers who preceded her; the magnitude of her heroism as a mother, according to him, can only be understood within the context of what mothers in the preceding centuries had lacked. He never quite says what that is, but in light of the book he just read and to which he is responding, what those mothers lack that Guber has in abundance appears to be the spirit of sacrifice that is necessary for the new nation. According to Ben-Gurion, she is willing to sacrifice her sons to the cause, it seems. Ben-Gurion's enthusiastic praise in the immediate aftermath of her sons' deaths, and his continuing recognition of her strength as a mother by virtue of her work for the nation despite her grief, served as the catalyst for not only her fame but also for the creation of a self-sacrificing mythology of Israeli motherhood within the culture of the newborn state.

But implied in Ben-Gurion's unqualified aggrandizement of Rivka Guber as the Mother of Sons is that Jewish mothers from other times and other places did not have the kind of fortitude or character that Guber demonstrates in her response to her sons' deaths. As we continue our exploration of Israeli salvage poetics, we must ask ourselves to what extent Guber

Rivka Guber (1902–81), Israeli stamp 1992.

concurred with his claim that she had emerged from generations of women incapable of making the kind of sacrifice she made. Where, indeed, did Guber come from and how did she represent that world in her writings?

Guber never attempts to "reinvent" herself, obscuring the person she once was. Even so, she is rendered symbolic within a nationalist culture and struggles to reclaim her particularity and her material existence in the face of that symbolic rendering. Guber owns her past as a part of her present despite strong externally imposed national incentives to divorce herself from it. Similarly, the trauma of her bereavement is largely hidden from the public eye in the public accolades heaped upon her, but in her autobiographical writings, as well as in her work on behalf of Holocaust survivors in Israel, she is able to reclaim that grief. Her variation on salvage poetics, is, therefore, a poetics of loss and grief and memory, a reclamation of all that which was supposed to have been "forgotten," but which she refuses to forget, both in her personal life and in her national consciousness.[4]

Guber, as the symbol of committed Israeli motherhood, risks the deprecation and ridicule that goes along with any discussion of eastern Europe, and certainly any valorization of it, in the early years of the state. I believe she accomplishes this precisely in her embracing of the role of maternal icon. After the publication, with Ben-Gurion's imprimatur, of *The Book of the Brothers* all her subsequent activities and writings were understood under the umbrella of her "motherhood." Indeed, her identity as national "mother" became a vehicle for delivering messages and memories that may not, under any other guise, have been acceptable in the early Israeli environment. Guber, crowned "mother" of modern Israel, fulfilled the expectations of good Israeli women. From her position as the Mother of Sons she was able, essentially, to reinvent the role of eastern Europe for herself as well as for others, salvaging it, in the process.

To illustrate the way in which Guber's crowning as the Mother of Sons served as the platform for her to speak of those things that the early state culture forbade, we need look no further than the speech she gave in 1961 on the very occasion of her being granted that appellation.

> In our Torah, which for us supersedes the concept of civilization, the greatest personalities of our nation—whose images are engraved in our souls—are crowned with the title of father and mother. For this reason, the three Hebrew words *'em, 'umah, ve-'emunah* stem from the same root. Our mother Rachel—beloved above all women—was buried, in her youth on the roadside, in a lonely grave. Legend laid a heavy burden upon her—never to rest in her grave and never to know consolation, until her sons had returned to their land. During all the bitter years of our exile, up till our time, the Jewish mother has been a symbol of home and homeland, in the eyes of her sons. She has preserved our age-old traditions, keeping alive the hopes of the nation. The mother was the honor and grandeur of the home: even in times of extreme oppression and suffering, she was not debased by the suffering, but on the contrary, she rose to great heights. I feel that this is the time and place to commemorate an unknown Jewish mother, one of numerous others, who lost their lives in the Warsaw Ghetto, after all the members of her family had been killed in her presence. This mother—Esther Sachs—has become for those who have heard of her, the mother of all the victims of the Holocaust, of the six million. All this because of a single letter, which reached her son in Israel, by miracle. He was the only survivor of his family and he had built his home here in Israel, even before the Second World War. This is how the letter begins: "Are you still alive, my son? Is there still someone in the world to call me mother?" The mother who had been bereaved of everything is looking to her son, not for support, but to have someone to live for. She is content to know that he is alive to call her "mother." The letter contains a horrifying description of pillage and mass murder, of children

wrenched out of their parents' arms, who know that they will never be returned to them. In conclusion, the mother writes: "After the pogrom your father said to me: 'Don't worry, Hitler cannot destroy us; we have a son in Eretz Yisrael.'"[5]

Honored in a special ceremony in Tel Aviv at the historic home of Chaim Nachman Bialik (1873–1934), the first modern national Hebrew poet, Guber links the three words: *'em* (mother), *'umah* (nation), and *'emunah* (faith). While the first two words (*'em* and *'umah*) do, indeed, share the same root (*'a-m-m*), the third word, *'emunah* (*'e-m-n*), does not.[6] This error could, in fact, be reflective of a linguistic error on Guber's part. But it is more likely that she is doctoring the grammar for the benefit of the message she is trying to convey, one in which mothers have sustained the nation with their faith for many generations. Their faith in what? As she articulates in the above passage, she considers the Jewish mother to be the metonymy of comfort and home even during periods of great suffering. The first of the two mothers she invokes as examples is the biblical figure of Rachel, who died in childbirth and was buried on the side of the road, near Bethlehem, as her family traveled back to Canaan, Jacob's homeland, from Paddan 'Aram, her own. In Jeremiah 31:15 we read: "Thus said the Lord: A cry is heard in Ramah: Wailing, bitter weeping—Rachel weeping for her children. She refuses to be comforted for her children, who are gone." Rachel, the symbol of the nation weeping for her children in exile, is presented by Guber as particularly unfortunate because she never actually saw redemption take place. Unlike Guber, who has lived the experience of redemption, returning to the land and raising sons there, the biblical Rachel must remain eternally weeping. Guber's second example of motherhood, nationhood, and faith is Esther Sachs, who died in the Holocaust, purportedly happy in the knowledge that her son remained alive in the Land of Israel. Just as Guber has accepted the title of the Mother of Sons, she essentially names Esther Sachs "the Mother of the Holocaust," serving as a mother to all its victims. This begs several questions. First, is it really an honorific to be the mother of six million victims? Second, don't those victims all have their own mothers to mourn them? What is the message that Guber is trying to communicate here? Being a mother of those sacrificed in the name of a larger national cause, as she was, becomes an honor. Guber sees Sachs in some sense as her parallel—another mother who has lost children. Yet Sachs's son is not lost at all, according to his mother; he is alive and well and living in Israel even as she dies a terrible death.

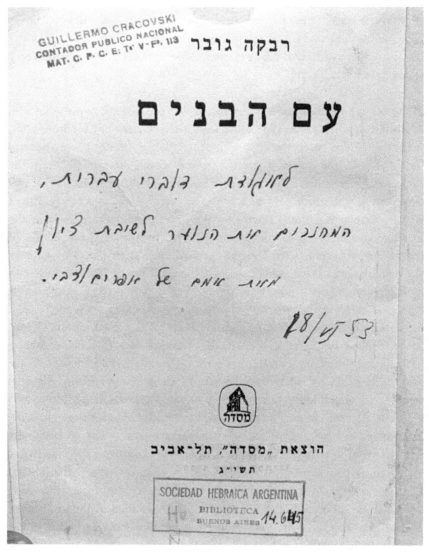

Personal signature of Rivka Guber from *'Im ha-banim*. She writes: "To the Council of Hebrew Speakers Educating the Youth for a Return to Zion. From the Mother of Ephraim and Tzvi."

Through her invocation of Sachs, by calling her the mother of all Holocaust victims, however, Guber highlights something that was not often acknowledged within the national culture of the pioneers. What was it like to leave everything behind in Europe and then, within a decade or two, see it go up in flames? What was it like to watch helplessly as families and friends and communities in Europe vanished during World War II? Perhaps Sachs would be more appropriately coined "Mother Among the Victims" because she was abandoned in Europe, first by her son when he emigrated, then, during the Holocaust, by the world.

Even though Sachs in her letter purportedly revels in her son's being in Palestine, and therefore safe during the events of the Holocaust, the only way to explain Guber's identification of Sachs as mother of all Holocaust victims is that somehow Sachs's son is a victim as well. He is a victim of the ideology that separated mothers from children in the name of building a state, the victim, perhaps, of the ideological forces that rendered eastern European Jewry and eastern European Jewish experience, and the Holocaust itself, anathema to the construction of a new nation for Jews. In Guber's eyes, Israel's existence serves as an antidote to Esther Sachs's fate in the Holocaust. It took her son away from her, just as it took Guber's sons from her. Guber's designation as the ultimate mother because she lost her sons is echoed by Sachs's designation as the ultimate mother because she lost her son—through Zionism and his emigration to the Promised Land. I would argue that Guber's invocation of the Holocaust at her award ceremony, and of Esther Sachs, testifies to her own sense of irremediable loss and to her confidence in linking the Holocaust to her own experiences as a grieving mother.

Throughout her work Guber equates motherhood in Israel with loss in the Holocaust. In her introduction to *'El mas'uot Lachish* (*The Signal Fires of Lachish*, 1961), which explores her experiences settling immigrants in the Lachish region and solidified her reputation as the Mother of Sons, she describes the interment of Herzl's ashes in Jerusalem:

> The casket was borne slowly in an open car. It was covered with a pall of white silk and nothing more. The pall itself was covered with letters embroidered in gold. The women of Vienna who survived the Holocaust of Europe embroidered a thousand words from *The Jewish State* with their own hands on the pall intended for the coffin of the man who envisioned the Jewish state. Herzl arrived in the country together with the first wave of the great immigration, and his casket was transported on wings of eagles. This is no legend.[7]

Concluding with an allusion to Herzl's most famous statement, "If you want it, it is no legend," which became the rallying cry of the Zionist movement in its earliest years, Guber tells us that the women of Vienna who survived the war are the ones who represent, for her, the meaning underlying the Jewish state.[8] They are the ones who embroider the words of Herzl on his bier. This juxtaposition of literature, Zionist ideology, women, death, and the Holocaust embodies what Guber does throughout her corpus. Speaking as a bereaved mother and as a woman, she writes as a memorial to her sons who died in the War of Independence, thereby presenting herself as the voice of a generation of immigrants who built the Jewish state with their own hands, against the backdrop of the Holocaust.

Despite her having been cast in an iconic nationalist role as the Mother of Sons even during her lifetime, what is striking about Guber's written corpus is the way that she voices the dreams and aspirations of a generation of Israeli founders while still maintaining a profound and respectful connection to her original homeland. This articulates itself in so many ways, large and small, it is hard to enumerate them here. I will offer just a few examples. At the end of her final book, *A Legacy to Impart*, are two proximate texts in a section titled "Goodbye to a Bygone Day," where she captures, first, the essentials of Zionist attachment to the land in Israel, then her own familial connection to eastern European Jewish farmers, and finally the connection between past, present, and future. In the first text she writes:

> Most of our years in the land were spent in agricultural work, which is strenuous physical labor. It wasn't at all difficult for us because we loved it. Sixty years of our life on the land, making our living off of the earth. We grew out of a society that was fulfilling the dreams of generations, raising its children to freedom, reviving our language, and returning human and national dignity to our people.[9]

Voicing all the ideals of the founding generation, Guber reminds her readers that she and Mordecai did the three most important things a Zionist could do: they established a farm on Jewish soil, living off of it; they gave birth to "native" children; and they revived the Hebrew language. All this is framed within the broader purpose of "returning human and national dignity to our people." On the same page, she asserts:

> Zholte, my birthplace, and all the Jewish colonies in southern Russia have been completely wiped off the earth, along with any memory of the Jews in the agricultural settlements. I have no hope of finding the cemetery where my father and my father's fathers are buried. Just one

man, a descendant of a neighboring village, Sdeh Menuḥah, a man who now lives in Ein Harod, Yisrael Ben Eliyahu, managed to visit the settlement where he was born and raised and left his parents and siblings behind. He got permission to visit from the Soviet government, as per the request of Bordov, the Russian ambassador to Israel. Ben Eliyahu found all the settlements settled by Ukrainian neighbors who murdered and then inherited. Out of the entire population of Sdeh Menuḥah all that remains is one communal grave. On it a monument bearing the Soviet symbol has been placed, and it is engraved in Yiddish and Russian with the following message: "Here are buried Soviet citizens from the village of Klinininsk—1,875 people—elders, men, women, and children—who were tortured and killed by the fascist executioners and their collaborators during the occupation, on September 10, 1941. . . ." Only a few remnants of the Jewish colonies have made it to Israel. . . . The scions of the Jewish settlements who were absorbed by the Land of Israel have continued the labor of their fathers. Among them were those who labored on behalf of the State of Israel on important missions. Most of them sent down deep roots in their birthland: in the Valley of Jezreel, the Jordan Valley, in the Western Galilee and in the Negev. To the descendants they bequeathed a commitment to the earth that they brought with them to the land of the fathers from the fields of the Jews in Ukraine. About the verse, "and you shall see and remember . . . and do" (Num. 15:39), the sages say: "Memory brings about deeds." Our faces are turned toward the eternal, and as we set off on our long journey we won't take anything along. If we were to leave our memories behind, our legacy to our inheritors would be significantly impoverished. Farewell to the past. I want to finish my remarks with the words of one of the founders and teachers of our generation, Shlomo Tzemah, a man of words and deeds who said: "I will bow down to this land and thank her for all the goodness she has done on my behalf. As much as I gave her, she gave me more."[10]

In these final words of her memoir, despite her rather conventional articulation of the fulfillment of Zionist ideals, Guber returns to a crucial theme that she repeats throughout her oeuvre: she came from a family of Jewish farmers who lived off the land for several generations in Ukraine. This contrasts with a more widespread image of the Jewish pioneer from eastern Europe as coming from a mercantile background, with absolutely no idea how to farm. We will also see this contrasting image in Yizhar's recounting of his father's failed experiences in Rehovot as well as in the literature of the moment. S. Y. Agnon's antihero, Yitzhak Kumer, in his classic novel *Only Yesterday*, for example, begins his journey as a pioneer on an agricultural settlement and ends up in an ultra-Orthodox neighborhood in Jerusalem[11]; Y. H. Brenner's hero in his classic *Breakdown and Bereavement* winds up flat on his back with malaria and sunburn after trying his hand at an agricultural vocation and ultimately, like Agnon's protagonist, settles in Jerusalem.[12] Indeed, rather than centering itself on Zionist heroes, the canonic literature of the Hebrew renaissance focuses primarily on antiheroes who cannot fulfill the agricultural ideals set by the Zionist ideologues that drew from A. D. Gordon's notions about settling the Promised Land through physical and farm labor.[13] Guber, on the other hand, reminds her readers that there were Jews from eastern Europe who were actually equipped for farm life when they arrived in Palestine. She, interestingly, was not one of them, and neither was Mordecai, because while her family were farmers, she never participated in farm life because she was sent off to school. Mordecai, too, was a gifted Hebrew teacher, not a farmer. But they nonetheless joined the farming effort—first in Rehovot, then in Kfar Bilu, and finally in Kfar Warburg—learning to farm and reminding Israelis that farming is not foreign to Jews from eastern Europe. When the Gubers gave up their farm in 1955, moving south to assist in the settlement there, their work with the immigrants in education and municipal management was probably far more suitable to their skill sets and their preferences.

In the above conclusion to her memoir, Guber holds the land up as her ultimate achievement. She claims to have worked it for sixty years, to have supported herself on it, and to have enjoyed every minute of the hard physical labor she experienced. She reminds us, however, that this pull toward the land was not born with her arrival in Palestine. Her family, her community, and others like her, grew up in the diaspora working the land. She acknowledges the terrible end met not only by her community but by the community next door and others in the area. At the end of this passage Guber quotes the book of Numbers in its articulation of the connection between memory and deed. Even as she says that she must bid farewell to a bygone world, she implores her reader (along with her grandson Yonatan to whom this book is dedicated) to remember. Even while voicing the Zionist ideals of farming the land, of raising native children, and of reviving the Hebrew language she reminds her readers to remember. That which she spends the vast majority of the book remembering for her audience, however, is not necessarily her experiences as a pioneer in early Israel but rather her life in the eastern European diaspora.

Affirming the words of Hebrew poet Saul Tschernikhovsky (1875–1943), that "man is nothing more than the landscape of his childhood," Guber dedicates three-quarters of *A Legacy to Impart* to the period preceding her twenty-third year.[14] While many other eastern European pioneers in Palestine and early Israel certainly continued to affirm the integrity of the world they had left behind, not many of them were national symbols of Zionist ideology the way Guber was. A couple of examples shed light on how her own connection to life in eastern Europe distinguished her from some other immigrants. In the case of Fania Oz, Amos Oz's mother, for example, nostalgia for the world left behind was fundamentally disabling and her longing for the world of her childhood in the face of the privations and compromises of life in Palestine led to her depression and ultimately her death. We will see something similar in our discussion of S. Yizhar's mother, whose map of the world oriented itself around the shtetl she left behind in eastern Europe, even more than half a century after her arrival in Palestine. Guber, however, does not view her earlier life in diaspora as an antidote to the disappointments of her life as a pioneer. Rather, this world left behind is something else, something whose destruction she acknowledges but whose contours and institutions she cherishes as a model to deploy in the present.

While often invoking her family's farming credentials as one way to express pride in her eastern European background despite Israeli vilification of it, she also invokes education in eastern European Jewish communities as a source of pride. For Guber, who is the driving force behind building an educational infrastructure in the Lachish region of southern Israel, education is an area of major importance. And yet, she focuses on educational structures in traditional eastern European society in ways that eclipse what she is really observing in the present or trying to discuss. In *The Signal Fires of Lachish* Guber shares the following reflection:

> The people of Israel have known how to create an educational climate in all the countries of their exile. I once heard Dr. Yom Tov Levinsky tell how a small child would be taken for the first time to the house of his rabbi in a village in Galicia fifty years ago. The date was set for Shavuot, on the holiday of the presentation of the Torah. The age of the beginners was between three and four years, "when the child knows how to speak." The pupils would bathe and be purified in a mikveh after a night

of vigil. His mother would dress the child in new clothes, and his father would wrap him completely in a talith—a prayer shawl—(that he might not see on the way a pig, a drunkard, or any other impure sight) and would carry him to the synagogue on his shoulder. There they would seat the new pupils in a row, and the rabbi would repeat the verse: "Moses commanded us a law, an inheritance of the congregation of Jacob," until they knew it by heart. He would then show them a tablet on which the letters of the alphabet were written. The tablet was spread with honey. The rabbi read out the letters and would let the children touch them and lick their fingers, as if to say: "the Torah is sweeter than honey." At the same time an "angel" would shower sweets on them from above. In the late afternoon the children would be brought to the rabbi again, this time to his house, where they would begin their regular studies. The melamed would take them for a walk, usually on the banks of a river. The children would crumble bread and throw crumbs into the water to feed the fish. In this way, the rabbi would give his pupils their first moral instruction: "One must not beat a dog, or chase a cat—be kind to dumb animals." People from Yemen and Morocco tell similar stories. The difference is that in their countries, this tradition has been carried on to this day. There is great perturbation among the Eastern immigrants at present. They are fearful of the results of modern education, and they ask in concern: "What kind of education is this that forbids one to chastise a child who has done wrong? And how is it that a woman is permitted to do the teaching?" The campaign for education has been no easier for the State of Israel than the military campaigns in which we gained victory. People say that the officers of the Israeli Army are in the habit of commanding their troops with the words: "After me!" instead of "Forward!" And that this is the secret of their success. But the state of affairs in the field of education bears no resemblance to the traditional behavior of the army. In this field, it is mainly the beginners and teachers with no experience at all who are sent to the firing lines, while most of the experienced and well-trained teachers entrench themselves in well-protected flanking positions.[15]

Highly critical of the educational environment in Israel where those on society's margins were deprived of well-trained teachers, Guber tells the story of toddlers' introduction to classical Jewish education in eastern Europe. She offers a kinder, gentler view of the heder system of religious education (particularly of boys) in eastern Europe, contrary to the modern

Hebrew autobiographers, fiction writers, and even poets who often vilified this system. Bialik, for example, wrote a famous poem about the deprivations of ḥeder study.[16] Guber, however, brings it as an illustration of the kind of educational system that her non–eastern European Jewish neighbors, friends, and students in the Lachish region might aspire to in Israel. She writes, "People from Yemen and Morocco tell similar stories. The difference is that in their countries, this tradition has been carried on to this day." Asserting that this system no longer exists for eastern European Jews, perhaps because of the destruction of eastern European Jewry geographically, or perhaps because she presumes that eastern European Jewish settlers in Israel have fallen into lockstep with more "modern" modes of education, she describes it in loving and reverential detail as an illustration of what still exists in other parts of the world.

Read carefully, this passage, both in what is present and what is absent, makes evident Guber's strong affiliation with Zionist ideology, which marginalizes immigrants from non-European countries in favor of an emphasis on eastern Europe as the lens for viewing all the cultures that have converged in Israel. Had she been trying to make a point about how Moroccans and Yemenites feel about Israeli education, one might wonder why she does not bother to get details about what actually happens in Morocco and Yemen. Not only does she not include such details, but she also attributes this story to a lecture she heard rather than to her own educational experience or to that of anyone in her circle of family or acquaintances. For Guber, because it is eastern European, this story is emblematic of something far larger than itself. It is far away, in both time and place, yet it exudes for her the kind of educational values she holds dear: the love that parents express when bringing their children to school for the first time, the love that teachers must shower on their young students, and also the sweetness of language and of tradition communicated to the student by sensory methods and not simply textual ones. The fact that Guber claims to be describing something that is still practiced by Middle Eastern Jews while she invokes an example from eastern Europe is indicative of Guber's Ashkenazi bias, despite her unflagging dedication to minority communities in southern Israel. Guber frequently voices, partly through vociferous renunciations of these attitudes but sometimes through her own tacit agreement, many of the Ashkenazi Israeli establishment's assumptions about the Middle Eastern Jewish immigrants; the consensus, by and large, was that these immigrants were "backward" in their approach to marriage, literacy, birth control, and social organization, among other things. While she is, on the one hand, sympathetic to their resistance to modern modes of education, the only illustration she can come up with for their actual educational orientation is an eastern European model. And even that model is simply a model for her, not a lived experience.

Aside from her strong Ashkenazi bias, what else does this passage reveal? It reveals an approach to eastern Europe that is certainly out of step with the general attitudes toward eastern European Jewish culture in Israel. She idealizes something that has been actively vilified—the education of young boys from the age of three in the sacred texts by ill-equipped and frustrated rabbis who were unable to pursue more lucrative careers.[17] She also uses an eastern European educational institution as the basis for describing contemporary Middle Eastern Jewish educational institutions. To explain the shifts that Guber makes here from authentic to manufactured memory, as do others in modern cultures, Pierre Nora uses specific terminology, comparing "*lieux de mémoire*," or "sites of memory," to "*milieux de mémoire*," or "real environments of memory."[18] He writes:

> Our interest in *lieux de mémoire* where memory crystalizes and secretes itself has occurred at a particular historical moment, a turning point where consciousness of a break with the past is bound up with the sense that memory has been torn—but torn in such a way as to pose the problem of the embodiment of memory in certain sites where a sense of historical continuity persists. There are *lieux de mémoire*, sites of memory, because there are no longer *milieux de mémoire*, real environments of memory.[19]

History, here, is displaced onto objects and locations that came to represent history without necessarily being "historical" or corresponding to personal memories. Museums, calendars, and memorials all become *lieux de mémoire* in Nora's conception.

For Guber, it seems, the eastern European heder is a site of memory but not an actual place in the real world. By superimposing this site of memory onto Moroccan and Yemenite immigrants, she keeps it alive but also uses it to perform a kind of cultural violence, replacing the actual subject of her discussion, eastern Jews, with eastern European Jews. Through this imposition of one cultural model onto another, Guber demonstrates a simultaneous allegiance to and transgression of early Israeli norms. Even as she valorizes the heder system that was so profoundly vilified within the Israeli imagination, at the same time she insists on looking at Middle

East Jewish communities through the lens of eastern European Jewish customs. This reflects a broader theme in her oeuvre, one of conformity to Israeli ideals even as she, in her continuing allegiance to eastern Europe as relevant and even exemplary, defies them. For Guber, Jewish eastern Europe is a thing of the past, not a reality in the present. As such, it is wholly unthreatening and she sees no need to divorce it from her reality or from Israel's. Her approach to its history is not one of shame and negation but one of pride in the ability to remember.

Guber's ability to remember, even when others do not, is evident in her work transcribing the stories of the survivors living at Kfar 'Aḥim. Here, again, she blends her Mother of Sons role with that of the act of remembering, or salvaging that which has been forcibly repressed. In *Village of the Brothers* she writes:

> There are no grown children in Kfar 'Aḥim but, with one exception, there are no grandparents either. And so we were elected "honorary grandparents" to the entire village. To this day, whenever Mordecai and I visit Kfar 'Aḥim, we are immediately surrounded by children and adults. The first boy born in the village, to Malka and Shimshon Gantz, was named Ephraim, after our elder son. One day, when he was still a toddler of about two, I was out in the main street of the village. The many children, all still very young then, gathered around me, skipping by my side. Each tried to catch hold of some part of me—a finger, a fold of my dress, the strap of my handbag. I had no idea that little Ephraim was also in that crowd, trying to fight his way to my side. When he saw that he would not be able to push his way through the others, he ran a little way in front of me, turned around, raised his eyes to me pleadingly. "But it's me," he stammered. "I'm Ephraim."[20]

Casting herself as the grandmother to a population whose stories she helped to commemorate, Guber reinforces the link between her role as "mother" and her role as rememberer, reminding us that for her, salvaging the past is intimately connected to her role in Israel as the Mother of Sons. The surrogate grandmother to the entire village, and the surrogate mother to little Ephraim, Guber inhabits a maternal role in nearly every aspect of her life. It is interesting, in the context of this discussion, to contemplate Guber's perceived role as "grandmother" or surrogate mother to a group of Holocaust survivors, which is what Kfar 'Aḥim was. These survivors, mostly young adults in their twenties and thirties, were too old to be her actual children in 1949 when the village was founded. Emphasizing the metaphoric nature of her grandmotherly relationship to them, she connects them to her own grandparents even as she adopts them as her grandchildren:

> Right from the start we felt very close—a special kind of closeness—to these sturdy Jewish men and women, most of whom had been born into families who had tilled their native soil in the Transylvanian mountains. They reminded me of the people of my own village in the Ukrainian plains, where four generations of my ancestors, farmers all, had lived and died. These Jewish villages in the Kherson region had all been totally wiped out in World War II.[21]

Taking this opportunity to remind us that eastern European Jews can be farmers, both in the present and the past, she introduces these survivors as members of her own ancestry, salvaging them just as she salvages her own past throughout her writing, even as she claims grandmotherly status among them.

Reinforcing, again, the connection for Guber between iconic maternity, memory, and salvage, she tells us about the remarkable parenting she heard about from some of these survivors, parenting that served to "salvage" entire families. Orphaned survivors who were "adopted," even as adults, by Rivka and Mordecai are often parents themselves, and their distinction, in Guber's writings, is their success in watching out for their children during the war. This serves to emphasize how important a role Guber believes that maternity plays in the act of salvage, be it historical salvage or the kind of salvage that takes place in the here and now, when confronted with disaster. In her book on Lachish she writes:

> One older woman stood out among the new settlers—the only one of them who had succeeded in bringing her three children safely to the country. The eldest child was sixteen. The children gave their parents every help. This strong family established a model farm. The mother had a habit of making excuses to justify herself—as though she were culpable by reason of her children still being alive! She would say: "I have to fear the evil eye: there are many people of our age here, but all of them except me are still young parents." The woman told me how she had watched over her children during the years of the war. They had been a family of farmers, the only Jewish family in a Transylvanian

Rivka and Mordecai Guber, Nehora 1959.

village. When the Second World War broke out, her husband had been sent to do forced labour in Russia, and the woman remained alone on the farm with her three small children. The village priest was one of the followers of the anti-Semitic Kousa, and he incited the peasants to loot Jewish property. When they robbed the woman of her cows, her chickens, and the farm equipment, she took her three children and stood together with them on the steps leading to the village church, on a Sunday. When the priest arrived, she addressed him: "You've taken both the head of the family and our means of livelihood away from us—take the children as well, for I can't support them any longer!" The priest answered scornfully: "Do you actually think that I have any interest in how you support them?" "If not," she said, "then how do you lead your flock? Is that the teaching of your religion and your faith?" The villagers were impressed by her words. They returned one cow and a few chickens and told her: "We're making you a present of this, only because we saw with our own eyes that you do the work yourself, like one of us." This clever, hardworking woman succeeded in protecting her children throughout the war, and in bringing them safely to Israel. But here, in the homeland, she did not succeed in keeping all three.... [Her son Benjamin] was killed by a mine near the Gaza Strip. Kfar 'Aḥim, whose members had known so much loss and bereavement made another sacrifice—the eldest son of the village. When we reached the silent village after dark and opened the gate of the well-kept farmyard, the father embraced us and said: "We, too, must taste of the bitter draught, our turn has come...." Inside the house, the mother sobbed the melody of the traditional lament, but with unfamiliar words: "How dear you are my country! Every foot of your soil is drenched with my son's blood."[22]

Like Guber, this woman, unnamed, lost a son to the State of Israel. Her story is told here as the story of the quintessential mother—a unique woman who managed to protect her children and support them even in the face of virulent anti-Semitism and community betrayal. A complex relationship exists between this woman and Guber, one in which Guber is a surrogate mother to this mother and yet this mother is part of a community that has, in turn, adopted Guber's own dead sons by naming their village after them—even in the face of the many dead who haunt their own histories, including their own children. The guilt and superstition that this woman feels in the face of her children's survival of the Holocaust in

Europe, as articulated above, seems to have been channeled by the community as a whole in their decision to commemorate Guber's children, but not their own. It is important to note here that she calls this woman by the name that Guber herself was called by Ben-Gurion, the Mother of Sons. This is a second example of Guber sharing with others the honorific of being a mother of a nation of sons killed in wars, the first being her allusion to Esther Sachs, discussed earlier. Guber's sharing of this title represents a way to communicate her own unbearable loss as well as the sense that the State of Israel and the ideology of aliyah, or ascent, to the Promised Land creates a kind of death through abandonment and separation. Guber writes:

> The members of Kfar Achim, who left behind them innumerable dead in a foreign land—whole communities that were obliterated—named their village after two brothers who were "sabras." The new settlers took this decision themselves. They fought for their right to the name with the government authorities, and first of all with the mother of the brothers, myself. I pleaded with them, claiming that that my sons' fate was one with the country's, and that it was a sin to distinguish the two from all those who fell in the War of Independence. But the members of the village stood by their decision. For several months they suffered financial distress and did not receive the usual loans, owing to their inability to sign documents with the village's legal name.[23]

Although it is clear that the members of Kfar 'Aḥim chose this name to honor Rivka and Mordecai for the children they lost, and not necessarily to honor their own sons, I would add that they are also honoring all their own lost by honoring Rivka and Mordecai, immigrants from eastern Europe themselves who had made it in Israel as they, the settlers of Kfar 'Aḥim, hoped to one day do. Rather than demonizing, rejecting, and silencing these survivors, Guber mothered and adopted them, and encouraged them to tell their stories of life before Israel in a way that no one else did, and perhaps no one else could. Guber represented for them the possibility of acceptance and love. But even Guber acknowledges the impossibility or the undesirability of canonizing the Holocaust dead in the Land of Israel through naming a village after them. Instead, it was the Israeli-born sons of Rivka and Mordecai who earned that distinction.[24]

Just as Guber, in sharing her role with mothers who lived through the Holocaust or even those who died in it, subverts the sacred position granted to her by Ben-Gurion that excluded all mothers who came before her, so too does she brazenly subvert the ultimate taboo by invoking Yiddish with love and pride and elevating it to the sacred language of truths. Yiddish, which was demonized on the streets of Palestine and campaigned against in popular culture, was the ultimate victim of Jewish nationalism. Twice in *A Legacy to Impart*, however, Guber presents Yiddish as a language capable of performing the inexpressible, thereby displacing the Hebrew she usually extolls and renouncing the sacred mission of reviving the language on which she frequently reflects. In the first instance, she tells us about a friend's daughter, Reyla Berman, who was deported from Ukraine to Auschwitz. Berman "wrote" a postcard reassuring her mother that conditions were good in the camp, a ploy used by the Nazis. Guber tells us that in place of a signature, Reyla signed, in Yiddish, the word *rateven* (save me), thereby communicating the truth to her parents. In another instance, after Guber gives birth to a stillborn child in Rehovot during the early years of her immigration to Palestine, she is sitting on a bench outside the hospital; suddenly the woman sitting beside her on the bench jumps up as she witnesses some hospital orderlies transporting her husband's corpse to the morgue. The woman cries out in Yiddish to her dead husband: "I have to tell you something, I haven't told you anything yet!" Guber concludes this piece with the following observation: "The dialogue of years had ceased. There was no one else to speak to." For Guber, Yiddish here is the key to a "dialogue of years," something not to be cheapened or denigrated. She also meditates explicitly on her attitude toward Yiddish in a description of her courtship with Mordecai and of her childhood home:

> I started getting letters from Mordecai all the time, whenever it was possible to send letters from Ekaterinoslav, love letters, written in Yiddish. Yiddish was, after all, my mother tongue, which all the Jews of Russia spoke in those days. My father used to read to us in Yiddish the stories of Sholem Aleichem on the long Sabbath nights in the winter alongside other long novels whose authors I can't recall. Perhaps he was the only father in Zholte who was able to provide high culture for his children. But with his successful daughter, Father insisted on speaking Russian. I thought of Yiddish as some kind of inferior language, a jargon. Many years passed until I realized that Yiddish is a national treasure.[25]

In this passage, Guber acknowledges that Yiddish was her native tongue, and even as she praises her father for passing on Yiddish culture to her by reading Sholem Aleichem on Shabbat evenings, she acknowledges that for a long time she viewed Yiddish as secondary to Russian. Summing up her changing perspective on Yiddish, however, Guber ends by stating that Yiddish has become, to her, a "national treasure." She reinforces her change of heart by describing a visit to B'nai Brak where the daughter and granddaughter of her community rabbi in Ukraine has settled after surviving the war. "We were moved by the quiet Jewish pride that permeated the room and radiated out of the rabbi's pleasant and modest granddaughter, who spoke excellent Yiddish. When I complimented her for this, she said, 'At our house they spoke Yiddish, not just because of my grandfather.'"[26]

In her writings, Guber is able to express her admiration for this girl who can speak Yiddish in Israel as well as the vilification of Yiddish that she herself felt and that had been expressed in Israel throughout its history. One example is when Ben-Gurion, in a famous controversy, criticized Rozka Korszak (1921–88), a survivor and organizer of the Vilna Ghetto uprising who arrived in Palestine while the war was still raging and shared her experiences in a public forum, in Yiddish. Ben-Gurion became upset as she told her tale. "Eventually and abruptly, he stormed out of the reception, claiming—in Hebrew—'The language grates on my ears.'"[27]

Even though Guber does express her appreciation for Yiddish, she also brings to the fore the Zionist perspective that its day was past, and the future was Hebrew. At the end of *Only a Path*, Guber writes about a man named Dr. Shimon Sachs (perhaps the son of Esther Sachs?): "The author tells how his name, Shimon, was adopted when he relinquished the German one given to him at birth, erasing it from his memory."[28] She writes admiringly of this commitment to the Hebrew language and the new land as expressed in his forfeiture of his original name, not just through the act of changing it, but through the act of "erasing it from his memory." Unlike Shimon Sachs, however, Guber does not erase from her memory her original name, place, or language. As the Mother of Sons, she, engaging in salvage poetics, recognizes the origins of the nation as well as its continuity with what preceded it.

Dorit Yosef writes of Rivka Guber that she told her story to the Israeli public in unmitigated tones of Zionist nationalism and contrasts this with more contemporary bereaved mothers in Israel who take the liberty to express resentment and even rage at the country that robbed them of their children.[29] I would agree that there is a significant tonal difference between

Guber's rhetoric of loss and that of bereaved Israeli mothers today. However, Guber's nationalism, I believe, while pronounced, was not unmitigated. Much of Guber's public story is constituted by her autobiographical writings about eastern Europe. It is here that she is able to maintain a place where she can uphold Zionist ideals but also honor her diasporic memory and her history, and the memory and history of so many others in Palestine and early Israel.

4

"A THIRD VOICE"

What Must Not Be Forgotten

While Rivka Guber served as an Israeli icon of Zionist motherhood, the mothers I discuss in this chapter were not icons in the traditional sense of the term. Rather, their children memorialized them in works of nonfiction that sought to grapple with an eastern European familial legacy that had been largely repressed in their own lives. Whereas Rivka Guber was able to talk of her own history in glowing terms from her iconic vantage point, the mothers represented here were not able to do so. Their children, however, do not work to rectify this situation for their mothers as much as they work to better understand their own histories. Nurit Gertz, with her mother, Dora (Deborah) Weinberg Gertz, in *'El mah she-namog* (Not from here, 1997) and Avner Holtzman in *Temunah le-neged 'einai* (An image before my eyes, 2004) present their eastern European–born mothers, Dora Weinberg Gertz and Leah Svirsky Holtzman, as the basis for reimagining the lives of eastern European Jews before the Holocaust. I say "reimagining" rather than "imagining" because in contemporary Israel eastern European Jewish life has been imagined for many years in a rather unfavorable light. Our subject here is how two native-born Israeli scholars of Hebrew literature attempt to move beyond the already imagined and into the realm of the reimagined. To borrow Marianne Hirsch's idea of postmemory, what we trace in this discussion is the nuanced presentation of each mother's voice within the context of her child's attempt to reconstruct a world that is of the highest personal importance, that is foundational to their experience both of contemporary Israel and of themselves (for more on postmemory, see chapter 6).[1] Each of these works of creative nonfiction in which eastern Europe is approached as a piece of both personal and Israeli history serves as an antidote to the concept of "what must be forgotten" in Israeli culture.[2] Both writers, in their engagement with their mothers' memories of eastern Europe, discover what must *not* be forgotten. In Gertz's work, what must not be forgotten is that the Israeli pioneers of the New Yishuv were Europeans, first and foremost. She comes to realize that to understand early Israel, even native-born Israelis like herself must not only go back in time but also transcend place and reach beyond Israel. In Holtzman's work, what must not be forgotten is that many new immigrants to Palestine came from deeply entrenched and richly endowed European communities that did not represent the antithesis of the new state but created its very foundations.

Neither of these books is formally a book of ethnography, as neither Gertz nor Holtzman is an ethnographer. But in my work on the construction of Jewish understandings of pre-Holocaust eastern European Jewish experience in both the United States and Israel, I have found ethnographic discourse to be a useful lens for considering attempts to both salvage and represent lost worlds. Barbara Myerhoff, the late preeminent ethnographer of American Jewish experience, introduced into ethnographic writing the concept of a third voice that has proven helpful in my understanding of both Gertz's and Holtzman's books. A "third voice," according to Myerhoff, is created "when two points of view are engaged in examining one life."[3] Neither wholly the voice of the ethnographer nor the voice of the informant, a third voice articulates the relationship that is expressed when the two come together to tell a life story.

Myerhoff, in her work with elderly Jews in Southern California, articulated concern over the balance she strove to achieve between her analytical, scientific voice and the voices of her informants. In her introduction to *Number Our Days*, she writes:

> As often as possible, I have included verbatim materials, heavily edited and selected, inevitably, but sufficient to allow the reader some direct participation. I have tried to allow many individuals to emerge in their fullness and distinctiveness rather than presenting a completely generalized picture of group life.... The format of this book is designed to meet several purposes. In addition to wanting to speak within it as a participant, and wishing to preserve particular individuals, I wanted to render the elders' speech.[4]

Highly cognizant of the literary concerns that came to redefine ethnographic discourse during her career, Myerhoff focuses here on the writing of ethnography and the place of the ethnographer as author in that process. At the same time, she is sensitive to the fundamentally social nature of the work that she does, particularly with the elderly whom she interviewed for much of her career.

The concept of a third voice becomes ramified and nuanced when it comes into contact with the work of Gertz and Holtzman, late in their careers, as they discover eastern Europe with the help of their mothers. Their narratives, as they develop, comprise an intersection of author and "informant" as well as of the cultural affinities and ideological echoes expressed in these cross-generational encounters. Gertz and Holtzman, whose attunement to the past informs not only their personal relationships with their mothers but also their identities as Israelis bears a similarity to S. Yizhar and Amos Oz, who at the end of their careers drew on their parents' lives to paint portraits of an earlier generation of Israelis who came to Palestine from eastern Europe (see chapters 6 and 7). Both Gertz and Holtzman, through a textual mediation of their mothers' memories and experiences, create an effect that transcends the sum of its parts. The third voice, a combination of each author's voice with that of his or her respective mother expresses itself radically differently in each work.

Coupled with consideration of the construction of a third voice in each of their works, looking at Gertz and Holtzman through the lens of Israeli salvage poetics we see how their books employ different artifacts around which each of them constructs a framework for salvaging the eastern European Jewish past. For Gertz and her mother, Dora, the act of remembering the past is mediated by the act of salvaging memory itself. Thus, memory becomes that artifact which must be held up, framed, and preserved. Indeed, in *'El mah she-namog* memory becomes a metonymy for eastern Europe itself. As long as Dora's memory can be preserved, eastern European Jewish experience before the Holocaust can be preserved. Once her mother's memory goes, eastern Europe will be forever gone from Gertz's life experience. Much of the book is a meditation on aging and memory, on a search for the last vestiges of that which, as the title of the book indicates, is fading away (*namog*, literally translated, means "faded").

Holtzman's artifacts are more materially defined in *Temunah le-neged 'einai*. Each chapter is organized around a photograph that he uses as a starting point for exploration and exposition on various aspects of prestate eastern European Jewish existence. The chapter I discuss here focuses specifically on the Polish Lithuanian town Święciany where his mother, Leah Svirsky Holtzman, was born and raised before the Holocaust; the representational artifact he uses is a single group photograph taken at the birthday party of her little sister, Hanale, on March 10, 1937 (see page 101). In this chapter Holtzman paints a portrait of a modern Jewish community, deeply rooted in the soil of eastern Europe, as he reaches back four hundred years in presenting its Jewish institutions, history, and ultimate destruction on September 27, 1941.[5] Holtzman's treatment of this photographic artifact does far more than salvage the memory of those pictured therein, most of whom were killed; it salvages the memory and history of a Jewish town. Holtzman describes Święciany in great detail as he depicts the intimate history of his mother's family alongside the broader history of the town they inhabited, the friendships they cultivated, and the opportunities available educationally, financially, and ideologically to those within the circle of their lives. For Holtzman, the birthday party photograph provides him with visual evidence of his mother's family and community while also enabling him to present a milieu and a moment unknown and unrecognized by an Israeli readership.

While Gertz does include photographs in the book's afterword, her primary artifact is not necessarily a photograph, the way it is for Holtzman. Gertz nevertheless develops a photographic conceit by naming each chapter similarly to how photographs are captioned in popular media with a place name and a year, for example: Italy, 1925; 'Ein ha-Ḥoresh, 1933; Białystok, 1939; Suwałki, 1907; Warsaw, 1918; Ostrów Mazowiecka, 1924. This convention of labeling photographs with place-names and dates detracts from the specificity of the photographic subjects, rendering the photographs more broadly ethnic than if particular individuals were identified therein.[6] In the case of *'El mah she-namog*, Gertz's title for each of her chapters begs the question of how general she wants to be in her collaboration with her mother—are her titles trying to represent her mother's past or the past of an entire generation? Gertz and her mother, Dora, engage in dialogues over Dora's writing to re-create a European context for the state's founders. While the end result is not exactly an "ethnography," what we are left with in the case of Gertz and her mother's collaboration is both an intimate encounter with Dora's past lives (and loves) and a powerful reminder of the European lives and experiences that preceded and populated modern Israel in its mythical founding generation.

Alongside the mechanisms of a third voice and of the artifactual basis of salvage poetics, one additional element in both Gertz's and Holzman's reimagining of eastern Europe with the help of their mothers can be found in the role they assign to literary history in their respective texts. Both authors' books incorporate literary texts, sometimes those of the modern Hebrew renaissance but also selected classics of European literature translated into Hebrew. As discussed in our earlier exploration of the Knesset's homage to Sholem Aleichem, Israeli society was to a great extent built on belles lettres (see chapter 1). Holtzman, indeed, is a scholar of the modern Hebrew renaissance, specializing in the work of M. J. Berdyczewski (1865–1921). Gertz, for her part, is a scholar of film but was trained in literary studies, and her grandfather Tzvi-Zevulin Weinberg (1884–1971) was a lesser known but important writer of the modern Hebrew renaissance.[7] In their books, Gertz and Holtzman rely on the Hebrew writers of this European era to bolster, confirm, and in some cases flesh out the narratives they are trying to write about a world that has passed on. As we will see, they also allude to works by Tolstoy and Proust at critical junctures, invoking European literature as a significant part of their mothers' intellectual and cultural worlds and contrasting this orientation with their own Hebrew one.

In Gertz's collaboration with her mother, Dora, the third voice that she constructs is explicit. She never lets us forget that *'El mah she-namog* is a collaboration between herself and her mother. What emerges is neither her mother's story nor her own story; it is the story of a relationship. One of the most important aspects of *'El mah she-namog* is the way that it presents itself as a work in progress. In her brief prologue to the book, Gertz writes:

> This book is made of three books, and maybe more. The first book is about an Arab house that was destroyed, in the hills beside Motz'a. I don't remember ever having been in that house. Maybe in my distant childhood, or maybe even before then. But not long ago I discovered it again. I thought that if I were ever to write a book it would be about the people who lived in that house and what happened to them. But because I don't know anything about the people who lived in that house and what happened to them, that book was never written.
>
> The second book I wrote with my mother. Thus, it is constructed of two books, not one. She wrote her memoirs about her studies and her move to a new land, and I wrote the opposite book: about the new land she moved to and the other lands she left behind.
>
> The second book was supposed to be the last book, but when I finished writing it, I discovered that beneath it there was another book.

That is to say, beneath this land, there was another one. So, we went to Poland and wrote the third book, which itself is made of two books, if not more. My mother wrote about the people with whom she spent her childhood and youth. I wrote specifically about those who abandoned her and died.

Thus, essentially, we have three books here, maybe more.[8]

In this fascinating presentation of a palimpsest of books, Gertz asserts that books and countries are parallel: "The second book was supposed to be the final book. But when it was finished, I discovered that beneath it was another book, that is to say, beneath this country there is another country."[9] The first book, the one that was never written, is a book about the occupation of Palestine by the Jews. The second book is the story of the education and aliyah of Gertz's mother. But when that one was completed, Nurit realized that a story she had never considered was lying beneath the surface of that book—the story of her mother's life before she reached maturity, her mother's world before she left eastern Europe and arrived in Palestine. Nurit does not make it clear whether the catalyst for the third book is her mother or herself, whether the impulse to go further back and farther away was stimulated by her mother's memory or by Nurit's experience of her mother's memory. The rest of the book—its second part (even though she considers it the third part in deference to the first book that was never written), when Nurit and Dora travel together to eastern Europe—is an exercise in the revision of Nurit's sense of her own personal history. It marks the transition, for her, away from viewing her distant past in an old Arab house and toward viewing that past in her mother's eastern European background. Gertz's narrative embodies the story of a generation of Israelis—the story of a people who were taught to be anchored in a particular place to the exclusion of all other places and to be anchored in a particular language to the exclusion of all other languages. It is the story of several magical disappearing tricks: the disappearance of the local population in that chosen land and the disappearance of all prior countries and prior affiliations outside of that chosen land. In the course of *'El mah she-namog*, as she works with her mother to preserve and document her memories, Gertz discovers the power of memory to reconstitute a past that was supposed to have been forgotten but which she realizes must not be.

The book begins with a section that contains three chapters, focusing, respectively, on Italy, 'Ein ha-Ḥoresh, and Białystok. In these three chapters we learn about Dora's life during the years in which she earned a doctorate in agriculture (Italy), moved to Palestine (Ein ha-Ḥoresh), and went back to eastern Europe to introduce her first child, Nurit's older sister, Dalit, to her in-laws (Białystok). The second part of the book contains three chapters as well. The first is situated in Sovalki, where Dora was born; the second in Warsaw, where her family relocated in Dora's childhood; and the third in Ostrów Mazowiecka, the hometown of Dora's mother, Motel.

Nurit's foray into the unknown of eastern Europe, as she writes in her prologue, is predicated on her mother's memories. Yet, from the very beginning of the book, the issue of memory as something that is fleeting and unreliable is evident. In the first part of her book, Nurit, it seems, only expects her mother's memory to extend to the boundaries of her life in Palestine and later in Israel and no further. But in the second half of the book, Dora demonstrates that her memory even reaches beyond the point in the early 1930s when she left eastern Europe to study agriculture in Italy.

Though memory is the artifact that catalyzes an engagement with the eastern European past for Nurit, she comes face-to-face with memory's intense fragility at the very beginning of her journey with her mother. Their first stop is Italy, where Dora is to meet Alessandro, her study partner and close friend from the years she spent in Portici earning her doctorate. Alessandro, still handsome, still youthful looking, has suffered three strokes and remembers absolutely nothing. In a video that Dalit (Nurit's sister) and Nurit are taking of Dora's encounter with Alessandro, the following conversation takes place:

Women picking oranges on Kibbutz 'Ein ha-Ḥoresh, ca. 1940.

"Do you remember how you helped our mother do her gardening projects?" my sister says, trying her luck. "Yes . . . yes . . . so long ago." "After all, you came from an agricultural family," my mother says, joining the fragmented conversation. "You were born in, where were you born, Alessandro?" He looks at her blankly. He can't remember place-names at all. His family, seated around him, try to help: "Alessandro, where were you born?" "There . . . in that place . . . in Paiza." He smiles a defeated smile. The word "Paiza" serves as a general term for place, village, city, native land, everything. "You were born in Salerno," his son tells him. "Yes . . . in Salerno," he remembers. "Do you remember the stories about your family? Do you remember?" Alessandro: "Yes . . . yes . . . it was so long ago, so long ago."[10]

Alessandro's failure to remember the details of his own background do not upset Dora nearly as much as his inability to remember the details of their relationship.

"Do you remember when I left Italy for Poland?" Now Mother and Alessandro are sitting together on the couch. Mother holds his hand and he regards her with a humiliated, sad smile and says, "We haven't seen each other for so long." This inspires her to try again: "Do you remember Venice?" "It's hard for me," he answers, but she won't give up. "In the train, do you remember?" He says, "Yes." And she suddenly gets frustrated. "So what did we do there? You tell me." And when she doesn't get an answer, she turns angrily toward her son and says, "Does he understand what I am saying? Does he remember?"[11]

Dora and Nurit's thematization of the fragility of memory continues throughout the book. Later, Dora and Nurit meet with one of Nurit's father's many mistresses, Stella. Stella claims that she never got money from him and that they never had an intimate relationship. When Dora and Nurit express skepticism, Stella feels embarrassed and admits that maybe she does not remember. Dora says to Nurit after their visit with Stella: "What kind of people are these? They don't know how to enjoy life at all. If you have such a beautiful love story, you should at least remember it. You should try to hold on to a little piece of it, some lovely particle."[12]

Dora remarks, in the Białystok chapter, on her relationship with Aharonchik, Nurit's father, in terms of memory as well. In reflecting on how much her fiancé in Poland, Lutek, loved her, and how much Aharonchik, the man she ultimately married in Palestine, did not, Dora insists that Aharonchik never called her by her name. "Why didn't he ever call me by my name? It was as if he was saying, may her name be erased. It was understood by me as if someone was trying to erase my name."[13] In Jewish culture when you "erase someone's name," it means that they are too horrible to even have their name articulated (like Amalek, or Haman, or Hitler). For Dora, her husband's purported refusal to say her name is a sign that he hates her. As the story of how Dora erroneously chose Aharonchik over Lutek draws to a close, Nurit makes an editorial remark:

> The chapter on Lutek is finished, and with it the sorrow. What was, was. Every morning the people of Motza can see her: walking on Rimon Street very slowly with a bag in hand, past the big garbage cans, toward the hill. On June 10, 1995, she writes in her journal: "As usual I walked to the hill and back. When I get to the bottom of the hill I think: If only I had a stick then I could climb up and see what is in bloom. The important thing is to keep my legs moving. They are always the first to go." But what is really beginning to go is the memory. "Memories are short lived," she emphasizes. Thus, every day the same question is asked again: "What are we writing now? What chapter are we on? We've already written about the kibbutz?" "Yes." "And I have already reviewed it and edited it?" "Yes." "What was in it?" "About Lutek and Daddy." I suggest that she go back to it and edit some more, but it is hard to edit when memory no longer connects paragraph to paragraph.[14]

Thus, the story of Lutek is finished because Dora can't remember any more. And, in fact, much of Lutek's story grew out of the fortunate circumstance of Dora's having kept all his letters to her. Her memory is aided by his begging for more letters, by his reassurance that he is almost ready to join her, by his concern over her reports about the free love practiced on the kibbutz. Dora knows that Lutek knew her name and called her by her name because all she has left of him are the letters he wrote to her, in which he writes, "Dear Dora."

A link is established in these ruminations about memory between the failure to remember and the willful desire to erase. This link is, it seems to me, the ars poetica of Gertz's book, wherein Dora begins to forget just as she realizes all that she has to remember. The original intention of the book was to stop remembering in 1939, with the chapter on Białystok, the final chapter of the first part of the book.[15] Nurit does not even think to ask her mother to go back to eastern Europe in her memory, as if for Nurit herself that part of her mother's history has been completely erased. But the writing of the Białystok chapter, which ends with Dora's last-minute escape from Europe in late August 1939, takes Dora all the way back to the birthplace and childhood of Nurit's grandmother. When Dora has finished narrating her escape from Europe after all flights have ceased and the last ship has presumably left the port, instead of moving forward in time with Nurit and talking about her return to Palestine (and Nurit's birth nine months later, in 1940), she chooses to take Nurit back in time, to the period that preceded Dora's departure for Italy in the early 1930s. She takes Nurit back to the village of her birth (Suwałki), to the city of her childhood (Warsaw), and to the childhood village of her mother, Motel (Ostrów Mazowiecka).

When they go back to these places and these times that Nurit never anticipated, some surprising things happen. In the final chapter of the book, when Nurit and her mother visit Ostrów Mazowiecka, Dora and Nurit find that the house they are looking for is no longer there. Dora refuses to believe it, and she

> searches in the town hall for some memory of her grandfather's wooden house. "After all, in 1924 before I went to Italy everyone was here. Even in 1939, when we were here for a visit, everything was still here. Even the town hall was here, just smaller." We try to find out if there are any Jews left. "Where is the Jewish cemetery?" There is no Jewish cemetery. They recommend that we go down to Branyeskvaygo St. where some old people live. Maybe they will remember.[16]

After unsuccessfully consulting with the town's elders, Nurit realizes that the only way for her to better understand her grandmother Motel's life is to rely on her mother's memory. Nurit had no relationship with her grandmother, she writes, even though Grandmother Motel lived in Israel while Nurit was growing up:

> She was just an old woman, with a face full of growths that were called *bukelekh*. She was sick and she spoke in Yiddish. For twenty years she lived in Israel and she did not speak a single word of Hebrew. What more did I need than this to love her? My only connection to her was through the word *essen*: she was always trying to push food into my mouth. Therefore, to be fair to her, I have to introduce her through one of my mother's first memories.[17]

What does Dora remember first about her mother? She remembers when her sister, Ruchele, age one, lay dying. A doctor came in, dressed in a soldier's uniform, either Polish or Russian. He tried to get a reaction from Ruchele, sticking her with needles, palpating her little legs with no response. Motel picked up Ruchele and took her to the window, saying, "Ruchele, look! The world is so beautiful, why don't you want to live?"[18] The memories that Dora shares with Nurit about Grandmother Motel are unexpected, in light of Nurit's alienation from her. They represent a highly artistic and generous sensibility: when the family got a piano, Motel pulled Dora aside and whispered to her that it was really for Dora; once Dora planned to attend a concert and Motel made a skirt for Dora out of Scottish plaid and fashioned a belt in the shape of a butterfly to go with it; Motel gave Dora a bottle of perfume so she would smell nice; and for the last three decades of her life Motel read *Anna Karenina* in Russian, with the help, first, of her older daughter's husband and, after he died, on her own.[19]

This memory of Motel's literary habits reminds us that it was far more common for an eastern European Jew to be involved in and invested in Russian literature than in the Hebrew literature of the moment. Nevertheless, Gertz does claim a stake in the Hebrew literary developments of eastern Europe via her grandfather and Motel's husband, Tzvi-Zevulin Weinberg, who was a Hebrew writer. His first attempt at publication was rejected by no less than Chaim Nachman Bialik himself. His autobiographical novel, *Bi-drakhim 'avelot* (Paths of mourning, 1942), serves for Gertz as her source on his life, and as Gertz documents her grandfather's lifelong infidelity to Motel, she identifies moments in Dora's life on the basis of what her grandfather was writing at that time, in particular his writings about a lost love, Simaleh (though he called her Friedeleh in his stories).[20]

In its very final moments, Gertz and Dora's text also pays its own profound debt to literary traditions other than Hebrew ones. In an allusion to madeleines—the cookies that serve for Proust, the novelist of memory, as the catalyst for memory—Nurit acknowledges the limitations of her mother's memory and turns to her own memory as responsible for the revival of lost worlds. Toward the end of the book, we read:

> Before we went to Poland, we traveled to Tel Mond. It was like a preparatory trip. Grandmother and Grandfather's house had been replaced by a modern one. Beside it was an apartment building. But we did find the neighbor's house—Davidowicz's: inside the new neighborhood, still hidden inside a huge tree, still standing. We went into

the garden: the house had sunk beneath the tree; in the courtyard were piles of branches and broken-up furniture, even inside the little fishpond. The doors were broken, but there was a veranda, and from the veranda there were stairs that took us to the garden. Suddenly, without any madeleine cookies, just like that, by themselves, the water started to flow from the little spigot of the pool, the courtyard was filled with color, the straw chairs peeked out from between the trees, and my grandfather and grandmother and other neighbors began moving around beside them and speaking. Mrs. Davidowicz went down the stairs of the veranda with a platter of bread, jam, and tea. And cookies. I could see her there, at Davidowicz's house. But I wanted to see her in her wooden house in Ostrów Mazowiecka, to smell the smell of the groats that would cook in the house of Rabbi Wolf Ber [Nurit's great-grandfather] when his wife was still alive, to see him standing there, white on white, in the light of the candles, and to hear the sound of his footsteps from above.[21]

The house in Tel Mond, her grandparents' house in Israel, has been destroyed, but magically their neighbor's house, which is still standing, comes to life, and Nurit is able to see her grandparents again. It is her grandparents in Israel, however, not her grandparents in Europe that Nurit is able to see. In Europe itself, Nurit experiences another wonderful revelation, similar to this one, when she and her mother are in Ostrów Mazowiecka looking for Reb Wolf Ber's house:

The street is empty. Reb Wolf Ber's house is lost beyond the fog, but beyond the silence I can see my mother's two cousins, Toivka and Frieda, peering out from her memory, dressed in the most fashionable clothes, with braids wound around their heads, riding on women's bikes whose wheels are decorated in colorful ribbons, and the whole street is looking at them, girls riding bicycles! It was really a novelty in those days.[22]

In Israel Nurit developed the ability to make visions appear, to bring the dead back to life. In Europe, she perfects that ability. While in Israel she needed the physical remnant of the Davidowicz's house to bring back her grandparents, in Europe she is able to do so without a house and without any personal memory of her mother's cousins, for she has never met them. Her mother's memory has combined with her own, and a third voice created; the memory of an Israeli woman merged with that of her

European-born Israeli mother has catalyzed a reimagining of eastern European Jewish life.

Holtzman's third voice is far less explicitly presented than is Gertz's. *Temunah le-neged 'einai* is divided into two parts. The first part comprises three chapters, each centered around a photograph. Chapter 1 focuses on M. J. Berdyczewski, as perceived by his wife, Rachel, and documented in her diary. Chapter 2 delves into the development of Y. H. Brenner (1881–1921) as a writer. Chapter 3 explores U. N. Gnessin (1879–1913) at the end of his life and the drama surrounding the erection of a headstone in his memory. These three chapters, as described in Holtzman's own introductory summation, encompass the rise and demise of an eastern European Hebrew literature in Warsaw. The second part of his book contains two chapters. The first discusses his mother's hometown—its background and its destruction—on the basis of a photograph of his aunt Hanale's birthday party in 1937. The second discusses his father's experiences with Zionism in eastern Europe on the basis of a photograph taken of his father's youth group, Dror, in 1947 at the Indersdorf refugee camp in Germany.[23] There, Holtzman's father, Haim, a young survivor, met Yitzhak Tabenkin (1888–1971), a founder of the kibbutz movement and the Labor Party, and was photographed with him.[24]

I explore the chapter pertaining to Leah, Holtzman's mother, and her hometown, for several reasons. First, it is sandwiched between the chapters

Aunt Hanale's birthday party, 1937. Courtesy of Avner Holtzman.

on three central literary personas and the chapter on a Zionist encounter. Second, it is strangely silent on the subject of his mother who, nevertheless, must have been his informant, because only she would have been familiar enough with all the personages and institutions in the photograph to be able to parse it. This is interesting when considered in contrast to his father's chapter, which follows his mother's in the second part of the book, where Holtzman leads with an identification of his father in the group photograph. Finally, this chapter on the birthday party photograph appeared in both an American and an Israeli context, highlighting, through the differences between the two versions, those very elements that define the Israeliness of the third voice that Holtzman develops in this chapter. Within the context of Israeli salvage poetics, this chapter about Holtzman's aunt Hanale's birthday party photograph is particularly fascinating because of the way that it expresses Holtzman's unique constellation of commitments: he represents Jewish Święciany over the course of several centuries as well its place in Zionist and Holocaust history while still maintaining his focus on the particular people featured in the photograph. His reticence to emphasize his own familial affiliation with the figures in the photograph is, perhaps, his clearest articulation of his salvage poetic impulse. His text represents a hybrid between his own history and the history of a place, and in straddling the English and Hebrew versions of the essay, between Israeli expectations and American ones.[25]

Whereas Holtzman's book as a whole is concerned with depicting Jewish eastern Europe through the lens of its major Hebrew writers, the birthday party chapter approaches Święciany very differently. In his discussion of his mother's hometown the only literary allusion is to a passage from Tolstoy's *War and Peace*. This allusion to Tolstoy situates this town outside the realm of Israeli literary history. After three chapters on three Hebrew writers, the absence of any allusions to the eastern European Hebrew literary milieu so lovingly and painstakingly developed for more than half the book is notable.

In the Hebrew rendition of this chapter, however, Holtzman explicitly cites Tolstoy's Hebrew translator: "*War and Peace*, volume 3, part 1, section 12, in Leah Goldberg's translation." For the Hebrew reader, this allusion to Leah Goldberg (1911–70), one of the best-known European-born Hebrew writers from the early years of the state, draws what would seem to be an unexpected amount of attention away from the allusion to *War and Peace* itself. Whereas the identity of Tolstoy's translator is left unnamed in the English version of this essay, in the Hebrew version it is important to Holtzman to acknowledge Goldberg. She is, indeed, the next generation after Berdyczewski, Brenner, and Gnessin, who were the focus of the first part of *Temunah le-neged 'einai*. Berdyczewski and Gnessin wrote exclusively in Europe while Brenner wrote both in Europe and in Palestine before he was killed in the Arab riots of 1921.[26] Goldberg, on the other hand, though she spent her early life in Europe, developed her writing life primarily in Palestine-Israel and represents for Holtzman, as the translator of Tolstoy's *War and Peace* with its allusion to Święciany, a critical bridge between Hebrew and Russian, between Israel and eastern Europe.

Goldberg's importance to Israeli letters cannot be overstated. She was the author of a widely read and revered poetic corpus, in addition to laying the foundation for a Hebrew children's literature. Finally, Leah Goldberg's influence on modern Israeli reading habits was immense because of her work as a translator of belles lettres from Russian, German, Lithuanian, Italian, French, and English into modern Hebrew. She translated works by Rilke, Mann, Chekhov, Akhmatova, Shakespeare, and Petrarch in addition to her magnum opus, Tolstoy's *War and Peace*.[27] For Holtzman, Goldberg provides an important link between Israel and Święciany because her translation of *War and Peace* has enabled him, a Hebrew literary critic, to access the only work of great literature that alludes to his mother's hometown in eastern Europe. Goldberg's translation provides a bridge between Russia and Israel, between Holtzman's mother's life and his own.

Core to the notion of salvage poetics, as we have discussed, is when writers, scholars, or artists take it upon themselves to frame and explicate a designated artifact of a disappearing world. Here Holtzman appoints the birthday party photo as his artifact and himself as the mediator of that artifact. It seems, however, that for him Goldberg's translation of Tolstoy is another artifact, the artifact that brings Święciany into mainstream literature and justifies its presence in the pantheon of writers he discusses in his book. While Berdyczewski, Brenner, and Gnessin may not have alluded to Święciany, Tolstoy did, and Leah Goldberg made it possible for Holtzman to access that reference. Thus, Leah Goldberg, for a fleeting moment, plays the role of mediator of an artifact for Holtzman the way that Holtzman does for us. For her, the artifact is Russian literature; for Holtzman it is a family photograph. Indeed, translations are often essential to the construction of a salvage poetics, as Maurice Samuel made evident in his treatment of Sholem Aleichem and I. L. Peretz for an American audience.[28] In order for Holtzman to do the work of salvage for his mother's community, he needs a translator as well. Leah Goldberg is that translator.

But is she? It is somewhat vexing that in this essay Holtzman's mother is alluded to only obliquely. Essential to his reading of the photograph in his own idiom, but invisible to the reader, Holtzman's mother, Leah, is the unspoken mediator of Święciany for him. His grandmother, Rachel Svirsky, who survived the war with her daughter Leah, may also have provided some of the more intimate details shared by Holtzman—extramarital affairs and the like. Avner Holtzman's gesture toward Leah Goldberg as Tolstoy's translator brings to light the very notion of translation as a conceit for the chapter as a whole. His mother and his grandmother are his translators, and yet they are absented. What kind of third voice does this create? Holtzman, in this chapter, takes special ownership over this photograph and its history, internalizing the details his mother has provided. His analysis moves from the domestic realm of the people present in his grandparents' dining room on a particular day, back into the realm of Jewish and Polish local history and forward into the realm of Zionism and the Holocaust. In the English version of the essay, he is concise, naming a few important rabbis who emerged from the town and alluding as well to anecdotal local history as it is represented in Tolstoy's novel. Yet the bulk of the English article is given over to a description of the people in the photographs, their relationships with the birthday girl and her family, some idiosyncratic and very particular observations about the way that some mothers dressed their children, the dysfunction in certain peoples' marriages, and the economic situations of certain members of the group. We read, for example, the following:

> Adjacent to Hanale, in the center of the picture, sits Lovka Pliner, age nine, in a dark suit with a white collar. His disabled father had received a government license to trade in cigarettes, and his mother also owned a small business—a shop for notebooks, pencils, and other writing utensils. Lovka was the youngest of three brothers, and very popular. Beside him, in a gray woolen dress topped by a star-shaped red collar, sits Mashele (Masha) Baran, age five, a soft, round-faced girl with light hair. She was the only child of Bronya Baran, who can be seen to her left casting a slightly melancholy glance. Mashele's father, Shmuel, had deserted wife and child sometime before to move in with Yedida Gut, who taught with him in the local Yiddishist school. Among the town gossips, why Baran preferred a clumsy-looking lover to his graceful and pretty wife was a subject of intense speculation.[29]

In a descriptive feat Holtzman presents titillating and detailed information about two different families in one short paragraph, giving us in the process a sense of their social milieu and their daily lives. The Pliners are business owners; the Barans are experiencing marital strife and are active in one of the four educational establishments frequented by the Jews in Święciany. (These establishments are detailed in the Hebrew version but not the English.) In the next paragraph is another description that becomes especially poignant when it returns at the end of the essay. The first allusion to Dudik Stein reads as follows:

> Bronya Baran's arm hugs the shoulder of Dudik (David) Stein, age seven. Dudik had lost his father as a small child; his mother, Lisa, née Levine, was a wide-backed woman, always dressed in black, who managed the flour and sugar warehouse she had inherited. Everyone knew that Dudik was the apple of her eye, and that she treated him like a prince. Among the local children he stood out by virtue of his appearance: since infancy he had been dressed only in suits, his shirts carefully ironed, his hair perfectly combed, his shoes brilliantly shined—a real little aristocrat.[30]

Emphasizing the connection between Dudik and Bronya, who is not his mother, by alluding to the fact that she has her arm around him, Holtzman underscores the deep friendships among the various people at the gathering. At the end of the essay, when Holtzman describes the fate of those at the birthday party during the Holocaust, he returns to Dudik's suit as he details a September 1941 massacre in nearby Poligon, where the majority of the Jewish population of Święciany was murdered:

> Among the victims of Poligon were the shy Rokhele Kreizer, age twelve, her father, Shlomo, and her mother, Batsheva. Rokhele's older brother, Hershele the artist, had managed to escape; he would be overtaken by death in the ghetto of Kovno in 1944. The twin daughters of the murdered Dr. Kovarski, the pretty Fira and the sad Lina, were likewise murdered at Poligon, together with their mother, Pola; so too was the delicate Rivele, together with her mother, Kreina. Dudik Stein, by now eleven years old, probably wore one of his fine suits in the march to Poligon; he was killed together with his mother, Lisa, who no doubt, as was her wont, protected him till the last moment. Guta Gurevitch, Hanale Svirsky's governess, also died there, as did the town photographer, Yankel Levine, gone to death together with his wife and three children.[31]

In the English version of his essay, Holtzman says that his goal is to "testify" through his description of this photograph "that all who gathered in that house, on that balmy spring day in 1937, once truly existed. For some of them, indeed, and especially for the innocent children among them, the picture may be the only such piece of material evidence—that, and these lines now penned in their memory."[32] For him, this essay, in English, is a work of remembrance, centered around the fate of this community in the Holocaust. Its focus almost entirely on the tragedy of the Holocaust that was to consume not only the individuals in the photograph but also their families, their community, and their way of life could have been written by any child of survivors in any country. It is not laced through with any strong indications of cultural affiliation or agenda. Published in *Commentary*, a journal of "conservative Jewish thought and opinion" founded in 1945 by the American Jewish Committee, this essay finds a comfortable place among American Jewish readers whose relationship to the Holocaust is just that—a relationship without the added Israeli baggage of an ideologically motivated demonization of the victims' victimhood.[33] The Hebrew version of the essay, significantly expanded, is dramatically different. Regarding Holtzman's treatment of Zionism, the English version of the essay is wholly limited to one allusion to the fact that as "secular, non-Zionist Jews imbued with Russian culture and responsive to the new Yiddish literature, the Svirskys were among the founders of the local Yiddishist school."[34] While this observation also appears in the Hebrew, the Hebrew version is far more attentive to the history of Zionism in the town of Święciany. It is also the Hebrew essay where the idea of a third voice becomes most apparent in Holtzman's construction of his salvage poetic.

In general, the Hebrew essay is oriented more toward telling the Jewish history of the town than focusing on a portrait of domestic destruction. Holtzman mentions, for example, that the local chief rabbi, Rabbi Moshe Avigdor Amiel, became the chief rabbi of Antwerp and then of Tel Aviv after leaving Święciany.[35] He sketches out the history of the decline of religious identification and the rise of Zionism and Jewish socialism (Bundism) among the town's Jews. He discusses the impact of the founding of a local branch of Ḥovevei Zion (Lovers of Zion), a forerunner of modern Zionism, in Święciany in 1885.[36] He notes the name of the first person to leave for Israel as part of that movement, Abraham Solomiak, and he mentions that ten families followed suit during the periods of the First and Second Aliyot (1882–1903 and 1904–14, respectively), while forty families contributed funds for the First Zionist Congress in 1897.[37] Holtzman also notes that in 1911 an anonymous author in the local Hebrew newsletter laments that the citizens of Święciany would pursue Zionism more enthusiastically if only the Zionist emissaries from bigger locales would spend more time recruiting there. The Bund, he points out, was always the more popular movement.[38]

In an interesting moment, Holtzman reflects on the beautiful natural environment surrounding Święciany and the role it played in the children's leisure time: "One might assume that the few who left for Palestine suffered with longing not only for their families, but also for the verdant landscape they left behind, which contrasted so significantly with the yellow-white desert they found in their new home."[39] Given that so few left for Palestine, it is interesting to contemplate why Holtzman would draw attention to this fact. Holtzman, who is focused here on the town's Zionist history, it seems to me, is drawing on the literary texts produced in the early years of settlement that also lamented the contrast between the beauty of the lush European natural environment into which most of these writers were born and the alternatingly arid and swampy country that they had long been taught to idealize from a safe distance, but that in close proximity was barely tolerable.[40] Holtzman's focus on Zionism in Święciany as a historical movement, but also as a projection of his own understanding of early Zionism based on early modern Hebrew literature, is at the heart of this chapter.

Holtzman's text is narrated omnisciently. He does not share his mother's voice, or his grandmother's voice, in the course of the chapter. Their presence in the photograph, however, is not only unmistakable, but notable. Why doesn't he quote them or attribute any of his information to them? He creates a voice in his chapter that is independent of their voices and removed from them insofar as his concerns, as an Israeli literary scholar, are not necessarily their concerns. Although he never actually states this, it seems reasonable to assume that he wants to see whether their stories match up with the stories he knows from Brenner, Berdyczewski, Gnessin, and others. He wants to investigate the history of Zionism in this town to better understand the movement in which his grandparents and their friends did not participate. His "testimony" in Hebrew reaches beyond the memory of the individuals in the pictures. It extends to those concerns that an Israeli audience would deem not only relevant but possibly even redemptive too. Even though so many of the town's residents "went like sheep to the slaughter," the town did have a Zionist presence. Even though the Jews had largely abandoned their religious practices, they had not exactly assimilated; rather, they had developed a Jewish secular culture, with sports clubs and Yiddish schools, with theaters and libraries. The story he tells is a testimony as much to his own Israeli environment as to the existence of the individuals in the photograph. The third voice here is the voice Holtzman's mother and grandmother intertwined with his own, not explicitly, but implicitly.

To conclude, for Holtzman, the third voice is his voice, which insists on the invisibility of his mother as the translator and on the narration of those things that would be of interest to contemporary Israelis—the history of Zionism in a town destroyed by the Holocaust. To his credit, in the Hebrew version of his essay Holtzman makes a point of reanimating the town and the life of the town in the prewar years for his Israeli audience, resisting the urge to view the Jewish world of his mother's hometown strictly in terms of its own destruction in the Holocaust. In the English version, by contrast, he limits his discussion of the town's history to the context of the Holocaust. Holtzman's focus, in the Hebrew, on the Zionist minority in the town further suggests that he is trying to recuperate the history of eastern European Jewry for an Israeli audience by emphasizing Europe as the source of Israeli Zionism's ideological roots. The third voice developed in Holtzman's text is thus the voice of an Israeli son who has incorporated his mother's (and grandmother's) voices into his own, sharing details that only they could have shared with him about a revenant of a bygone world. The description of Aunt Hanale's photograph has become Holtzman's very own description, independent of the voices of his forebears. He has successfully incorporated an eastern European perspective into his Israeli one, creating the possibility, moving forward, for an Israeli discourse on eastern Europe that does not demonize or distance but that acknowledges and understands.

For Gertz, the third voice, while following a very different course, ultimately takes on very similar dimensions. At the book's end during her Proustian reveries, when Gertz conjures first the image of her grandparents' home in Tel Mond and then the image of her maternal great-grandfather's home in Ostrów Mazowiecka, she leaves her mother's memories behind and claims them for herself. They become incorporated into her own experience of the past and into her own sense of herself. Unresolved for her is that first book she had planned to write, the book about the abandoned and destroyed Arab house in Motz'a, because she could not identify a reliable informant to assist her in reconstructing that world from memory. Now that she has salvaged her mother's memory and come to understand the continuities between eastern Europe and Israel in the pioneer generation, perhaps that Arab house will spur her next project—the identification of someone whose memory can lead her back to an earlier time in Israel-Palestine, one in which the house in Motz'a was inhabited by a Palestinian family.

II

RECONSIDERING THE NEGATION OF THE DIASPORA

5

"HOUSES OF STUDY"

Salvaging the Texts of Jewish Tradition

Transitioning now to canonic works, beginning with perhaps the most canonic of modern Hebrew writers, S. Y. Agnon, I return to an investigation of the nuances of the representation of eastern Europe from the perspective of someone who was born and raised there. S. Y. Agnon draws on his own experiences as someone who left that world far behind but returns to it to perform a critical act of salvage. That salvage takes on the form of a uniquely literary and textual engagement with the Jewish traditions of scholarship and intertextuality. In S. Y. Agnon's *Oreaḥ natah la-lun* (*A Guest for the Night*, 1939), texts and textuality stand at the interstices between the real and the imagined, between the ethnographic and the literary. The decline of Torah study becomes a metonymy for the very real cultural attrition experienced by Jewish communities in transition. Here I focus specifically on an *intertextual* salvage poetic—a poetic found in Hebrew literature just before midcentury that posits intertextuality as a means of institutional and cultural salvage of a disappearing way of life. Our case study is Agnon's *A Guest for the Night* because of its explicit thematization of return to a culture in precipitous decline, through a presentation of early twentieth-century Galician Jewry as not enamored of texts, but actually constituted, sustained, and defined by them.

The classic example of a text that turns Jewish culture into a book can be found in Abraham Joshua Heschel's *The Earth Is the Lord's*.[1] Heschel's essay, first delivered as an oral address in 1945 at the YIVO Institute for Jewish Research's annual conference not only focuses on the scholarly world of traditional Judaism as if it were pervasive in all strata of society, it also deploys a conceit of textuality, which presents the culture itself as a text. Heschel, for example, calls *shtetlakh* "sacred texts opened before the eyes of God, so close were their houses of worship to Mount Sinai."[2] He observes: "Yet the Jews did not feel themselves to be the People of the Book. They did not feel that they possessed the Book, just as one does not feel that one possesses life. The book, the Torah, was their essence, just as they, the Jews, were the essence of the Torah."[3]

Like Heschel in the aftermath of the Holocaust, Agnon views postcataclysmic Jewry in light of Jewish texts. Though published on the eve of World War II, indeed within days of the war's beginning, Agnon's novel was an explicit response to the destruction of World War I.[4] What is of interest here is the way in which Agnon, focused on the depiction of the eastern European Jewish world in the aftermath of a major war, deploys a textual thematic and an intertextual poetic designed to salvage the losses sustained. The particular form of salvage evident here posits the text as being the culture itself and therefore is not to be understood as a practical attempt to document or preserve particular texts. Rather, the sacred text is used as a conceit for a culture and as a model for future modes of representation that exist on the border of the ethnographic and the imaginative. For Agnon in *A Guest for the Night*, the intertextual salvage poetic is played out in a presentation of two textual institutions: one physical and one rhetorical. The physical institution is the old *bet midrash*, or house of study, and the rhetorical one is the *dvar Torah*, or the sermon.

In their readings of this novel, literary critics Arnold Band and Gershon Shaked allude to an important moment toward the novel's conclusion where, for the first time, the narrator acknowledges that he is an author: "Against my will I have mentioned that I am an author [*sofer*]. Indeed, the nomenclature of authorship [in Hebrew] comes from the notion of a 'scribe' [*sofer*] of the words of Torah [*divre Torah*]. Yet, since they call all authors now 'sofrim,' I do not hesitate to call myself an author."[5] Both Band and Shaked translate *divre Torah* here as words of Torah in a textual sense. It is also possible to understand *divre Torah* in this context as oral words of Torah, or the act of sermonizing.[6] As the protagonist prepares for his homeward journey to Jerusalem, he begins to worry about the money he has left after his long sojourn in Szibusz, his hometown. He reflects on the financial hardships of authorship, identifying himself, in the process, as an author. In contrast, however, to reading this text as one in which the narrator has failed to reveal himself as an author until now, perhaps throughout the text he has been alluding to his own authorship, in the traditional sense, as a homiletical orator or deliverer of *divre Torah*. This type of authorship is emphasized in his intertextual practice of allusions to traditional Jewish texts such as the Bible, Talmud, and Midrash but also in the more particular sense of the *divre Torah*, or sermons, that he composes, transcribes, and delivers at certain junctures in the text. Expressed here is the fact that the narrator actively attempts to preserve the institution of the *bet midrash*, the place where the words of Torah, or *divre Torah*, are studied in textual form, alongside the institution of the *dvar Torah*, or the sermon, where the words of Torah are transmitted in oral form.

Throughout *A Guest for the Night* Agnon meditates on what he calls the "imaginary real," an apt expression of the principles underlying the salvage poetics he deploys throughout the novel: "Since the people of my town cannot imagine that a man should describe things as they really are, they believe I am a shrewd fellow who talks much and evades the main point. At first I tried to tell them the truth, but when I found that the true truth deceived them, I left them with the imaginary real."[7]

This notion of the imaginary real is further developed in a conversation with Hanoch, a laborer who plays an important role in the protagonist's rejuvenation of the *bet midrash*, and whose death, later, will make him an important symbolic figure for the protagonist:

> This Hanoch has a weak mind, and he does not grasp anything that is higher than his cap. Nevertheless I talk to him about matters of the utmost significance and explain them to him. If he does not understand, I elucidate with a parable. But even so, he does not understand my meaning in the least, because a man needs a little imagination for that. "Do you know what imagination is, Hanoch?" I ask him. "I don't know," says he. "If so," I say to Hanoch, "sit down and I will explain it to you. Imagination is something through which everyone in this world lives: you and I and your horse and your cart. How can that be? Well, you go out to the village because you imagine that your income is assured there. The same applies to your horse and the same to your cart, for without the power of imagination the world would not go on living. Happy is the man who uses his imagination to feed his household, and woe to the man who uses it for vanities, like those who present dramas and farces."[8]

At first, we are presented with a description of "imagination" as an alternative to the "real." Indeed, Agnon was writing at the twilight of the

Hebrew renaissance, which valorized the capacity of the Hebrew language to represent "things as they are."[9] Hebrew literature had, until the modern Hebrew renaissance, been limited primarily to epic representations of the ancient world, rendered in a language comprising biblical pastiche. During the period of the renaissance, writers began to try to write about "real" things, or contemporary matters, in an unencumbered language, or a language that tried to break the fetters of allusion and liturgical diction. The idea of realism, or in some cases even naturalism, of representing speech in its natural rhythms and society in its contemporary habitat, pervaded Hebrew letters. Here Agnon complicates this idea of representing things as they are, or the real, by combining it with the imaginary.

In the first text quoted above, Agnon's narrator introduces the idea of an imaginary real to accommodate the limitations of his neighbors' sense of propriety. Agnon's narrator cannot really tell the truth in terms that they can accept. Perhaps he has the advantage of being simultaneously both an insider and an outsider and therefore is able to observe things and express things that someone with only one vantage point cannot. Or perhaps because of the copious suffering that took place during the war and in its aftermath, the senses of the town's inhabitants were dulled and their horizons limited. In any case, Agnon's protagonist-narrator must adapt the real to make it palatable to his peers, and he calls it an imaginary real.

In the second text above, as Agnon attempts to define "imagination" for Hanoch before his untimely disappearance and death, he links imagination inextricably with the bare necessities of life. We can survive, he argues, only because we imagine what we will do next based on the continuity of our lives. Thus the real and the imaginary are linked in an assertion of the essential role of the imaginary in effecting a successful mastery of the real. This dance of real and imaginary in Agnon's rhetoric certainly articulates an important qualification of the valorization of representing things as they are but also asserts a basic principle of salvage poetics: a fundamental commitment to documentary (the real) within an aesthetic frame (the imaginary), which places the documentary and the aesthetic in tension with one another.

In a continuation of his presentation of the imaginary real to Hanoch, Agnon's narrator asserts that there are "higher" powers of imagination (*dimyon ha-'elyon*) and "simpler" powers of imagination (*dimyon pashut*). The higher powers are to be used for the work of living, as described above, but the simpler powers are to be used for the act of going to the theater:

Happy is the man who uses his imagination to feed his household and woe to the man who uses it for vanities, like those who present dramas and farces. Once I went into a theater where they were showing a kind of drama. I said to my neighbors: "I know the end of this drama from its very beginning." And what I said was fully confirmed, because all I had to do was mirror one thing with another. And this I did through the power of the simple imagination, but if I had used the higher imagination, I should have been proved wrong for most plays are made with the simple imagination because the authors have not been privileged to possess the higher imagination. I see, Hanoch, that you do not know what theaters are, so I will tell you. A theater is a house to which respectable householders go. And why do they go there when they have houses of their own? Because sometimes a man tires of his own house and goes to another house. That other house, the theater, is like this: People perform there who have never seen a house in their lives, but they pretend they know everything that there is in a house; so they show the householder all that there is in their own houses, and the householders are delighted and clap their hands and say: Fine, fine. Surely, they should know that it is not fine, because it is not true. But there are two groups, and each believes that what is shown in the theater is true of the other. Yet there is one man who does not believe this for that man is at home in both houses and knows what is to be found in each of them.[10]

Agnon's presentation of the theater as a foil to the domestic space, and his articulation of different levels of imagination that are deployed in each, further complicates the clear separation between the imaginary and the real that Agnon presented earlier. Here the theater, the ultimate simulation of the real, whose purpose is to convince its audience to suspend its disbelief, is presented as a product of what he calls a more "simplistic" imaginative faculty. At the same time, the common home is presented as a product of the higher imaginative faculties, because, according to the statement above, it is base to take people out of their homes to entertain them with and to show them their own lives. The impulse to see one's life dramatized and to applaud it when one could just as well have stayed home and experienced one's own life on one's own terms, is a narcissistic foible of human nature that need not be humored, according to this statement by Agnon's narrator. The very desire for realism, for the aesthetic depiction of things as they are, is under attack here, for what constitutes realism if not the desire to see an aesthetic adaptation of the familiar?

The scenario of a departure from home for a glimpse of one's own life in the theater strongly resembles the premise on which *A Guest for the Night* is based. The narrator has left Palestine after the destruction of his Jerusalem home in the Arab riots of 1929 to recollect himself in Szibusz, his hometown. Is Szibusz being likened here to a theater? Is the narrator criticizing his own desire to view what he would imagine to be his truest self in the city of his childhood and young adulthood because, in fact, it is as if he is expecting some kind of performance that is based on the simplistic imaginative faculty? The Szibusz the narrator seeks out is, indeed, not the real Szibusz, because the Szibusz he seeks out no longer exists. The inhabitants of Szibusz whom he encounters during his sojourn there are performing in a play of his life that he is directing. But what he really should be doing, the protagonist asserts of himself throughout the novel, is to go back to his real home, his new home, the home in Palestine that he fled to revisit his childhood home. According to the narrator, the protagonist's imaginary Szibusz conflicts with the real Szibusz in the same way that the institution of the theater reflects a problematic reflection of the real life of human beings.

This link between the imaginary and the real, between real considerations of the future based on the past and the inner workings of the human spirit, as expressed through this meditation on the imagination, provides a rare glimpse into the salvage poetic underlying not only Agnon's novel *A Guest for the Night* but for his literary corpus as a whole. His attempt to represent a real world, but within the contours of his individual imagination, is more than a creed of fiction writing. It is a creed of a particular moment in the history of Hebrew literature during the Hebrew renaissance. In the maelstrom of an era of tremendous social destruction and cultural change, people began to write in a modern style. For the first time Hebrew writers were writing about the world in which they lived in a usable and malleable language. Indeed, they were creating that idiom as they wrote in it. That world, however, was changing dramatically through modernization, world wars, and migration. The impulse to claim the privilege of a creative language, of the individual imagination, in a world that had long limited the expression of individual creativity in the Hebrew language (in deference to rabbinic authority and notions of collective responsibility) ran up against the impulse, once again, to do a service for the collective—to represent a world teetering on the brink of oblivion. What was that world? It was a world of Torah study, of prayer, of religious communal authority.

For Agnon, it seems, the creative imagination, the faculties that are to be utilized in the development of an imaginary world, are secondary to the

Buczacz postcard with view of synagogue.

creative faculties that are to be used in an encounter with the real. The old *bet midrash*, which serves as the psychic locus of the novel, becomes the center of an imaginary real to Agnon. It is the place where the protagonist retreats when he finds that he is essentially alone there, the place whose key is entrusted to him by people who no longer have any use for traditional Torah scholarship, the place where the protagonist becomes a kind of spiritual leader and provides physical succor to all those who have no warm place to go and no safe place to rest. It is, as it were, a theater for the homeless protagonist to play at being home once again. But to no avail. Like the theater, as an expression of the so-called simple imagination, the *bet midrash* provides a digression from home, but nothing more.

In *A Guest for the Night*, the *bet midrash* is no longer a significant part of Szibusz for most of its inhabitants. Since World War I, the interest in Torah study and the culture of prayer and scholarship have diminished and nearly disappeared. But what the protagonist manages, very nicely, to do is to reinhabit the place that defined the life of the town for him as a child, to reanimate it for himself, and to use it as a base for his engagement with the rest of the town. From the *bet midrash* in Szibusz he is able to establish a relationship with Hanoch, the emblem of loss as the story unfolds. He is able to establish a relationship with Reb Hayim, an exemplum of humility and former splendor—an unrivaled Torah scholar and community agitator in prewar years, who is taken prisoner while doing his army service during the war and returns to the town a broken man. In fact, Reb Hayim claims to no longer have any knowledge of the scholarship that made his reputation during his early years. When Hanoch, the wood gatherer for the *bet midrash*, vanishes with his horse, Reb Hayim takes over the job of collecting wood. Each man, in his turn—the simpleminded, kindly Hanoch and the brilliant, traumatized Reb Hayim—acts as the wood gatherer and sexton for the *bet midrash*, assisting the narrator in his rehabilitation of that institution, symbolically rebuilding the *bet midrash* with their wood and actually repopulating it by heating it and attracting impoverished townspeople to it during the wintertime.

A prayer quorum is formed in the newly repopulated *bet midrash*, and people again begin, alongside the narrator, to study the sacred texts therein. Reb Hayim helps Hanoch's widow feed her children, and even teaches the children to pray, both the Kaddish in their father's memory and other prayers that Hanoch, simple as he was, was unable to teach them during his lifetime. At the end of the novel Reb Hayim passes away as well.

The two major figures circling the narrator-protagonist in *A Guest for the Night*, Hanoch and Reb Hayim, who enable the protagonist to imagine the continuing viability of the *bet midrash*, are removed from the story as it progresses. Both Hanoch and Reb Hayim represent the "higher" imaginative faculties, as defined earlier by the narrator. They are engaged in the struggle for survival, with even Reb Hayim, a former luminary, sleeping in a shack and using the narrator's coat as a blanket on his deathbed. For Agnon's alter ego, however, Hanoch and Reb Hayim serve as proof of both the reality of his memory of childhood and the truth of his memory of the town. Both help him to bring the *bet midrash* back to life, at least for the winter. But with their deaths, and with the narrator's departure from the town, it becomes apparent that the narrator's sense of the real was only imagined, that his Szibusz is not the Szibusz of the present and cannot be brought back to life, even in the imagination of its native son.

The very name "Szibusz" (a clever play on Agnon's native Buczacz), in Hebrew, *shibush*, means a textual elision or bastardization that has been preserved and transmitted, thus becoming canonic. The narrator's memory of Szibusz is, in itself, a bastardization of the real thing, but it is all that will remain, it seems, when committed to posterity by the narrator turned author, in the crucial moment of revelation, quoted above, but which warrants rearticulation here: "Against my will I have mentioned that I am an author [*sofer*]. Indeed, the nomenclature of authorship [in Hebrew] comes from the notion of a 'scribe' [*sofer*] of the words of Torah [*divre Torah*]. Yet, since they call all authors now 'sofrim,' I do not hesitate to call myself an author."[11] Here, the sacred *sofer* evolves into the modern *sofer*, just as the narrator becomes an author.[12] In so doing, he memorializes Szibusz by textual means, through writing about it, but in its own traditional idiom, through the words of the Torah, or in the form of a *dvar Torah*, a sermon. His exchange of one kind of authorship for another in his confession as an author can be understood as an engagement with the notion of modern authorship as a variation on a different kind of authorial tradition in Judaism—the composition and delivery of sermons, or *divre Torah*. His *divre Torah*, therefore, throughout the novel, are a confession of authorship that demands that we consider authorship as an oral institution, not strictly a textual one, even in modern times. Here the narrator synthesizes two senses of authorship into one—drawing on the traditional Jewish author as a *sofer* of *divre Torah* and the modern *sofer* as a literary author—thus not simply preserving but improving on the traditional institution of *divre Torah* through the transcription of an oral performance.

Similar to S. Ansky's statement about his quest to mobilize native Jewish art forms in the production of a modern Jewish art, salvage poetics also includes an element of preservation and mobilization. How do you use your literary (or other) art to mobilize, improve on, and preserve a culture that is in rapid decline? The imagination, the imaginary real, as Agnon puts it in *A Guest for the Night*, is essential in a daily struggle for survival. We now turn to how that daily struggle for survival may be applied to the broader struggle for survival expressed in a body of literary and other aesthetic work produced at the turn of the twentieth century and responding to the decline and destruction of its subject matter.

Invoking sermons, Agnon narrates and frames the inner workings of Jewish homiletics as that artifact that can facilitate the salvage of a lost culture, the culture of the house of study, or the *bet midrash*. In the two discrete sermons presented below, Agnon pursues the subject of "houses" or "homes."[13] This fixation on houses as the thematic centerpiece of this institution of the *dvar Torah* functions tellingly within the culture of the novel and within the culture of modern Jewish salvage poetics. As discussed earlier, throughout the novel Agnon presents Jewish textual culture as the culture to which he or the protagonist returns from the Land of Israel in the years following the destruction wreaked on the Galician Jewish communities during World War I. He does not find many familiar personages or familiar homes in his hometown. In fact, he has nowhere to spend the first night of Passover. But he finds comfort, familiarity, sustenance, and purpose in his rejuvenation of the old *bet midrash*. Similarly, in the very act of preaching to his fellow townsmen, he reintegrates into their consciousness an awareness of those texts that, to his mind, defined his childhood and his memory of the town that they continue to inhabit. In other words, he is trying to reintegrate his townsmen into the horizon of his town as he remembers it, through words of Torah and institutions thereof—the old *bet midrash* and the *dvar Torah*. Thus, both the *bet midrash* as a physical repository of Jewish texts and the *dvar Torah* as a rhetorical repository of the same together represent the home to which Agnon's protagonist is trying to return.

The unnamed protagonist and narrator of *A Guest for the Night* not only takes on the physical rehabilitation of the *bet midrash*; he also takes on the role of the spiritual guide, or the "preacher." Invited to give a sermon in the *bet midrash* by the men who join him there on a winter Shabbat evening, he presents the sermon lucidly, virtually anatomizing it for us as he proceeds. The first paragraph begins:

> I opened a Pentateuch, and I glossed the weekly Torah reading, beginning with the verse "And Jacob awoke from his sleep," and he was afraid and he said, "How terrible this place is. This must be a house of God" [Gen. 28:16–17]. This is not like Abraham who said, "God will appear on a mountain," or like Isaac, of whom it is said, "And Isaac went walking in a field" [Gen. 22:14 and 24:63]. Rather, Jacob emphasizes the house. And so I sermonized about three methods for worshipping God. The first is the man who seeks out God in high places, or highfaluting ways, like on a mountain and goes through his life with lofty ideas and intentions. The second is the man who seeks out God as in a field, for the way of a field is to plant seeds in it, and to harvest them, and there is a good scent there, as it says, "See, the scent of my children is like the scent of a field" [Gen. 27:27]. The third, which is God's favorite, is to approach him as one would approach a house, as it is written in the case of Jacob our father, God's favorite among the forefathers. He blesses himself and praises himself saying, "My house is a house of prayer" [Isa. 56:7]. As is written in the Zohar: A mountain and a field are places of freedom, but a house is a guarded, respectable place.[14]

The narrator then proceeds to discuss three periods in the history of Israel as understood metaphorically through an engagement with the three concepts just introduced: mountains, fields, and houses. First there was a period

Buczacz synagogue.

when the sages imagined that we do not need houses or fields. Rather, Jews should "lift their eyes toward the mountains," because mountains represent freedom and nothing is more beneficial than, or as desirable as, freedom (Ps. 121:1). During the second period, the field is valued over the mountain: "And she went out to the field to ask after her father" (Judg. 1:14). The third time, the time we are now living in, when we are exhausted from wandering up and down mountains and across fields, is a time of houses, where we find rest. The merit of the three forefathers can be found in the nature of the three exiles: Abraham redeemed us from Egypt, Isaac redeemed us from Babylonia, and Jacob will redeem us from our present exile. We should most aspire to emulate Jacob, as in "the house of Jacob, let us go and walk in the light of God" (Isa. 2:5). And Jacob said, "And I will return in peace to my father's house," and of him it is said, "And God will be my Lord" (Gen. 28:21).

Throughout this discourse, Agnon brings a series of proof texts and maintains a simple structure of triads: three forefathers, three locales, three exiles. Each of the triads invokes other triads within it: (Abraham = mountain = Egyptian exile); (Isaac = fields = Babylonian exile); (Jacob = house = contemporary exile). The preacher-narrator begins his sermon with a text from the Bible and ends with an allusion to the present moment, wending his way through a variety of texts from the Torah and Prophets, and even venturing into a Kabbalistic text rendered entirely in Aramaic.

The triumph of the "house" over the other two locales woven through the sermon is an allusion to the general theme, throughout the novel, of the narrator as a "guest" for the night in his own hometown. His physical house has been destroyed in Arab riots in Jerusalem, and his wife (called a man's "house" in the Talmud) and children (or "builders" of houses) have gone to Germany to be with his in-laws. For his part, the narrator has returned to his own hometown but has no home to speak of because his own immediate family is gone and most of the people he once knew were killed in World War I, have died of old age or grief, or have emigrated. He returns, time and again, to the notion of his own homelessness, of his having no home to return to in his chosen Palestine and no home to inhabit in Szibusz. He creates a home for himself in the *bet midrash*, not a home to merely dwell in, because he never really dwells there, but a home to study and teach in, and to eat in when his innkeeper's wife, Mrs. Sommer, neglects to cook for him. His notion of a home, therefore, is a place of texts, a place of textual traditions, and a place of community. By inserting this and other fully fleshed out sermons into his novel, Agnon not only furthers his thematics in a variety of different ways, but he also preserves a mode of discourse, in this case, the homiletical sermon.

Elsewhere in *A Guest for the Night* Agnon delivers a sermon in a slightly different style, with a similar thematic. Once spring has set in, the narrator finds that his rejuvenation of the old *bet midrash* as a house of study and prayer has not withstood the test of the seasons. In the winter, when there was a fire blazing in the grate, it was not hard to attract a daily prayer quorum of ten men, a minyan, and even to bring in some students of the Talmud or Jewish legal codes. But with spring the narrator cannot seem to get the required quorum, even on the Sabbath. On one particular Friday night, the narrator sits in the old *bet midrash* waiting for an audience to hear his gloss on the weekly Torah portion. Three men sit with him, yawning by the stove:

> I perused my book, and cocked my ears to hear if people were coming. Half an hour passed and no one arrived. I said to myself, "Why don't the people who are sitting here ask me to teach them?" Now, even if they ask, I won't answer them. Because they were quiet, I said to myself: "If two people sit together and they share words of Torah, the holy spirit hovers between them. Whether there are many people or few, words of Torah must be spoken. Even if only one of them wants to hear words of Torah, it is forbidden to keep them from him." While I was talking to myself, they slipped away. This man felt strange with a bellyful of Scripture verses and sayings from the sages, and no one wishing to hear them. Moreover, on other Sabbaths I did not prepare anything, but whatever God put in my mouth I would speak, and for this Sabbath I had prepared many comments.[15]

So the narrator decides to recite the *dvar Torah* to himself, before he leaves the empty *bet midrash*. It begins, like the previous *dvar Torah*, as a transcription of an actual rhetorical performance:

> The portion for that week was the one beginning: "These are the regulations of the Tabernacle," and what I wanted to say was connected with the last verse of the portion: "For the cloud of the Lord was upon the Tabernacle by day, and fire was on it by night, in the eyes of all the House of Israel, throughout their journeys" [Exod. 38–21 and 40:38]. We should be precise in interpreting "In the eyes of all the House of Israel"—do houses have eyes? And what does Rashi of blessed memory want to teach us, when he explains that the journey also includes the places where they encamped? And I went back to the verse "And the glory of the Lord filled the Tabernacle, for the glory of the Lord was not mingled with the cloud" [Exod. 40:34]. Then I went back to the beginning of the portion, "These are the regulations of the Tabernacle, the Tabernacle of Testimony." Why was the Tabernacle mentioned twice? Because in this passage they were told that the

Tabernacle was destined to be destroyed twice: the First Temple and the Second Temple. And we may ask: Was it for the Holy One, blessed be He, at this moment, when Israel had joy and gladness, to inform them of such an evil thing? But this is explained by the word that follows: "Testimony" [Exod. 38:21]. It is a testimony to all the people of the world that there is forgiveness for Israel, and these are the tidings. Since the Lord poured out his wrath on the wood and the stones, but Israel remained in existence, we learn that the Tabernacle, which in Hebrew is *mishkan*—was Israel's pledge—in Hebrew *mashkon*; and that is why it is written, "the Tabernacle of Testimony" for it was a testimony and a pledge for Israel. And these are ancient matters.[16]

After one or two more points, based on close readings of the Tabernacle texts, the narrator begins to summarize his method and his message, instead of presenting a transcript of the sermon: "Finally I went back to the beginning and explained a number of scriptural texts about which I raised questions, and touched on a number of topical ideas which are already implied in our eternal Torah."[17]

What we see here in Agnon's approach to this sermon is twofold. First, as in the earlier sermon, he presents a biblical verse as his starting point, and as in the earlier sermon, he focuses on the issue of a "house." Unlike the earlier sermon, what he models for us here is a gloss not on the Bible, but on Rashi, a medieval commentator and the most important and most frequently studied rabbinic voice on the Torah and the Talmud, who interprets the biblical verse in a way that seems strange to Agnon's narrator. From Rashi's interpretation that the cloud's accompaniment of the Children of Israel on all their journeys includes all the places that they encamped, the preacher arrives at the conclusion that "encampment" is an allegory for the historical future of the children of Israel—that God's glory will accompany them on their journeys, even into future destructions and exiles. The Tabernacle with which the cloud is associated in the starting verse of the sermon becomes a figure for the destroyed First and Second Temples.

Once this is clearly articulated, with a concluding note on the notion of the tabernacle being a Tabernacle of Testimony (*mishkan 'edut*), an institution that testifies to God's forgiveness of the Jewish people because God allowed the destruction of the physical temples but the Jewish people survived, Agnon shifts into a more summary mode of sermonizing. The transcription becomes an overview, and the sermon is no longer a mimetic performance in the text, but a diegetic description.

The earlier sermon, delivered to a group of interested congregants in the *bet midrash* on a different Shabbat evening, during the winter, is transcribed from beginning to end. We are told that that sermon was delivered upon the request of those who had gathered in the *bet midrash* for the evening prayers, and that marks the first time the narrator takes on the role of preacher and teacher within the context of the *bet midrash*, of which he is now the proud possessor of the key. At this juncture, his role as keeper of the key is defined, at least for him. He is not simply a janitor, a gatekeeper, or a hanger-on. His role is to foster a return of the *bet midrash* to its former intellectual glory, overseeing, or at least facilitating, the scholarship that can still be pursued there because the books have remained. All that is missing are the people to study the books and the encouragement to do so.

The second sermon, in contrast, delivered to an empty *bet midrash*, is a cross between performance and meditation, with the first half being a performance, and the second half a meditation. Or even more poignantly, the first half exemplifies the role of the narrator as a character in the novel, and the second half reminds us that he is a narrator whose omniscience drives the novel even when he is not an actor in the story. In other words, the homodiegetic nature of the narrative, in which the narrator plays a role as an actor in the narrative, is emphasized because we are presented with a sermon both as it is delivered, mimetically, as well as diegetically.

Critics have discussed the figure of the narrator in this novel, emphasizing the autobiographical nature of the "return" described herein, as Agnon did return to Buczacz in 1930, even if, as Dan Laor argues, for a much shorter time than the year described in the book.[18] Arnold Band rightly warns his readers not to assume that there is too close a correspondence between the author Agnon and the unnamed narrator of *A Guest for the Night* even if at selected moments the narrator reminds us that he is an author.[19] Agnon plays here with his readership by insisting on not naming his narrator, by having the narrator share with himself many biographical details, and most importantly, by having his narrator, as he does in the second sermon, control both the mimetic and diegetic levels of the story. If he is both performing the sermon and anatomizing the sermon, if he is both inside the institution being represented, and outside of it, representing it, it is harder to distinguish Agnon the author from the authorial narrator presented in his novel. Like the daughter of a rabbi returning to her hometown throughout Dvora Baron's literary corpus and serving as a homodiegetic narrator, so too does Agnon's narrator serve as a tricky alter ego designed to maximize the autoethnographic premise of the work at hand.[20] Posing as the author himself, Agnon's narrator emphasizes more than just the "realism" of the novel. His seemingly autobiographical presence in the novel and his isolation within the culture he thought he would be revisiting on familiar terms emphasize the gap between the actual and the expected, between that which is observable in life and that which can be depicted in a literary text.

Agnon's *A Guest for the Night* gives us a glimpse of the kinds of changes, imposed from without, and evolving from within, experienced by Jewish communities throughout Galicia, particularly during the interwar period. Commensurate with the massive physical, communal, and economic destruction wreaked on the Jews of Galicia during World War I, the culture of Jewish scholarship, of ritual observance, and of local familial networks was in serious decline. Agnon's presentation of sermons in *A Guest for the Night*, alongside his thematization of the narrator's attempts to recuperate the old *bet midrash*, does not pave the way for a general articulation of the cultural changes undergone by the Jewish communities of Galicia since his departure about two decades earlier. Rather, Agnon creates an intertextual salvage poetic both through allusions to traditional Jewish texts and through a presentation of textual institutions. In so doing, he engages in a subtle narratological negotiation in which he has his alter ego, the narrator of the text, pose as a kind of native informant, or a participant observer, not only lamenting the loss of textual institutions but intervening in that loss as well.

Far from his newfound home in Jerusalem, the Agnonian narrator/author's position in *A Guest for the Night* vis-à-vis the Israeli salvage poetics we have been tracing is unique. He leaves Palestine not simply to visit a moribund relic of the past in his hometown of Szibusz, but to rehabilitate it. Through the *bet midrash*, the narrator seeks to reignite an interest in the textual life of his hometown, in the commitment of its inhabitants to the study of Torah and the performance of sermons. By doing so, he hopes to push his hometown beyond the traumas of the First World War and to reclaim it. He fails, however, to do so, leaving Szibusz as he found it. Going back to Palestine at the end of the novel, the narrator/author is by no means triumphant. He is, rather, intensely mournful, enacting more of an exile than a homecoming. While within the ideology of the literature of the Yishuv, any movement toward Palestine is to be understood as an aliyah, or a rising up toward the ancestral homeland, in the case of *A Guest for the Night*, the journey to Palestine is a failure of sorts, an abandonment of Szibusz and its ancestral hold on Agnon. In our chapter 7 discussion of Amos Oz's literary genealogy, Agnon returns as a European literary ancestor whom Oz could not expunge from his consciousness and his writing. As we continue our exploration of Israeli salvage poetics and the journey back to that which was supposed to have been forgotten but could not be, we will keep Agnon's literary depiction of his exile from Szibusz on the horizon of our analysis.

6

"SUDDENLY THERE IS SINGING"

Musical Worlds and Salvage Memory

For S. Y. Agnon, intertextual allusions served as the keys to salvaging the culture of eastern European Jewry in the aftermath of both the First and Second World Wars. As an eastern European–born Hebrew writer in Palestine and then Israel, Agnon was one of the last canonic writers to write about eastern Europe unapologetically. The next generation of Hebrew writers, those born largely to eastern European parents, who grew up with the State of Israel, wrote about what they lived and knew: life in the new state, the experience of war, the struggle to break away from the ideologies and legacies of their elders. One such writer was S. Yizhar. When he began writing, belatedly, about eastern Europe, Yizhar chose music as his salvage artifact. Only in his late-career writing did Yizhar, who was born in Palestine to Russian-born Zionist pioneers Ze'ev and Miriam Smolenski, turn his focus to his eastern European origins; his early books focused primarily on his identity as a native-born Israeli in a young country—in fact, early on he was viewed as the quintessential first-generation native-born Israeli author. His first story, "Efraim Goes Back to Alfalfa" (1938), is considered the first "Israeli" story, written by a native-born Israeli about an Israeli subject: the culture of the kibbutz. In 1959, a year after he published *Days of Ziklag* (1958), his massive novel that tracks the psychic experience of a group of soldiers encamped in a stronghold during the 1948 War of Independence, Yizhar was awarded the prestigious Israel Prize for literature.[1] Writing about Israeli communities (the kibbutz) and the experience of the first generation of Israeli soldiers, Yizhar's "Israeliness" as a writer was complemented by his focus on the natural Israeli landscape. *Hirbet Hizeh* (1949), his novella about the fate of a Palestinian village during the War of Independence, and his short story "The Prisoner" (1949), about the ambivalence of a young soldier tasked with brutalizing a peaceful Palestinian farmer during that same war, were both canonized in the Israeli school curriculum and contributed immeasurably to Yizhar's reputation as being an early voice of conscience for Israelis.

In *Mikdamot [Preliminaries]* (1992), however, S. Yizhar revisits his childhood experiences. Distinct from Yizhar's usual preoccupation with the Arab-Israeli conflict and the representation of Israeli culture and landscape, *Preliminaries*, written after a decades-long silence, is emblematic of a generation of native-born Israelis who have come, at the end of their lives, to question their own unspoken origins through an exploration of their pioneering parents' psychic worlds and histories. In a complex negotiation of his usual fixation on the Israeli landscape, Yizhar in *Preliminaries* moves away from questions of Palestinian-Israeli territorial relations and into the question of the ideology of the "negation of diaspora," or *shlilat ha-galut*. This is not to say that he does not engage with Palestinian-Israeli relations in this book. Indeed, he does. However, I maintain that this theme so primary to his earlier work is really secondary to the salvage poetics discernible here.

Preliminaries is a coming-of-age and birth-of-the-artist story. In it, the protagonist's consciousness of language and of the increasingly broadening spheres of his life—first himself, then his family, his community, and finally his nation—is at the forefront. We follow him from earliest childhood until his thirteenth year as the child of Zionist pioneers who left their families and culture behind to build the State of Israel. His mother's homesickness and his father's frustrated desire to become a farmer of an unforgiving land in an impossible economy color the young protagonist's life as the family moves from settlement to city, from community to community, chasing after the dream they cannot seem to fulfill. The older he gets, the further and further away from his parents' eastern European psychic worlds he grows. But as a young child the protagonist learns the geography of his mother's Ukrainian village at the kitchen table even before he becomes familiar with that of Palestine. For his part, his father transmits to the child an awareness of the layers of Jewish intellectual and religious history unwittingly, peppering his discourse with allusions to the Psalms and the Talmud, to the daily liturgy and Hasidic melodies, despite his avowed Zionist secularism. In this novel the young child absorbs myriad echoes of his parents' eastern European background, in their manner of speaking, their dreams of the past, their longings, and their disappointments. As he grows, the child finds in music a replacement for that which was aggressively "forgotten" of his parents' eastern European past. By embracing Mozart and Schubert, the child seeks to broaden the limited geographical and cultural horizons of the nascent Jewish state and to fill in the empty spaces left by his parents' repression of their history and culture.

As we continue to navigate the tension in Israel between a postvernacular interest in Yiddish and eastern Europe and a salvage poetic inclination to preserve a culture more comprehensively through a reframing of its artifacts, our discussion of Yizhar will identify a new category of Israeli engagement with its eastern European legacy, "salvage memory," which combines salvage poetics with postmemory, whereby children absorb their parents' trauma via artifacts of their parents' past lives. Salvage memory is most frequently identified in the second generation of Israeli pioneers—that generation whose parents, like Yizhar's, came to Palestine at the turn of the twentieth century to establish the State of Israel. This generation still has some access to the languages, texts, and memories of their parents, even if their parents have chosen not to share them because of their fealty to the antidiasporic ideologies of the Yishuv and the early state. Yizhar, despite having spent most of his life and literary career identifying as a first-generation Israeli, at the end of his life finds himself identifying strongly as a second-generation pioneer.

In Marianne Hirsch's formulation of "postmemory," the generation born to survivor parents after the Holocaust, or the "second generation," inherits its parents' traumatic memories through artifacts such as photographs.[2] These children of the second generation do not remember the Holocaust, but they cannot escape its "memory"; because they were raised by traumatized parents in its aftermath, their parents' memories are, to some degree, their own. In the Israeli context we have been exploring, the first generation of children born in the nascent state of Israel, which is simultaneously the second generation of Zionist pioneers, inherit memories of the diasporic world not just left behind by their parents but often actively repressed and negated by them too. Just as children of Holocaust survivors were often not told directly about their parents' experiences but had to either sleuth them out or live with their own ignorance of something so central to both their parents' and their own lives, so too did Israeli children of pioneering parents often develop a postmemory that acknowledged the world their parents had come from and its significance to their own lives, but without sufficient knowledge to really comprehend it.

When Israel and Israelis began to grapple with the legacy of the negation of the diaspora—all that which was deliberately "forgotten" by the culture of the Jews in Israel—Israeli writers such as Yizhar (and, as we will explore in the next chapter, Oz) began, later in their lives, to contemplate the emotional landscapes of their childhoods. Echoes of eastern Europe figure prominently in their later writings, not as a fully fleshed-out attempt to reconstruct a world "over there" but rather as an attempt to reconstruct a psychic world "right here." They each reflect in their own way what it was like to grow up with Yiddish-speaking parents in a climate where Yiddish was identified with everything that was deemed dysfunctional about Jewish life in the diaspora. They represent, to varying degrees, what it was like to have no extended family in Palestine-Israel and to live with the knowledge that their parents felt terrible remorse over having left everyone behind to pursue Zionist ideals that were to a large extent unfulfillable and to an even larger extent actively hostile to everything that had nourished and supported those ideals. Their parents had grown up on promises of "next year in Jerusalem" and had chosen Zionism within a European context. When they arrived in "Jerusalem," however, they learned that they were expected to not only renounce but also disdain the culture that had given birth to their Zionist aspirations. What impact did this experience have on their children? Salvage memory is created in a situation where there is both an awareness of trauma, loss, and fissure and a sense that continuity is inevitable: Can children of immigrants have no awareness of and no interest in the world that forged them?

Because Yizhar and others of his generation were the repositories for their parents' dreams and aspirations, because they were supposed to be the living embodiment of Israeli nativism, of the "New Jew," the legacy they were bequeathed by their parents extended to questions of the relationship between personal history and collective ideology. No matter how much the Israeli establishment hated Yiddish, Yizhar was raised by a mother whose first language was Yiddish and who sang Yiddish lullabies to him. No matter how much Israel resented the history of diaspora and its scholarly and religious appurtenances, Yizhar's father was profoundly familiar with the Jewish liturgy and could not help but recite Psalms when under duress. Yizhar grew up with Yiddish and with Psalms always in the background; he grew up with an awareness that something was missing, that something was just out of reach. What was it? He cannot remember it because it is not his to remember. But what he can do is write a novel in which a precocious child and his pioneer family search for a "place" in the world.[3]

Musical Worlds and Salvage Memory 135

Let us proceed, then, with our focus on music as that artifact that helps constitute the salvage memory developed in *Preliminaries*. The depiction of music in *Preliminaries* has been the subject of much critical discussion, most notably in Ariel Hirschfeld's detailed analysis of the novel's music-like composition.[4] In this chapter I focus on the role that music as theme plays in Yizhar's engagement with his eastern European forebears as a young child.

Early in the text, Yizhar's protagonist discovers the joy of music:

Singing. Sudden singing. Suddenly there is singing. Suddenly a choir starts singing. Suddenly there is the sound of a choir singing. From the windows of the school, and suddenly everything is full of the sound of singing. . . . Suddenly with voices filled to the right height for singing voices, with full, clear singing, with many voices singing together fully, not in a single line but with many lines together, wonderfully intertwined like a pipe they have thickness and bulk and a full roundness, and it enters into him warm and strong and smooth and full and whole and round and rich, or as though lots of horses are suddenly bursting out of a gate and galloping in the open, or like the wind unleashing a running wave over a field, he doesn't know what it is like, and there is no like, unless it is a sudden vast view from the top of a mountain, no not that either, just that it is beautiful, wonderful, so very, yes, so very beautiful. He does not know that it is a youth choir, and he does not know that it is accompanied by a harmonium and he does not know that it is beautiful, yes, beautiful, only later he may begin to know.[5]

Here we see that the child protagonist and the adult narrator coexist in *Preliminaries*, through a variation of free indirect discourse wherein the child perspective filters the narrative while the adult narrator makes infrequent appearances to remind us of the gap between his present perspective and that of himself as a child. We read, for example, at the beginning of the passage, "Singing. Sudden singing. Suddenly there is singing," with its overtones of a childlike perseveration, and "he does not know that it is a youth choir," with its adult expression of hindsight. Dan Miron calls this adult voice a "future perfect modality" or an "immanent future."[6] Much of this divide, between the past and its future, and between the present and its past, revolves around the issue of finding words to describe certain feelings or certain experiences, such as this overwhelming response to music. An example of this effort to find words appears in the continuation of this passage, when the adult narrator tells us, "later perhaps memory will find words and he will know how to tell it true, not now, like blue or green that exist on their own without words to say."[7] Reporting the child's reaction to the music, the narrator continues:

> He is simply open now and is filled with abundance, he simply chokes back tears from the choking overfullness—not even this because this is later—now it is just the fulfillment, the knowledge of the fullness that is being filled, the knowledge of more than he can know there is, just opened up to be filled by this filling abundance, for which he seems to have been waiting forever, with all his six little years, closed in by the limits of his little capacity.[8]

The profound impact of this music on the child's sense of self—his becoming free, with the help of this music, from all the noise and pressure of his ideologically charged nationalistic environment—becomes the book's ars poetica; Yizhar writes with an "abundance" that is felt by the child in the Schubert chorale he heard on that fateful day so long ago, a sense of the birth of a "world," in all its "thickness and bulk and a full roundness."[9]

In Proust's *Remembrance of Things Past*, we read: "And no one will ever know, not even oneself, the melody that had been pursuing one with its elusive and delectable rhythm."[10] Music here is the vehicle for a very particular type of memory, a memory based on forgetting, like the postvernacular acknowledgment that our link to a culture is more forgotten than remembered. Not even the Proustian protagonist, the figure of the authorial self, can remember what the melody is that he hears incessantly running through his head. But it is there, and it follows the narrator's consciousness forever. Sandra Garrido and Jane W. Davidson, in a study of music, nostalgia, and memory argue that "music is one of the strongest triggers of nostalgic memory."[11] A loaded term, "nostalgia" can certainly be construed as a component of what makes Yizhar choose music as the narrative and emotional link between himself and eastern Europe in the early part of his novel and between himself and western Europe in its later parts. But nostalgia usually refers to something that we have experienced in our own lifetimes, and what Yizhar presents are two things that exist for his protagonist "elsewhere," outside the parameters of his own life and experience. Garrido and Davidson write: "In addition to music's power to trigger personal memories and feelings of nostalgia, culturally acquired associations mean that music can prompt 'memories' and a longing for time periods or places they only know about secondhand. . . . Music can evoke a nostalgic yearning for eras and lifestyles never personally lived through by the listener."[12] This property of music is essential to Yizhar's deployment of it in a salvage memorial context in *Preliminaries* and is also that which links salvage poetics to the concept of postmemory here.

Nostalgia, like that discussed by Wood and by Garrido and Davidson, is often associated with the search for a lost "world," over either a temporal or a geographical distance. What does a world mean to the protagonist of *Preliminaries*? At the conclusion of the passage from *Preliminaries* cited earlier, we read:

> Schubert? "Rose among the heather"? German folksongs? Chorales? In three voices, accompanied on the organ? Who knows? What difference does it make? Only that it should all be full, that it should all flow, that it should all be like a hosepipe, totally round, and you all open, only that they should not stop, the people singing the children singing the school choir singing. And suddenly there is a world.[13]

The rhetoric of locating a world in music resonates here with the widely used rhetoric of the loss of a world in the destruction of eastern European Jewry in the Holocaust. Yizhar's child protagonist, time and again, beginning here, articulates his quest for a world and his successful location of one, primarily through music. In an American context, mediators such as Roman Vishniac, Abraham Joshua Heschel, Maurice Samuel, and Irving Howe also search for a world, but they do so, using different modalities like translation, photographs, and paintings. For the child protagonist of *Preliminaries*, this world is less sharply defined as something that is lost; rather, it is something that is constantly being destroyed and coming into being through his own powers of observation and emotional assimilation, culminating in his successful identification of a new world in music. For Yizhar's protagonist, worlds are lost and found rapidly, primarily in conjunction with musical sounds. In his description of the 1921 Arab riots, his perspective merges with that of his mother, as they wait for his father to return from Jaffa with milk for the children, and we hear about a world that is lost, then saved: "One fine day they suddenly got together in their masses and attacked the settlement in a wild screaming mob with ululating women ready to loot and plunder, a terrible, savage, uncivilized, murderous mob, until finally after shots and shouts and the intervention of mediators they returned home and the world was saved."[14] The ululating women create their own kind of destructive music as they move in to loot and plunder, but the world is "saved" when their voices are silenced.

At another juncture, the narrator is invited to share in his mother's world:

> And so that the child will not be cut off from what she lost when she left behind the forest and the river she draws for him on the oilcloth on the empty kitchen table three clear dots that are the triangle at the heart of the world: here is Bromel, here is Luck, and here is Bretschke, Volhynia District, she tells him, all of them on the River Styr or its tributaries, all in the dark forest, members of her family lived in all of them and everyone she knew made a living from those wonderful, calm, sweet forests, until she cannot refrain from picking the child up, he weighs nothing at all, and hugging him and squeezing him firmly but gently to her heart, and kissing him noisily.[15]

Because of the periodic filtering of the narrator's consciousness through his parents' consciousness (usually his father's, but sometimes his mother's), there is some uncertainty as to who considers the triangle between Bromel, Luck, and Bretschke to be "the heart of the world." Perhaps this is a genuinely shared perspective—between the mother and the child. Being the heart of her world, it is also the heart of his world, at least early on. And that consideration is crucial for the child's quest for abundance and wholeness and worlds, as he identifies in his first experience of the Schubert chorale performance. Why is he so moved? Why does he seek out worlds? Because, I would argue, he feels that there is something missing in the universe he inhabits, something beneath the surface that he must seek out. This missing something can be easily identified as a natural allusion to the painful disorientation of childhood before the child has found his own path and embarked on his own journey. But I believe that in *Preliminaries*, part of what constitutes the child's own path and journey as a second-generation pioneer is the culture on which the State of Israel was built. What is missing? The eastern European culture that his parents and their peers brought with them to their Zionist ideologies, to their establishment of the state.

For the child, one crucial access point for this world, and also for other worlds, is music, and in a particular instance the music upon which "words" are built for him becomes the basis for a world:

> He does not hear every word. Nor does he always understand what they are saying. But, almost certainly, he can always hear the music of their

words, when they are just words and when they are real. Even when they are all talking together excitedly or shouting together excitedly or trying to get a word in, although they are always silenced, and in the end there is always one who succeeds and talks and the others listen. . . . It's only from the music of their voices that you can hear that it's just make-believe, and that they are just pretending to talk when they are actually saying nothing.[16]

For the child protagonist, there are worlds that can be accessed only through music, truths that can be accessed only through the music behind words. Despite his distrust of words, as we explore what worlds mean to this precocious child and how they are linked with his evolution into a writer of the early Israeli experience, it is important to consider how music and worlds connect to his vocation as a writer.

Yizhar's writing is a function, from very early on, of his felt obligation to serve as a witness, and it becomes an archive of all that he, an observer of worlds, sees and hears within the penumbra of his parents' home and community. Early on, as a two-year-old about to embark on arguably the biggest trauma of his life, we read about his experience of a world of insects and dirt while he waits for his father to finish plowing:

Daddy child dust heat and round-about. Thin tiny body in a shirt and shorts that are too large for it, made by Mummy who sings as she sews and sings as she holds her work up to see, she has no one to show it to, so that it always turns out too large, and they will have to wait for the child to grow and fill out the space that is still empty now, and in the meantime with his thin arms and thin matchstick legs he moves things in the dusty ground and soaks up the frail greyness into his inner being, perhaps so that someday they might do something, so that he may tell them precisely as they were, and so that he might show them to someone who has the patience, all these things that do and don't have any substance apart from being this world from close up.[17]

As this very young child experiences this world, it is the "someday" and the "so that he may tell them precisely as they were" that signals something writerly in the child's future; the language of mimesis that he employs here is the very same language that was used in the rhetoric of the early modern Hebrew writers. In the eagerness to escape the fetters of a language that was entirely textual and that had not been used to represent the lived lives of Jews for several millennia, the writers of the modern Hebrew renaissance wanted to represent "things as they are." In the adult narrator's representation of his child self's reverie in the dirt, he shares these literary aspirations of the generation of writers that just preceded his own. For them, things as they are, however, was the representation of the Jewish street in the cities of Europe. For him, things as they are is life in the Land of Israel, and for the young child, it is clods of earth.

As he grows, this sense of his role as a future author salvaging worlds through words develops. In describing his parents' friends and their visits with them in the child's presence, we read:

> And there is also Mr. Munchik, who here among friends is simply called Eliyahu, and his subject is anything to do with business and economics, he is the one whose house on the seashore was built by a team of women working to contract and his son Yigal is a friend of the shadow lying on the ground near the door, who has enough light to read his book and enough darkness for them not to notice that he is not missing a word of their conversation, where were it not for him it would vanish at once and nothing would be known of it, it would remain in the darkness that begins literally at the end of the veranda, because right after that start those sand dunes that are cooling down fast, and from which now, as you look, a vague dim glow comes, as though they have not been completely extinguished.[18]

Like the young girl in Malkah Shapiro's narrative, which we explored earlier, who for the sake of narrative verisimilitude positions herself as witness to the conversations of men and boys in situations that would normally be barred to a girl, here the child feels acutely his own responsibility toward posterity (see chapter 2). What is it that he wants so badly to record and to preserve? How, in his adult life, as an author, would he do that?

On the cusp of his literary birth, expressed through his desire to become ears and eyes of a whole generation and to turn that into text, we read the child's encounter with Schubert as an acknowledgment that music, for him, precedes language in meaning-making, that words can never substitute for the truth that is music. In fact, as we have also seen, music reveals the emptiness of words, their remarkable lack of reliability. As he struggles to express, for us, the power of music for him, we witness the child's discovery of both the power and the limitations of metaphorical language in the context of his description of how music makes him feel: "[A]s though lots of horses are suddenly bursting out of a gate and galloping in the open, or like the wind unleashing a running wave over a field, he doesn't know what it is like, and there is no like, unless it is a sudden vast view from the top of a mountain, no not that either."[19] Here Yizhar does not present just one image but rather a cascade of images, a buildup of language, as if we are witnessing the birth of an idea; here the child is trying to figure out what the music reminds him of and he cannot settle on anything—it is like a horse galloping, but not really, like a crop waving in a field, but not really, like the view from the top of a mountain, but not really that either. There is a sense in this stutter, this surrender to the ineffability of the child's experience, that the protagonist is always on the hunt for something beneath the surface of daily experience, for the worlds we have already described. And this quest plays itself out primarily in terms of music. The protagonist searches for meaning in language not from the words themselves, but from the music behind the words. He distinguishes between the "real" and the "make-believe" with the help of the music he discerns in the voices of his interlocuters.

For the child protagonist of *Preliminaries*, his father's music and his father's musical proclivities are woven together with his own early memories of trauma and fear. The fabric of forgetting seems to be covering up, for him, those worlds that he so desperately seeks. He longs to "remember" something that is not within his capacity to remember and only finds access points through music connecting him specifically to his father's history and the texts and prayers he brought with him from eastern Europe to the Land of Israel:

> Then, imperceptibly, as happens sometimes, he becomes aware that he is soundlessly humming some melody, a soundless sobbing, some ya bam bim bam, some kind of Hasidic tune from long ago, twenty-six years Daddy has been here, with one gap, yet he's still there, where he was in his first sixteen years, with that old bim bam, so heart wrenching, yet so antiquated and stupid, and the moment you realise you stop in embarrassment, peer around to see if anyone has noticed, aware of how inappropriate and wrong it is for this time, and embarrassing, even though this snatch of song has not melted away or dried up, it is still soundlessly sobbingly sobbing away inside him, he does not touch and no one will touch this thing of his that is inside his innermost inside, this ya bam bim bam oy yo yo oy of his.[20]

"Daddy" walks around with a Hasidic melody forever reverberating in his head. He is embarrassed by it because it smacks of his life before Zionism, but he cannot repress it. This musical inclination, the constant Hasidic melody inside his head returns again and again throughout this text:

> Tam teidel, tam teidel, tam tam, Daddy used to sing shyly, one of his Hasidic singsongs, and in a kind of ecstasy under his moustache, that hid many things, and much shyness, but not his sad smile, or his emotion, as he sang in a singsong with pure devotion, when he thought he was alone and no one could see him, stopping suddenly when he was caught by surprise. And Daddy would take him on the festivals to the local synagogue, hand in hand, both in their best clothes, and there he would wrap himself in his faded prayer shawl, and even showed others the place in the prayer book, and everything there was tiresome and endless and boring and unreal, and Daddy read in correct Hebrew what the others round about deformed with their chanting, pretending, almost as though they were in disguise, and at the end they walked home in a leisurely fashion, as though they were just passing the time, because that was the way it was done, but God was not there. He was just a little boy who understood nothing, but he knew that there was something here that was not right.[21]

Here we see another articulation of the child's need to go beneath the surface of things, to look for the music behind the words, as he experiences prayers devoid of God and his father's proficiency with the prayer book when the others in the synagogue are confused and lost. This deeper engagement is something that he and his father share. The Hasidic melodies and the traditional Hebrew prayers are the child's first music, and the Schubert becomes the child's second music—the music that opens "worlds" to him.

Salvage memory, in *Preliminaries*, serves as a reflection of the search for the essence of the protagonist's psyche—the melodies, languages, texts, and affiliations that lay just beneath the surface of his experiences as a first-generation Israeli. Salvage memory, in other words, creates a reminder that not only is he a first-generation native-born Israeli but also a second-generation pioneer. In the blending of the perspective of the first-generation native-born Israeli child and the second-generation pioneer, we observe, particularly, the blending of consciousness of parent and child. Through that blending, we are introduced to the musical and literary fabric that make up the child's experience from his earliest remembered encounters. Salvage memory brings together the two musics described above—his father's and Schubert's—which, in turn represent his quest for something beyond his lived experience but situated in his postmemory. In our first glimpse of the child, for example, we read:

> How can he know that he is actually sitting here inside a theatre, that tiny theatre in which the greatest show on earth is being performed, the spectacle of the new Jew in the new Land, a show whose main point is the Jew working the land as a free man, independent, neither exploiting nor being exploited, and that the program of *ha-Po'el ha-Tsa'ir* is being put into practice and realized here, categorically, an exploit so exciting, stimulating and thrilling that people far away, hearing of it, abandon homeland, parents, home and studies and moneymaking, and with a light haversack in which the only heavy items are the same two books, the Bible on one side and Tolstoy on the other, stuffed among clothes that are unsuited to the climate and the work, get up and go, almost pushing away their weeping relatives, they shoulder their bag and they set off, eating up the distances by cart train and boat, until they land singing on the shore of Jaffa that welcomes them with a jet of heat, misery and worklessness and they quickly escape to Petach Tikva and Rishon Le-Tzion, or walk hungry but singing to the Galilee, when suddenly the rumour spreads that workers' farming communities are going to be set up in the land, in Kinneret and at Ben Shemen and here, the Zionist Organization will pay the cost of the materials and they will earn their livelihood by their own labour. And it will be a co-operative. The curtain is going up and the thrilling show is about to begin.[22]

The story of his father's immigration at the age of sixteen, carrying the Bible in one hand and Tolstoy in the other, abandoning his weeping relatives and making his way through an indifferent and sometimes hostile terrain, is presented as a theater performance. This is a show for the world to watch—the story of the fulfillment of the Zionist dream. But it is presented from the vantage point of a tiny human about to be stung by hundreds of wasps because his father needs to do his plowing so that he can participate in the reclamation of the wilderness, the domestication of the Promised Land. Following the stinging, we read a dramatization of rushing the child to the doctor in the neighboring village as he fights for his life, with the mother's Yiddish lullabies, and the father's recitation of psalms woven into a recounting of their respective immigration stories. The distinct consciousness of the mother is represented in the following way:

Then he knows not how Mummy is there, he is in her arms, and people, all around, how did it happen, what is it, run and harness, get moving, just get moving, quick, an ambulance, quick and catch that mule and from the plough to the cart, only be quick, people, be quick, and where's the other mule, here's Mummy in her arms already, *Mein Kind*, Mummy, *Mein Kind*, wrap him in something and she kisses him and counts where, and breathes kisses near the edge of his breaths, he is sobbing with pain, fainting, give him something to drink, everything's swollen, the face, how can it be so, choking and swollen and here all around, and Mummy more to her heart, *Oy Gott Gottenyu*, wrapping him all up and to her heart, *Mein Kind*, wrapping and squeezing.[23]

The repeated Yiddish phrases—my child, my child, oy dear God, my child—appear here as the mother joins the father and the child just after the disaster and they begin their journey on a rickety cart to the doctor, pulled by a reluctant donkey. The father's consciousness is articulated differently:

Like a nettle rash and terrifyingly swollen, as though there's no pulse in the pulse, only the sobbing of the pain that is beyond fainting, because he has not uttered a single cry beyond that first, terrible one that rent the world and the air and the sunlight, and at once his voice is silenced, from the pain and the swelling and Daddy is already at his side, already he's lifting him up, what is it, my boy, what is it, already waving them away with his hand and kicking them away with his foot, and flapping his hat, without being afraid of them, already running, where does it hurt, ruling out a snake or a scorpion and knowing already that it's them, the wasps, the damned wasps, from the hole in the ground, on which he had put his baby to sit and amuse himself while he finished this strip, the last one, oh the strip of the field of this place that doesn't exist yet, of this Co-operative Workers' Association of the Herzl Forest Project, of HaPo'el Hatza'ir. Are they three people together now (or four, with the older boy, seven years old, who had been left behind), or three one of whom is guilty and needs to explain and apologise and even promise? So long as, so long as, God, so long as, I lift up my eyes, whence my help, out of the depths I cry to You, O Lord hear my voice, let Your ears be attentive to the voice of my supplication, and in a suddenly murderous voice, Get along there, faster, you beasts, faster, quick.[24]

Here, in free indirect discourse with the father (he is called "Daddy" with a bow to the child's own idiom), we learn about the physical state of his child after having been stung by the wasps, and about Daddy's own role in bringing this injury about. Working for the association of the Herzl Forest Project, Ze'ev Smolenski is plowing the land and needs to finish his "strip" while babysitting for his younger son, and he has placed his child on the ground to keep him out of the way. The child's trauma story, of being stung and transported to the doctor, is interwoven with the father's story of immigration in a subtle allusion to the idea that the father's immigration is the child's trauma. This shared consciousness with his father persists for much of the first half of the novel as the experience of the pioneer-immigrant and the experience of his child are presented as inextricably tied together.

In this post-Zionist moment, the paragons of Zionism, such as Yizhar, are claiming the right to salvage that which was meant to be forgotten. How does Yizhar do this? He chooses an artifact, as did Maurice Samuel in his selection of the Tevye stories, or Abraham Joshua Heschel in his selection of Hasidic tales, and he weaves it into his narrative of early childhood. This is not a reconstruction of the Pale of Settlement but a new attentiveness to the elements of his parents' background that come to him through the years as he reflects on his own identity as a paragon of place, as the quintessential sabra, as the native author of a native Hebrew bound

Postcard of Rehovot, Jacob Street, ca. 1893.

to the Land of Israel. In the words of poet Saul Tschernikhovsky, if "man is nothing more than the landscape of his childhood," how does that landscape extend beyond the one land to others?

Preliminaries, which begins with the question "And where was the first place? The very first?," traces the consciousness of a child from earliest awareness, through adolescence, as he grows into his love of literature and music and develops a sense of self despite the intense collectivity of his environment. He works hard to differentiate himself from the struggles of his parents—his father's desire to embody the Zionist ideologies he espoused, his mother's longing for a settled homelife that might reconstruct the eastern European Jewish home she left behind as a teenager when she immigrated to Palestine. Organized around the stations of his childhood, the novel tracks the child's consciousness from place to place—from Rehovot to Neve Shalom to Tel Aviv to Tel Nordeau and finally to Be'er Yaakov. Like the travelogue that closes the biblical book of Numbers, which lists forty-two stops in the desert (Num. 33), Yizhar's book is something of a travelogue as well, a list of places that his family traveled through on their quest for a permanent home in Palestine. The child's emotional and artistic growth is developed in conjunction with all these places.

But the valence of place is different in *Preliminaries* than one would expect based on Yizhar's earlier work. It is not the place of *Hirbet Hizeh* or *Days of Ziklag*, where the psyche of the individual becomes bound up with every nook and cranny of the landscape. Here place is anchored in something other than the Israeli landscape. Yizhar's narrator cannot be pinned down to any single location. He is always looking beyond the land, for some kind of music, some kind of reverberation beneath, above, behind the land, like the "music" behind the words of those with whom he speaks. The teenage protagonist exemplifies the dilemma of the wandering Jew even in the Promised Land. He seeks out ways to fill his being with something larger than the smallness and sadness of a daily life on the sand and finds Schubert and Beethoven, Dostoevsky and Dickens, to enlarge his horizons, to deepen his sense of self.

Moshe Shamir (1921–2004), a peer of S. Yizhar's and a fellow writer from *dor ha-medina*, the statehood generation, wrote what has been considered the most oft-quoted first line in modern Hebrew literature: "Elik ba min ha-yam" (Elik came out of the sea.)[25] Taken from *Be-mo yadav* (*With His Own Hands*), Shamir's novelistic tribute to his older brother, Elik, who was killed in the War of Independence, his introduction of his brother as having come from the sea represents the approach that was meant to be taken by pioneers of the Jewish state. Their children were created, as it were, from nothing, and they were meant to inhabit the state fully, organically, naturally, and natively. Their parents' points of origin were to be meaningless to them. They were born not of flesh and blood that made the journey to Palestine from the texts, prayers, and languages of the Jewish diaspora. Rather, they were born of the sea, emerging like primordial creatures from a place without history to create a new history for themselves, a history of emplacement, not displacement. It was anathema to the founders of the state to continue the Jewish legacy of displacement and so the easiest thing to do was to forget all memory of what came before.

At the end of their lives, the generation of Israelis "born from the sea" have eschewed their obligation to participate in the erasure of all that preceded them. For Yizhar, as we have explored, the child protagonist did not "come from the sea." He came from his parents who came from Russia. And those parents, Miriam and Ze'ev Smolenski, brought to Palestine a cultural memory that Yizhar's protagonist can no longer see or hear in plain day but that he seeks out, beneath and behind the surface of the mundane place that the longed-for place has become. He is looking for a world in *Preliminaries*, and that world, freed from the dogmas and repressions of nationalist myopia, can be found in his earliest childhood experiences of his father's Hasidic melodies and his mother's oilcloth maps. It is the world of the eastern European foundations out of which the modern State of Israel developed.

7

"STORIES FULL OF BLACKBERRIES"

Literary Genealogies and Acts of Salvage

As we continue our discussion of canonic writers "reconsidering" the negation of the diaspora in their later works, we turn to Amos Oz's *Sipur 'al 'ahavah ve-ḥoshekh* or *A Tale of Love and Darkness* (2002). While eastern European–born S. Y. Agnon focused on sacred texts as his salvage artifact, and S. Yizhar focused on music, Oz's focus is on the European oral folktales shared by his mother, Fania Mussman Klausner (1913–52) alongside the traditional Jewish liturgical and mystical canon presented to him, orally, by his teacher and poet, Zelda Schneurson Mishkovsky (1914–84). The oral legacy of these two women brought eastern Europe back into his consciousness, facilitating a reorientation of his own literary genealogy within the schema of Israeli literary historiography. We begin with a glimpse into Oz's treatment of his own genealogy and then work our way over to the oral artifacts he identifies at the heart of his own salvage poetic model. Early in the novel, Oz describes a social gathering:

> On winter evenings a few members of my parents' circle used to get together sometimes at our place or at the Zarchis' in the building across the road: Hayim and Hannah Toren, Shmuel Werses, the Breimans, flamboyant Mr. Sharon-Shvadron, who was a great talker, Mr. Haim Schwarzbaum the red-headed folklorist, Israel Hanani, who worked at the Jewish Agency, and his wife Esther Hananit. They arrived after supper, at seven or half past, and left at half past nine, which was considered a late hour. In between, they drank scalding tea, nibbled honey

cake or fresh fruit, discussed with well-bred anger all kinds of topics that I could not understand; but I knew that when the time came, I would understand them, I would participate in the discussions and would produce decisive arguments that they had not thought of. I might even manage to surprise them, I might end up writing books out of my own head like Mr. Zarchi, or collections of poems like Bialik and Grandpa Alexander and Levin Kipnis and Dr. Saul Tchernikhovsky, the doctor whose smell I shall never forget.[1]

Oz's novel-cum-memoir about growing up in Mandate Palestine and divided Jerusalem as the only son of two European refugees presents us with a fascinating chiasmus relating both to actual parents and literary progenitors. In it, he paints a portrait of the founding fathers of Hebrew literature in a familial light, humanizing and defamiliarizing them, by casting them more as extended family members than as literary models. At the same time, he describes the ways in which his own nuclear family, and specifically his late mother, become the source of his literary genius even as they fail to nurture him as a son. In this chapter I trace this crossover, from canonic literary genealogy to family and from family to literary genealogy. Through this crossover, Oz embraces his mother, whose life was defined by her frustrated literary aspirations as his greatest literary influence while refusing to acknowledge the influence of Hebrew literature's giants on him as a Hebrew writer of the next generation. This movement from family to literary progenitor and from literary progenitor to family branches out in a variety of ways that illuminate the role of women in what seems on the surface to be a misogynist oeuvre, and the role of eastern Europe in what, on the surface, appears to be the work of the quintessential sabra. As we have observed throughout this study, salvage poetics can be identified in a variety of different formats. Here what we will see is the way in which preserving the voices of eastern European–born Israeli women, such as Oz's mother or the poet Zelda, serves for him as a means of salvaging the threads of eastern European folk expressions and Jewish religious literature within the Israeli literature of the statehood generation.

In the generational literary historiography of Israeli belles lettres, Amos Oz has long been identified as a poster boy for the literary generation of *dor ha-medina*, the statehood generation of Hebrew writers, who were mostly born in Palestine and whose first language, by and large, was Hebrew.[2] Therefore, by genealogical default, Oz, alongside Yaakov Shabtai, A. B. Yehoshua, Yoram Kaniuk, Yehoshua Kenaz, and others,[3] was the natural inheritor of the *dor ha-teḥiya*, the generation of the modern Hebrew renaissance, who heralded from eastern Europe. Included in that earlier generation, as is well known, were Chaim Nachman Bialik, S. Y. Agnon, Saul Tschernikhovsky, and Dvora Baron, all of whom immigrated to Palestine in the first half of the twentieth century. Critical lip service is given as well by Israeli literary historiographers to earlier Hebrew writers who did not make it to Palestine but who set the tone and tenor of the Hebrew renaissance, most notably Sholem Yankev Abramovitsh (Mendele), M. J. Berdyczewski, U. N. Gnessin, and M. Z. Feierberg.

This presentation of Oz as subverting his own literary placement by affiliating himself literarily with his family falls into a common discourse within modern Hebrew literary historiography. Modern Hebrew literary history is generationally foreshortened in that generations overlap with one another, rendering "succeeding" generations effectively parallel with one another, primarily because, as we have discussed, Hebrew literature played such an important role in inventing Hebrew-speaking culture and vernacularizing the language for use within a newly invented Hebrew social environment. Oz, as a younger member of the statehood generation is considered, simultaneously, the natural inheritor of someone like S. Yizhar, discussed in chapter 6, a generation older than him but also a native-born Israeli author, as well as the writers born in Europe who created a modern Hebrew literary idiom, such as S. Y. Agnon, discussed in chapter 5. The accumulation of literary ancestors in a literature barely one hundred years old can serve as a major burden for someone like Oz whose first book was published in 1965, less than twenty years after the establishment of the state and only a little over a century after the publication of the first Hebrew novel in 1853. The nuances of the Hebrew language in modernity changed so dramatically and so quickly, and are still changing for that matter, that the idea of literary ancestors feels almost ridiculous; the "grandfather" of modern Hebrew literature, Mendele, for example, was not really a "grandfather" to what was considered the next "generation" of Hebrew writers, led by Chaim Nachman Bialik, because Mendele was less than forty years Bialik's senior. But the designation of literary "generations" plays a very specific national purpose, particularly in new nations like the modern State of Israel: it creates a "tradition." And traditions can feel, at times, like a vise that must be thrown off. Here what we will see is that Oz throws off the literary tradition in favor of one of his own choosing, one anchored not in the eastern European literature that is teleologically oriented toward the creation of a national culture but rather a European literature oriented toward an eastern European legacy that defies Israeli national ideologies. As the creators of literary canons designate "generations" of writers, they assign each generation the responsibility to carry the torch of the one that preceded it. There is an implicit understanding that the second generation is in some way responsive to the first, aligned with it, but departing from it in subtle ways that do not negate the sense of indebtedness and influence that defines the second generation. In his study of canonicity in modernist Hebrew poetry, Michael Gluzman discusses inclusion and exclusion at a time of Israeli nation building, paying especially close attention to the different affiliative vectors that grow out of a close analysis of canonic writers' attitudes toward their place in the canon. Instead of fathers and mothers who bequeath literary obligations to their children, he identifies, in the tradition of Russian formalist Viktor Shklovsky, the selection of aunts and uncles by the younger generation—from among the preceding generation and beyond.[4] In so doing, Gluzman elaborates on the following questions: Why should literary generations embrace their schematization wholeheartedly? How does accepting one's placement as a generation of inheritors overdetermine one's literary path in debilitating ways? How does our reading of writers within canonic genealogies limit the scope of our critical understanding?

More than anything else, *A Tale of Love and Darkness*, like Yizhar's *Preliminaries*, is a *Künstlerroman*, a novel of artistic becoming. In it, Amos Oz situates himself at a nexus of literary influences that is constituted primarily by two major threads: a familial thread and a national literary one. The two, however, as described above, function at odds, with the national literary thread taking on a familial genealogical role in his literary conception of himself and his familial thread taking on the role of literary genealogy. The excerpt that opened this chapter provides a beautiful illustration of the progressive overlap between the familial and the literary threads that Oz introduces in his novel and paves the way for the displacement of the national literary by the familial, to dramatic effect.

In his description of winter nights during his childhood, when his parents got together with neighborhood friends to discuss politics and literature, Oz equalizes well-known literary figures with lesser-known personalities that populated his early life. Shmuel Werses, the well-known critic of Hebrew and Yiddish literature, is placed alongside Dr. Shlomo Breiman, administrator and instructor of modern Hebrew literature at the Hebrew University, and his wife.[5] Chaim Nachman Bialik, the foremost Hebrew national poet, is situated alongside Grandfather Alexander, who could barely write in

Hebrew. And Levin Kipnis, a writer of Hebrew children's books, is aligned with Saul Tschernikhovsky, another Hebrew national poet. For the child Oz, Grandfather Alexander was as important a poet as Bialik, and Levin Kipnis was as inspiring an author as Tschernikhovsky. The most important indication of Oz's unorthodox equivalencies can be found, however, in the final line of this passage, where Tschernikhovsky is identified as memorable not by virtue of his poetry but by virtue of his smell. And this smell keeps returning as Tschernikhovsky's leitmotif in Oz's account:

> Almost sixty years have gone by, yet I can still remember his smell. I summon it, and it returns to me, a slightly coarse, dusty, but strong and pleasant smell, reminiscent of touching rough sackcloth, and it borders on the memory of the feel of his skin, his flowing locks, his thick mustache that rubbed against the skin of my cheek and gave me a pleasant feeling, like being in a warm, dark old kitchen on a winter day. The poet Saul Tchernikhovsky died in the autumn of 1943, when I was little more than four years old, so that this sensual recollection can only have survived by passing through several stages of transmission and amplification. . . .
>
> But in the picture in my mind, which my parents' recurrent searchlight beams may have helped me preserve but did not imprint in me, in my scenario, which is less sweet than theirs, I never sat on the poet's lap, nor did I tug at his famous mustache, but I tripped and fell over at Uncle Joseph's home, and as I fell, I bit my tongue, and it bled a little, and I cried, and the poet, being also a doctor, a pediatrician, reached me before my parents, helped me up with his big hands, I even remember now that he picked me up with my back to him and my shouting face to the room, then he swung me around in his arms and said something, and then something else, certainly not about handing on the crown of Pushkin to Tolstoy, and while I was still struggling in his arms, he forced my mouth open and called for someone to fetch some ice, then inspected my injury and declared:
>
> "It's nothing, just a scratch, and as we are now weeping, so we shall soon be laughing."[6]

As a young child at his uncle Joseph Klausner's house, Oz fell down. Saul Tschernikhovsky, who was visiting Klausner, picked Oz up, held him, comforted him, and reassured the young parents. Oz's association with this great poet of the modern Hebrew renaissance is a familial, domestic one. His memory of him is not text centered but sense oriented. Oz even goes out of his way to deny any literariness in the encounter, saying that he certainly was not discussing Tolstoy or Pushkin with the great poet (the fact that Oz was about three years old probably played a significant role in that discursive choice). Tschernikhovsky is embodied as hands, a mustache, a smell. He is a man to the young boy, not a poet. Acknowledging that this memory was certainly influenced by his parents' awed retelling of the day that Oz was scooped up into the great poet's arms, we return to the earlier quote and consider the position of the child protagonist as narrated by the adult. One could argue that Oz, by focusing on the poet's smell and not his poetry, is only giving us access to the experience of the preverbal, or at least the preliterary, child. But Oz goes out of his way, in further reflections on this experience, to decouple Tschernikhovsky from any kind of literary consciousness: "So far as I can remember, no witty aphorism worthy of immortalization was exchanged on that occasion between the giant among the poets of the formative Generation of National Revival and the sobbing little representative of the later so-called Generation of the State of Israel."[7] In this passage, Oz acknowledges Tschernikhovsky's literary identity, but he denies any kind of passing of the torch. Even as he names their canonic literary positions with respect to one another Oz repudiates that relationship. In a final statement on Tschernikhovsky, Oz elaborates on his identity vis-à-vis Oz as a fatherly, comforting figure but not necessarily as a writer:

> It was only two or three years after this incident that I managed to pronounce the name Tchernikhovsky. I was not surprised when I was told that he was a poet: almost everyone in Jerusalem in those days was either a poet or a writer or a researcher or a thinker or a scholar or a world reformer. . . .
>
> But he was not just any old doctor or poet. He was a pediatrician, a man with a disheveled mop of hair, with laughing eyes, big warm hands, a thicket of a mustache, a felt cheek, and a unique, strong, soft smell.
>
> To this day, whenever I see a photograph or drawing of the poet Saul or his carved head that stands in the entrance of the Tchernikhovsky Writers' House, I am immediately enveloped, like the embrace of a winter blanket, by his comforting smell.

Here Oz first minimizes Tschernikhovsky's stature by asserting that during his childhood everyone in Jerusalem was some kind of intellectual (a poet, a writer, a researcher, and so forth). Then he downplays the importance of being a poet altogether saying that "he was not just any old doctor or poet." Although we would expect Oz to say, "He was Tschernikhovsky!" instead he says, "He was a pediatrician," as if being a children's doctor is what made him special to the exclusion of all else. Also, characterizing him by his smell, size, body, and warmth, Oz does not represent him literarily. Even the final statement, "To this day . . . ," addresses Tschernikhovsky on the basis of photographs, drawings, and sculpture, not on the basis of language. And what do these images bring up for Oz? "I am immediately enveloped, like the embrace of a winter blanket, by his comforting smell." As before, this is clearly a fusion of Oz's parents' association with Tschernikhovsky as a literary giant and his childhood reminiscences of him as simply a man, or even a kind of parent—comforting, sentient, warm. It seems that Oz assigns to Tschernikhovsky the role that he would normally assign to a mother—nurturing him after a fall.

Tschernikhovsky is not the only canonic writer of the modern Hebrew renaissance that Oz neutralizes and defamiliarizes by bringing him into the familial fold. In describing his father's father, Alexander Klausner, Oz brings him into a circle of literati, with unexpected results:

> As he made his way around the sun-washed streets of Odessa, a harbor town with a heady atmosphere colored by the presence of several different nationalities, he made friends of various kinds, courted girls, bought and sold and sometimes made a profit, sat down in a corner of a café or on a park bench, took out his notebook, wrote a poem (four stanzas, eight rhymes), then cycled around again as the unpaid errand boy of the leaders of the Lovers of Zion society in pre-telephone Odessa: carrying a hasty note from Ahad Ha'am to Mendele Mokher Seforim, or from Mendele Mokher Seforim to Mr. Bialik, who was fond of saucy jokes, or to Mr. Menachem Ussishkin, from Mr. Ussishkin to Mr. Lilienblum, and while he waited in the drawing room or the hall for the reply, poems in Russian in the spirit of the Love of Zion movement played in his heart.[8]

Who from the generation of the Hebrew renaissance does Grandfather Alexander not hang around with in Odessa? He seems to have been something of an intimate with Bialik, Mendele, Ussishkin, Lilienblum, and even Ahad Ha'am! But Grandfather Alexander, whom we encountered in this chapter's opening passage as a counterpoint to Tschernikhovsky, himself writes only in Russian! Grandfather Alexander, in other words, claims an association with these writers, but not on literary terms by any means.

By associating in this intimate way with the Hebrew greats, Grandfather Alexander becomes one of them, as it were, and they become a part of Oz's family.

This pattern of naturalizing, defamiliarizing, and rendering familial the giants of the Hebrew renaissance continues with Bialik:

> Once, it may have been in the late 1950s, a fine new ten-lira note came into circulation bearing a picture of the poet Bialik. When I got hold of my first Bialik note, I hurried straight to Grandpa's to show him how the state had honored the man he had known in his youth. Grandpa was indeed excited, his cheeks flushed with pleasure, he turned the note this way and that, held it up to the lightbulb, scrutinized the picture of Bialik (who seemed to me suddenly to be winking mischievously at Grandpa, as if to say "*Nu!?*"). A tiny tear sparkled in Grandpa's eye, but while he reveled in his pride his fingers folded up the new note and tucked it away in the inside pocket of his jacket.
>
> Ten liras was a tidy sum at that time, particularly for a kibbutznik like me. I was startled:
>
> "Grandpa, what are you doing? I only brought it to show you and to make you happy. You'll get one of your own in a day or two, for sure."
>
> "*Nu*," Grandpa shrugged, "Bialik owed me twenty-two rubles."[9]

The young Oz excitedly shares the new currency with his grandfather because he knows about Grandfather Alexander's association with Bialik. And how does Grandfather Alexander relate to this recognition of the icon that is Bialik? He calls in his debts. Not only does this vignette domesticate Bialik, as was the case with Tschernikhovsky in Uncle Joseph's house, but it renders Bialik somewhat ridiculous.

Oz establishes yet another familial connection in this novel, this time with both Bialik and Tschernikhovsky, in the following reference to a literary salon in Odessa established by Oz's grandmother Shlomit (his father's mother and Grandfather Alexander's wife):

> Occasionally Bialik would drop in for an evening, pale with grief or shivering with cold and anger—or quite the contrary: he could also be the life and soul of the party. "And how!" said my grandmother, "Like a kid, he was! A real scalawag! No holds barred! So risqué." . . .
>
> The poet Tchernikhovsky, too, might burst into the salon, flamboyant but shy, passionate yet prickly, conquering hearts, touching in his

childlike innocence, as fragile as a butterfly but also hurtful, wounding people left, right, and center without even noticing. . . .

Tchernikhovsky stoked his spirits with a *glazele* or two of vodka, and sometimes he would start to read those poems of his that overflowed with hilarity or sorrow and made everybody in the room melt with him and for him: his liberal ways, his flowing locks, his anarchic mustache, the girls he brought with him, who were not always too bright, and not even necessarily Jewish, but were always beauties who gladdened every eye and caused not a few tongues to wag and whetted the writers' envy—"I'm telling you as a woman (Grandma again), women are never wrong about such things, Bialik used to sit and stare at him like this . . . and at the *goyish* girls he brought along . . . Bialik would have given an entire year of his life if only he could have lived for a month as Tchernikhovsky!"[10]

Ventriloquizing his grandmother in her description of Tschernikhovsky and Bialik, we see another form of domestication. Bialik, morose, depressed, and jealous of his fellow poet's sexual prowess and masculinity, is described in keeping with Oz's father's and uncle's favoring of Tschernikhovsky's "masculine" poetry as opposed to Bialik's "effeminate" poetry. Providing Oz's grandmother Shlomit's perspective on these famous poets as squabbling teenage boys illuminates a further aspect of the kind of defamiliarization and familial naturalization that Oz performs on the writers of the modern Hebrew renaissance.

Rather than just continuing to refer to Oz's uncle Joseph Klausner in passing, I will offer here a more thorough treatment, within the context of the genealogical crossover between literary generation and family. Uncle Joseph was a famous member of early Zionist literati on the Yishuv and played a major role in Oz's sense of both his family and his literary development. His grandfather Alexander's brother, Joseph Gedalya Klausner (1874–1958), was a historian and editor during the period of the modern Hebrew renaissance, curating and cultivating a nationalist literary and political discourse at the Hebrew University in the early decades of the twentieth century. About twice a month on Saturday afternoons, when Oz was a young child, he and his parents would walk across Jerusalem from Kerem Avraham to Klausner's home in Talpiot, where Oz would observe the cohort that surrounded his uncle. Despite his clear affiliation with all the most important and most visible members of Hebrew literary society in the first decades of the twentieth century in Palestine, or perhaps because of the cult of personality that organized itself around him, Oz's great-uncle Joseph refused to use this power to assist his flailing nephew, Oz's father (Aryeh Leib Klausner). Within the context of actual familial ties, Uncle Joseph did very little to further the aspirations and ambitions of his nephew, who sought an academic post in literature at the Hebrew University: "While Uncle Joseph definitely encouraged my father, who was one of his star pupils, he never chose him, when the time came, as a teaching assistant, so as not to give malicious tongues anything to wag about. So important was it for Professor Klausner to avoid aspersions on his good name that he may have behaved unfairly to his brother's son, his own flesh and blood."[11] At this interesting interlude in the text, we see that family does not guarantee literary continuity; in fact, Oz suggests here that family associations with great literary figures may actually impede one's literary progress. While relating to his father throughout the memoir as a somewhat limited man, Oz does sympathize with him in this.

The generation of the modern Hebrew renaissance is presented by Oz as intimately intertwined with his family. Grandpa Alexander was buddies with Bialik and knew Lilienblum intimately. Grandma Shlomit understood the animosity between Bialik and Tschernikhovsky from the perspective of a woman with a husband and two sons who was deeply familiar with the ways of men. Tschernikhovsky's smell remains with Oz from childhood. Joseph Klausner, on the other hand, his actual uncle, demonstrated very little warmth, very little allegiance toward his own family members. He was so enamored with himself he could not see a way to assist in his nephew's suffering—something that was clearly within his power. All this is to say that Oz explicitly develops a literary genealogy in *A Tale of Love and Darkness* that does not take us in an expected direction, and Oz does not admit any serious literary allegiance to most of the renaissance generation.[12] With the exception of Y. H. Brenner and S. Y. Agnon, whom he begrudgingly acknowledges as literary influences, Oz seeks his inspiration elsewhere.

But what of Oz's actual familial genealogy and its impact on his writing life? Certainly, Klausner's impact was one of alienation. In Oz's own preference for Brenner and Agnon, he rejects his uncle's evaluation of writers who were "stuck in the diaspora," who cried and moaned and engaged in sophistry and solipsism, as he saw it. Oz's father's variation on this theme is described in the book as follows:

> My father, who at Agnon's request translated the article "Buczacz" for him from a Polish encyclopedia when Agnon was writing *A City and*

the Fullness Thereof, would twist his lips as he defined him as a "diaspora writer": his stories lack wings, he said, they have no tragic depth, there is not even any healthy laughter but only wisecracks and sarcasm. And if he does have some beautiful descriptions here and there, he does not rest or put down his pen until he has drowned them in pools of verbose buffoonery and Galician cleverness. I have the impression my father saw Agnon's stories as an extension of Yiddish literature, and he was not fond of Yiddish literature. In keeping with his temperament of a rationalistic Lithuanian *Misnaged*, he loathed magic, the supernatural, and excessive emotionalism, anything clad in foggy romanticism or mystery, anything intended to make the senses whirl or to blinker reason—until the last years of his life, when his taste changed.[13]

When Oz was a child, then, it seems that his father championed the negation of the diaspora. His uncle, Joseph Klausner, however, promoted Zalman Shneour (1887–1959), a Hebrew and Yiddish poet who never lived in Palestine or Israel; Uncle Joseph also rarely, if ever, wrote about Hebrew writers active in Palestine. Just as Oz tempers his representation of his father's dislike for Agnon by acknowledging that his attitude toward Yiddish and the diaspora changed at the end of his life (in fact, his father ultimately wrote his dissertation, in London, on I. L. Peretz [1852–1915]), it is important to view with a grain of salt the antidiasporic rhetoric Oz remembers from his family members during childhood.[14] These champions of the "New Jew" came from Europe. They were educated in European universities. They were raised in European languages. Oz's familial genealogy was a European genealogy.

It is this genealogy outside of Palestine and Israel, outside of the renaissance generation, that we will now consider here as we continue our discussion of the familial-literary chiasmus we have been tracing. Amos Oz's family—mainly his mother, as we will discuss—created the central axis of his literary consciousness. In a 2010 review essay on *A Tale of Love and Darkness* and S. Yizhar's *Preliminaries*, I focused on the European background that both authors acknowledge in their late-life novel-cum-memoirs, arguing:

> In *A Tale of Love and Darkness* and *Preliminaries*, Oz and Yizhar negotiate the countervailing powers of the self and the nation, depicting their psychological development alongside the political development of the State of Israel whose heavy mantle they were forced, as the children

of Zionist idealists (to a greater or lesser degree), to bear. Implicit in each text is a profound awareness of the burdens of growing up as a first-generation Israeli with spiritual and intellectual leanings toward a kind of aesthetic and consciousness that cannot be confined to a single landscape or a single language. Each of these writers, reflecting on his position as a native-born "Eretz-Israeli" Jew to East European immigrants within an imminent Israeli landscape, plays with the expectations heaped upon him—the embodiment of the Zionist ideal—against a backdrop of longing (as in Yizhar's case) or ambivalence (as in Oz's case) for broader, richer, and more culturally resonant European homelands left behind.[15]

Written as I was just beginning to conceive my notion of salvage poetics, my essay on Yizhar and Oz gingerly approached the possibility that these emblematic writers of the statehood generation were "returning" to their European origins late in their lives just as S. Ansky, the great ethnographer of the Pale, "returned" to Judaism after a failed attempt to join the Russian socialists, or Vladimir Medem, baptized at birth, "returned" to Judaism when he formed the Jewish Bund.[16] In all these cases, what we observe is a "return" to a culture and a means of acknowledging that culture as a turning point in these men's careers. For Ansky it was ethnographic, for Medem it was political, and for Oz it was literary. What are the parameters of Oz's particular return to Europe in *A Tale of Love and Darkness*?

As we continue our exploration of the different types of genealogies developed by Oz in *A Tale of Love and Darkness*, and particularly the fact that he designates the literary generation preceding his as members of his family, I would like to posit here that his mother, Fania Mussman Klausner, whom he lost to suicide as a child, becomes the key figure in his literary genealogy. His mother, in other words, takes on the role of a literary predecessor without any of the maternal qualities you would expect to see in his description of her, while Tschernikhovsky (alongside other canonic Hebrew literary figures) takes on a maternal role, with his pungent smell, his warm hands, and his ability to comfort and heal. Fania, Oz's mother, is at the center of a constellation of forces that come together for him as he engages in his own sort of salvage poetic in *A Tale of Love and Darkness*.

What is Oz salvaging? Eran Kaplan argues that *A Tale of Love and Darkness* serves as a kind of found text on Zionism's formative years, both in Europe and Jerusalem, as told by Oz. Citing Yigal Schwartz, Kaplan writes:

Literary Genealogies and Acts of Salvage 161

Amos Oz at work. Courtesy of Alamy, World History Archive.

Throughout most of his artistic and public career, Oz occupied a prominent place at the forefront of Israeli high art. He was one of the main pieces on exhibit on the Israeli artistic and intellectual scene. But, as Schwartz has revealed, for many readers of *A Tale of Love and Darkness* it is the real objects and real places described in the book that have registered most deeply with them. As opposed to traditional novels (including Oz's own earlier work), Oz does not draw on personal memories or the memory of personal objects in order to take them on a psychological journey with universal (middle-class) insights. Rather, Oz seems to lead his readers to specific memories and objects that serve as modern-day talismans to a specific social group.[17]

In a similar vein, Iris Milner views this book as part of the "back to our roots" movement that contemporary Israelis, many of whose grandparents Hebraized their names upon emigrating from Europe and spoke only Hebrew to their children, are now promulgating.[18] *A Tale of Love and Darkness* was thus written at a moment when it became acceptable to reclaim one's European roots, and it provided a portrait of first-generation Israelis for their children and grandchildren. Centered as it is in Jerusalem of the 1940s, however, it presents a very particular spin on European culture, one that is geographically situated in the Promised Land even as it provides windows into the world that preceded it. Irving Howe, in his depiction of nineteenth-century eastern European Jewish culture in his 1976 American classic *World of Our Fathers*, situates his overview of that world primarily on the Lower East Side, or the New York in which Howe himself was introduced to that culture through his family home and his parents' generation.[19] Oz, through his rich description of Jerusalem and his anchoring of his background storytelling about his grandparents within that milieu, uses a similar strategy. He introduces us to European Jewry through his accounts of the early Israelis in his own family who came from that world and raised him in Jerusalem.

In addition to the culture of Zionism in Jerusalem, on the Yishuv, and in Europe between the world wars, Oz is salvaging, it would seem, the stories told over and over again by his mother to Oz as a child. Of this, Oz writes: "I spent my whole childhood in Kerem Avraham in Jerusalem, but where I really lived was on the edge of the forest, by the huts, the steppes, the meadows, the snow in my mother's stories, and in the illustrated books that piled up on my low bedside table: I was in the east, but my heart was in the farthermost west. Or the 'farthermost north,' as it said in those books."[20]

Many critics have acknowledged the role of Oz's mother in his literary psyche, particularly in his early works that grapple with depressed young women in soulless marriages (Hannah Gonen in *My Michael*, Mrs. Kipnis in "The Hill of Evil Counsel"), but very few have acknowledged the active place of his mother's stories, her storytelling, within his literary genealogy. There are countless descriptions throughout *A Tale of Love and Darkness* of the stories that Oz's mother told him during his childhood and the impact they had on him: "My mother liked telling me stories about wizards, elves, ghouls, enchanted cottages in the depths of the forest, but she also talked to me seriously about crimes, emotions, the lives and sufferings of brilliant artists, mental illness, and the inner lives of animals."[21]

Elsewhere, Oz acknowledges the fear that his mother's stories instilled in him: "Surely my mother would never have been so crazy as to tell a terrible story like that to a four- or five-year-old child?"[22] But he forgives her and embraces these stories immediately after this assertion:

> My mother's stories may have been strange, frightening, but they were captivating, full of caves and towers, abandoned villages and broken bridges suspended above the void. Her stories did not begin at the beginning or conclude with a happy ending but flickered in the half light, wound around themselves, emerged from the mists for a moment, amazed you, sent shivers up your spine, then disappeared back into the darkness before you had time to see what was in front of your eyes. . . .
>
> Her stories were full of blackberries, blueberries, wild strawberries, truffles, and mushrooms. With no thought for my tender years my mother took me to places where few children had ever trodden before, and as she did so, she opened up before me an exciting fan of words, as though she were picking me up in her arms and raising me higher and higher to reveal vertiginous heights of language.[23]

Oz's mother is said by Oz to have spent her free time reading Turgenev, Chekhov, Agnon, and Gnessin. One of the signs for Oz that his mother was descending into despair and depression was when she stopped reading: sitting by the window with a book upside down in her lap, gazing outside. But the stories she tells her young child are not drawn from the classic belle lettres of European literature. They are folktales and fairy tales, tales of the European landscape and its ghosts and sorcerers. Even the stories that she told Oz about her own life, and the stories her sister, Sonia, told Oz about her upbringing alongside Fania in Rovno, all resembled these ghost stories and folktales. The house they lived in was inhabited by a variety of different personages—mainly mothers and daughters—who had been abandoned by men and lived beneath the radar of society; they subsisted in quiet desperation like madwomen in the attic; it was unclear where their income came from, and they created an undercurrent in the house of dark brooding and salaciousness.

This brings to mind Art Spiegelman's meditation in *Maus* on the loss of his mother's wartime diaries. After her suicide when Spiegelman was in his early twenties, his father destroyed her diaries in a fit of grief and rage. Thus, the only stories we know about the experience of Spiegelman's mother during the war, because she refused to speak of it to her son, have to be mediated by his father's stories. Spiegelman turns on his father when he hears of what his father has done to his mother's diaries and calls him "murderer," which to some extent he is, having taken Spiegelman's mother's story—all that is left of her after her death—and destroyed it.[24] Whereas Spiegelman lost his mother's stories, Oz still has those of his mother; and, as we read his recollections of the stories his mother told him as a child, we hear a kind of abstracted variation on her life. We see the resemblance between the folktales she used to tell him when he was a child and the stories about her that Aunt Sonia told Oz when he was an adult—stories of magic and the fears it invokes, of grief and the possibilities it inspires. These stories are all Oz has left of his mother and to a large extent it is their tonalities—the darkness, the emotionality, the lyricism—that make their way into his work, particularly in his meditations on Jerusalem—a dark, divided space caught up in the emotions of its inhabitants—or in his depictions of despair and madness in both his works that focus on Jerusalem and on kibbutz life.[25] He is not only salvaging his mother's stories in *A Tale of Love and Darkness*, but he is also salvaging the language she bequeathed to him: the tone and tenor of psychological despair and unexplored landscapes that "reveal" to him "the vertiginous heights of language."

Robert Alter, in his reading of this book, beautifully correlates two scenes that further illuminate this understanding of the place of Oz's mother within Oz's literary genealogy. The first he identifies is the scene of inspiration where the child Oz recognizes his calling as a writer:

> You will never forget this evening: you are only six or at most six and a half, but for the first time in your little life something enormous and very terrible has opened up for you, something serious and grave, something that extends from infinity to infinity, and it takes you, and like a mute giant it enters you and opens you, so that you too for a moment seem wider and deeper than yourself, and in a voice that is not your voice but may be your voice in thirty or forty years' time, in a voice that allows no laughter or levity, it commands you never to forget a single detail of this evening: remember and keep its smells, remember its body and light, remember its birds, the notes of the piano, the cries of the

crows and all the strangeness of the sky running riot from one horizon to the other before your eyes, and all of this is for you, all strictly for the attention of the addressee alone.... Slowly there descends over all a deep dim blue-gray color like the color of silence with a smell like that of the repeated notes on the piano, climbing and stumbling over and over again up a broken scale, while a single bird answers with the five opening notes of *Für Elise*: Ti-da-di-da-di.[26]

Oz, like many other child protagonists in classic *Künstlerromans*, has an epiphany in which his vocation becomes clear. Here, for Oz, it is the environment in which he grew up, the eastern European smells and tastes and sounds of immigrant Jerusalem, that will inspire him. But this moment of inspiration does not end here, Alter points out. In the very last lines of *A Tale of Love and Darkness*, after his mother's suicide, Oz invokes a bird, Elise:

My mother fell asleep, and this time she slept with no nightmares, she had no insomnia, in the early hours she threw up and fell asleep again, still fully dressed, and because Tsvi and Haya were beginning to suspect something, they sent for an ambulance a little before sunrise, and two stretcher bearers carried her carefully, so as not to disturb her sleep, and at the hospital she would not listen to them either, and although they tried various means to disturb her good sleep, she paid no attention to them, or to the specialist from whom she had heard that the psyche is the worst enemy of the body, and she did not wake up in the morning either, or even when the day grew brighter, and from the branches of the ficus tree in the garden of the hospital the bird Elise called to her in wonderment and called to her again and again in vain, and yet it went on trying over and over again, and it still tries sometimes.[27]

Oz's re-creation, from his imagination, of his mother's last night and last morning is marked by the same song he heard during his epiphany: "Für Elise." Oz ends the book in the present, with himself listening to the song he heard at those two watershed moments in his life—his vocational epiphany and his mother's death. The two are intimately connected in his life, not simply because of the trauma but because his mother opened his eyes to language and made him the writer that he is.

This attention to the mysteries of language as rendered in the words of an important female figure in his life is duplicated in his lyrical homage to the poet Zelda, one of his earliest teachers as well as a crossover figure who inhabits both a familial and a literary genealogy. Of her, he recalls: "She would call stars the 'stars of heaven,' the abyss was 'the mighty abyss,' and she spoke of 'turbid rivers' and 'nocturnal deserts.' If you said something in class that she liked, Teacher Zelda would point to you and say softly: 'Look, all of you, there's a child who's flooded with light.'"[28] While Zelda may have been speaking lyrically, she may also have been speaking archaically, being as she was an Orthodox Jew from eastern Europe who made her home in Jerusalem writing poetry and teaching children. She found her spoken idiom, like those writers in the generations that preceded Oz's, in texts, and she turned it into a kind of poetic vernacular. But there is more to the charms Zelda had for Oz than that. She opens the world of the Hebrew renaissance writers to him in a literary way that no one else ever could, not even his grandfather Alexander, uncle Joseph, and grandmother Shlomit, who hobnobbed with those very writers. In describing the way that he and his friends stayed at school for hours upon hours beyond the end of the school day to hear Zelda tell stories, Oz uses the language of Bialik himself: "[W]e seemed forgotten under the wings of Teacher Zelda's stories."[29]

Even while providing a link to the writers of the European renaissance, Zelda, in Oz's narrative, is enveloped within a domestic economy as well, like Tschernikhovsky, whose warmth and comforting smell Oz remarks on throughout the book. The summer after second grade, he wanted to spend as much time with her as possible and tells us, "I had willingly volunteered to help her with her morning chores. I ran off to the shops for her, swept the yard, watered her geraniums, hung her little washing out on the line and brought in the clothes that had dried."[30] In representing his participation in her domestic life, Oz brings her into the genealogy of Bialik and Tschernikhovsky, Ahad Ha'am and Mendele, humanizing her and defamiliarizing her. But he also characterizes her similarly to how he characterizes his mother, as someone whose language excited and inspired him, who shared orally a European corpus of literature that would have a lasting effect on his writing:

> She would read to me what she might have been intending to read anyway that morning: Hasidic tales, rabbinic legends, obscure stories about holy kabbalists who succeeded in combining the letters of the alphabet and working wonders and miracles. . . .
>
> . . . Day by day she raised the crossbar of my comprehension. I remember, for example, that she told me about Bialik, about his childhood, his disappointments, and his unfulfilled yearnings.[31]

Whereas the corpus his mother introduced him to were fairy tales and folktales from Europe, Zelda, a cousin of the Lubavitcher Rebbe Menachem Mendel Schneerson, introduced him to a different body of work—the work of Hasidut, rabbinic legend, and the Zohar. For Oz, who had emerged from a wholly secular family, the exposure to these texts in oral form "raised the crossbar of his comprehension" and affected his choice of theme and language immeasurably. Like his mother, Zelda was able to communicate her rarefied experience of the Hebrew language to the young boy:

> Teacher Zelda also revealed a Hebrew language to me that I had never encountered before, not in Professor Klausner's house or at home or in the street or in any of the books I had read so far, a strange, anarchic Hebrew, the Hebrew of stories of saints, Hasidic tales, folk sayings, Hebrew leavened with Yiddish, breaking all the rules, confusing masculine and feminine, past and present, pronouns and adjectives, a sloppy, even disjointed Hebrew. But what vitality those tales had! In a story about snow, the writing itself seemed to be formed of icy words. In a story about fires, the words themselves blazed. And what a strange, hypnotic sweetness there was in her tales about all sorts of miraculous deeds! As though the writer had dipped his pen in wine: the words reeled and staggered in your mouth.[32]

In an interview published in the *New Yorker*, Oz discusses his lifelong fascination with the deployment of language as a tool for the mimetic representation of human experience, particularly in a Hebrew idiom that is still, to this day, developing vernacular muscles.[33] Having been raised only in Hebrew by a father who was proficient in seventeen languages and a mother in eight, he had always felt the pinch of the limitations of his native tongue. When asked, however, in the pages of the *Paris Review* why he chose to write in Hebrew, Oz scoffs at the absurdity of the question.[34] How could he write in any other language? Hebrew is his native tongue, he says. But that does not mean that he is impervious to the power of other languages, to the possibility of language taking on a kind of sentience that Hebrew in the early days of its renaissance may not have possessed. Zelda's Yiddish inflections and presentation of language that was gleaned from religious texts taught him about Hebrew's "echo chamber," about the possibilities inherent in this ancient language that could be put to good vernacular literary use.[35]

One other figure played an important role in Oz's journey beyond the State of Israel and the limitations imposed on him by the expected literary genealogies: S. Y. Agnon was central to Oz's consciousness of his writerly vocation. As a child, as we have already seen, Oz would visit Agnon with his parents after having spent Saturday afternoons at his uncle's literary salons (Agnon lived next door). In contrast to Tschernikhovsky, Bialik, and Mendele, Agnon was not incorporated by Oz into the Klausner extended family in *A Tale of Love and Darkness*. We have already seen that Oz's father, and by extension his uncle Joseph Klausner from whom Oz's father gleaned his political and literary sensibilities, viewed Agnon as fatally "diasporic" or European in style and theme. What, however, did Oz's mother think of Agnon?

> "That man sees and understands a lot."
> And once she said:
> "He may not be such a good man, but at least he knows bad from good, and he also knows we don't have much choice."
> She used to read and reread the stories in the collection *At the Handles of the Lock* almost every winter. Perhaps she found an echo there of her own sadness and loneliness. I too sometimes reread the words of Tirzah Mazal, née Minz, at the beginning of "In the Prime of Her Life":
> "In the prime of her life my mother died. Some one and thirty years of age my mother was at her death. Few and evil were the days of the years of her life. All the day she sat at home, and she never went out of the house.... Silent stood our house in its sorrow; its doors opened not to a stranger. Upon her bed my mother lay, and her words were few."[36]

Oz's mother, whom Oz describes in this book as having been an astute observer of the human character, saw in Agnon a kindred spirit. His stories were distinguished by psychological depth even when rendered in a pseudo–folk idiom that would seem anathema to that kind of depth. In Agnon's *Bidmi yameha*, the story of the death of a young mother who had found very little emotional satisfaction in her life, Oz finds an appropriate literary means of expressing the angst and sadness of his mother's life. Indeed, Agnon himself, in a letter to Oz, refers to Oz's mother in the language of *Bidmi yameha*: "She stood upon the doorstep, and her words were few."[37]

Despite his fascination with Agnon, Oz discusses having resisted Agnon's influence in the following way:

> For several years I endeavored to free myself from Agnon's shadow. I struggled to distance my writing from his influence, his dense, ornamented, sometimes Philistine language, his measured rhythms, a certain

midrashic self-satisfaction, a beat of Yiddish tunes, juicy ripples of Hasidic tales. I had to liberate myself from the influence of his sarcasm and wit, his baroque symbolism, his enigmatic labyrinthine games, his double meanings, and his complicated, erudite literary games.

Despite all my efforts to free myself from him, what I have learned from Agnon no doubt still resonates in my writing.

What is it, in fact, that I learned from him?

Perhaps this. To cast more than one shadow. Not to pick the raisins from the cake. To rein in and polish pain. And one other thing, that my grandmother used to say in a sharper way than I have found it expressed by Agnon: "If you have no more tears left to weep, then don't weep. Laugh."[38]

In this description we see traces of his attraction as well to Zelda—in her Yiddish and her Hasidut—and to his mother, in her casting of shadows, in her polishing of pain. Agnon is the one canonic writer, the one Hebrew renaissance writer, that he could not push out of his own literary genealogy and into the Klausner family clan. Rather, Agnon comes to be included, in *A Tale of Love and Darkness*, in the constellation of women who introduced the joys and mysteries of language into his writerly soul.[39] Indeed, when we consider Agnon's alliance in Oz's literary universe with his mother and Zelda, we cannot help but consider Oz's complicated engagement with women in *A Tale of Love and Darkness*.

The observations of both Karen Grumberg and Natasha Wheatley, which discuss the place of women in Oz's corpus, expand our conception of Oz's relationship with his mother and with women more broadly. This relationship combined his mother's absence on an emotional level, overwhelmed as she was with mental illness and then committing suicide while Oz was still a child, with the role she played as a literary progenitor. Grumberg discusses Oz's attempt to exorcise his mother's ghost in *A Tale of Love and Darkness*; and Wheatley, his pained approach to memory as an old female friend who approaches him and, Medusa-like, tries to attack him.[40] Writing is his form of resistance, the only way he can get away from her:

> It's like a woman you have known for a long time, you no longer find her attractive or unattractive, whenever you bump into each other, she always says more or less the same few worn-out words, always offers you a smile, always taps you on the chest in a familiar way, only now, only this time, she doesn't, she suddenly reaches out and grabs your shirt,

not casually but with her all, her claws, lustfully, desperately, eyes tight shut, her face twisted as though in pain, determined to have her way, determined not to let go, she doesn't care anymore about you, about what you are feeling, whether or not you want to, what does she care, now she's got to, she can't help herself, she reaches out now and strikes you like a harpoon and starts pulling and tearing you, but actually she's not the one who's pulling, she just digs her claws in and you're the one who's pulling and writing, pulling and writing, like a dolphin with the barb of the harpoon caught in his flesh, and he pulls as hard as he can, pulls the harpoon and the line attached to it and the harpoon gun that's attached to the line and the hunters' boat that the harpoon gun is fixed to, he pulls and struggles, pulls to escape, pulls and turns over and over in the sea, pulls and dives down into the dark depths, pulls and writes and pulls more; if he pulls one more time with all his desperate strength, he may manage to free himself from the thing that is stuck in his flesh, the thing that is biting and digging into you and not letting go, you pull and you pull and it just bites into your flesh, the more you pull, the deeper it digs in, and you can never inflict a pain in return for this loss that is digging deeper and deeper, wounding you more and more because it is the catcher and you are the prey, it is the hunter and you are the harpooned dolphin, it gives and you have taken, it is that evening in Jerusalem and you are in this evening here in Arad, it is your dead parents, and you just pull and go on writing.[41]

In this passage, Oz fights off a female aggressor through writing. Why must this aggressor be female? Throughout his memoir he displays his fear of women—caregivers and strangers molest him, pursue him, damage him. As a child, he succumbs to them; then, as an adult, he resists them, for example, by developing literary conceits about the horrors of critics in the guise of women who can't keep their hands off him and tear him to pieces. What he betrays here is anxiety not over his mother's early death but over her impact on his writing life. For the first time, in *A Tale of Love and Darkness*, by bringing his mother into the circle of Zelda and Agnon, Oz acknowledges the fact that while his mother did not play the role of a mother in his life, having died when he was so young and having been depressed and disengaged through so much of his upbringing, she did play a significant role in his literary development. The wild woman who tries to harpoon him in the passage above is, perhaps, his mother begging him to acknowledge her. His resistance to her, through writing, betrays his anxiety over her impact on his writing.

Oz's depiction of his mother as the backbone of his literary genealogy as opposed to his familial genealogy, in conjunction with his designation of the writers of the Hebrew renaissance as extended family members instead of literary antecedents, indicates an attempt to salvage many things that converge here. First, there is his mother herself who died in his youth; then there are her stories, her allegiance to European literature and landscapes; there is the kind of Hebrew that could only grow out of continuity with European Jewry—its sacred texts and vernacular language; there is European Jewry itself and the writers who continued to write in its cadences and rhythms, like Zelda and Agnon; there is Jerusalem as a shelter for European Jews in the early years of the state and the culture that existed there.

His mother, Oz says near the end of his narrative in a description of his father's criticism of the types of stories she told the young Oz, "in her usual way, challenged the walls of censorship."[42] Salvage poetics are about defying censorship—the censorship imposed on the voices of a culture by the violence of historical circumstance. Oz's allegiance to his mother's literary traditions and her memory, narrated near the end of his life in *A Tale of Love and Darkness*, presents a uniquely poignant variation on the anxiety of influence. While Oz may have resisted explicitly acknowledging his mother's literary influence on him throughout his writing career, he brought her back in this late, monumental, salvage meditation.

POSTSCRIPT

A Yiddish Postvernacular in Israeli Literature

Starting in the final decade of the twentieth century, the attitude toward Yiddish in Israel, notoriously negative, began to shift. In 1990 the Knesset passed the Yiddish and Ladino Heritage Law, which inspired a special 1993 session of the Knesset, convened to pay homage to Yiddish "after years of denial and negation" on the part of the state. The National Authority for Yiddish Culture, whose aim is to "spread knowledge of Yiddish culture in all its forms . . . and promote, aid, and encourage contemporary artistic and literary expression in Yiddish," was subsequently established in 1996. On a more popular front, since the founding of the nonprofit organization YUNG YiDiSH in 1993 by Mendy Cahan, intended to "preserve and transmit Yiddish culture," there has been a flowering of interest in Yiddish throughout Israel. This is evident in the establishment of Yiddish programs at all the major Israeli universities, in the activism of Yiddish cultural centers such as the Sholem Aleichem House and the Leyvik house, and in Israeli high schools where students can now take a matriculation exam (*bogrut*) in Yiddish.

Yet, despite all this recent enthusiasm for Yiddish in Israel, the language is far from having been revived there as a vernacular.[1] Rather, it has become largely a postvernacular language.[2] Jeffrey Shandler coined the term "postvernacular" to describe the status of Yiddish outside the ultra-Orthodox Jewish communities in America and western Europe. In his *Adventures in Yiddishland* Shandler notes that in those more secular places, Yiddish has become less a language than a symbol, or marker, of a relationship between a lost world and a found one. Postvernacular Yiddish culture, according to Shandler, is a stand-in for the world of eastern European Jewish life, enabling contemporary Jews to perform their Jewishness within what they perceive to be a historically resonant framework.[3] But the Yiddish language itself, as a spoken idiom, is missing from the equation. Yiddish is an authorizing spirit, a linguistic idea, but not a usable or used language. David Grossman's *'Ayen 'erekh 'ahavah* or *See Under: Love* (1986) presents a unique variation on a rising postvernacular Yiddish consciousness in Israel at the turn of the twenty-first century.

As discussed in the initial chapter of this study of Israeli salvage poetics, the creation of a postvernacular Yiddish in contemporary Israel reflects an attempt to salvage the demonized language, if not in actual speech, then in spirit. In my reading of Iczkovits's *The Slaughterman's Daughter*, I argued that salvage poetics express a commitment to salvaging eastern European pre-Holocaust Jewish culture in a way that a postvernacular Yiddish does not. Salvage poetics and postvernacular Yiddish can be said to exist on the same spectrum, with slightly different end goals. Postvernacular Yiddish is focused on affiliation and affect, with people wanting a sense of Yiddish for purposes of personal identification with a bygone culture without the commitment of intense language study. Salvage poetics, on the other hand, reflect a deeper commitment to the representation of a lost culture, to the salvaging of its memory through an engagement with its artifacts. There is certainly an element of identification implicit in salvage poetics, an element of personal urgency that motivates the construction of a salvage poetic text; it reflects, I would argue, a more carefully constructed engagement with a world destroyed than does the development of a postvernacular. At the same time, postvernacular Yiddish consciousness in Israel may be a step in the right direction, a step toward a reconsideration of the role of eastern Europe in Israeli cultural and national history.

Several contemporary scholars have discussed the ways in which Hebrew literature, particularly in the early years of the state, can be better understood both formally and culturally, when its Yiddish undercurrents, its authors' Yiddish linguistic proclivities, are recognized and analyzed. According to Shachar Pinsker, in much Hebrew literature from the 1940s through the 1980s Yiddish significantly influenced the kinds of Hebrew texts that were produced. This was true, certainly, in the first half of the twentieth century among eastern European–born writers, but even later, as well, in the work of writers such as Yaakov Shabtai (1934–81).[4] My reading of *See Under: Love* presents a slightly different mapping of the relationship between Hebrew and Yiddish in a Hebrew fictional text. What follows is a model not for how actual Yiddish is incorporated into Hebrew literature, but the next stage of the process—how an approximation of Yiddish, an acknowledgment of its intensely postvernacular status, is worked into modern Hebrew literature. In *See Under: Love* we see a quest for Yiddish that looks toward Hebrew renaissance texts and early Hebrew translations of classic Yiddish literature. In other words, David Grossman approximates Yiddish in this novel by using Sholem Aleichem as a postvernacular icon (as did members of the Knesset in 1993), recognizing Yiddish as a source language for Sholem Aleichem's fiction and making intertextual references to earlier Hebrew writing that resonates with Yiddish for the first generation of native-born Israelis. However, Grossman mostly sidesteps Yiddish as an actual language within his novel. Like Iczkovits in *The Slaughterman's Daughter*, who alludes to Mendele's homodiegetic narrative conventions in Yiddish but actually models himself narratologically on Agnon's Hebrew corpus, David Grossman in *See Under: Love* alludes to Sholem Aleichem but ventriloquizes the early modern Hebrew writers of the Jewish Enlightenment, the Haskalah, and the modern Hebrew renaissance in their pastiche of biblical Hebrew.

To be sure, many readers have noticed the skill with which Grossman mimetically represents the Yiddish-inflected Hebrew of some characters in *See Under: Love*, particularly in the 1950s Yiddish-speaking milieu of part 1, and even the ways in which Grossman works some Yiddish into the text itself. However, my focus here is not how Grossman articulates Yiddish in contemporary Hebrew but instead how he approximates Yiddish through two primary models of salvage poetics. David Grossman's variation on salvage poetics in *See Under: Love* is evident first, through his incorporation of Sholem Aleichem's *Motl Peysie dem ḥazens* (Motl, Peysie the cantor's son) into the horizon of Momik's fantasy about reclaiming his parents' pre-Holocaust childhoods and second, in his presentation of a series of short stories authored in Europe by a character in the novel—Anshel Wasserman, the protagonist's great-uncle. These stories, presented in the novel as having been published in the eastern European Hebrew press under the title "The Children of the Heart," employ a prevernacular, literary, European-based Hebrew. This Hebrew in *See Under: Love* is used by Grossman to invoke an eastern European Yiddish-speaking milieu. Therefore, the argument here is unique in that I do not seek "traces" of Yiddish in Grossman's Hebrew. Rather, I seek to understand how traces of an earlier Hebrew literature can function in lieu of Yiddish within a postvernacular linguistic economy.

As our exploration of Israeli salvage poetics draws to its conclusion, this discussion of David Grossman's novel *See Under: Love* should serve as an apt case study of the relationship between many of the discussions that have been woven together in this book. Momik, the protagonist of *See Under: Love*, which is set in 1950s Jerusalem, is a child of Holocaust survivors whose traumatized parents try to protect him from their past. In so doing, they push him to the brink of insanity as he attempts to make sense of his present without any knowledge of his family history. Bella, a friend and neighbor, also a survivor, gives Momik some information about the war, and he also pieces together some history from library books. But Momik mostly learns about the world where his parents grew up and the event that destroyed their world by listening closely to the stories told in his presence by the Holocaust survivors in his neighborhood. These stories are supplemented by strange, sometimes disruptive behaviors on the part of his neighbors that accentuate this child's understanding that he is surrounded by damaged people. His parents, for example, ritualize eating in such a way that Momik cannot bring himself to eat in their presence. Hannah Zeitlin, a neighbor, runs naked in the streets at night, reliving sexual traumas she has experienced. His great-uncle, Anshel Wasserman, his grandmother's brother, whom he calls "grandfather," tells stories about "Herr Neigel," "Kazik," and a host of other mysterious characters that the child pieces together for himself into a portrait of the world "over there."

As we have seen throughout this study, the repression of the past in Israel was not unique to Holocaust survivors. It was part of the nationalistic fabric of early Zionism. The health and success of the new nation was predicated on "forgetting" the past—its languages, regions, complexes, behaviors, and values. In *See Under: Love* this kind of repression is translated into the experience of a child of Holocaust survivors to devastating effect. Momik, throughout his life, attempts to re-create the concentrationary universe that his parents have withheld from him. As a child, he creates a "Nazi beast" out of neighborhood animals; as an adult, he writes an "encyclopedia" that narrativizes and explicates the fragmented stories of his "grandfather."

Tom Segev, in his 1991 blockbuster, *The Seventh Million*, explores the relationship between Israelis and the Holocaust, arguing, as is evident in the book's title, that the first generation of Israelis as a whole constituted a population traumatized by the Holocaust, and Israeli society built itself around that trauma. Indeed, David Grossman's *See Under: Love* makes a similar claim. While it is focused on a single child within a single family, it is telling a story that we have been telling throughout this discussion of Israeli salvage poetics—the story of an attempt to identify a vocabulary, to imagine a past, that has been aggressively blotted out. Momik is able to piece together the world that preceded his own through a systematic process of investigation and inference.

Salvage poetics, as we have discussed, are a "series of devices by which texts or images are mediated, translated, explicated, personalized and/or valorized in an effort to create an accessible description of a lost culture."[5] They represent "a streamlining of popular desire on the part of an audience and specialized linguistic and cultural knowledge on the part of authors."[6] What does it take for a contemporary Israeli author to create a salvage poetic text? It takes an urgent sense of the need to understand one's own personal history and the desire to use an expressive medium to articulate that process of discovery.

For some of the authors we have explored in "Recalling Eastern Europe," the first half of this book, those who came from eastern Europe and who sought to represent that world for an Israeli audience—Ita Kalish, Malkah Shapiro, and Rivka Guber—we see a process of bridge building and mediation, a process of reconciling what they know to be true of their audience's knowledge base with what they know to be true of their subject matter. For them, it is less a process of learning about eastern Europe that they are documenting in their works, as much as it is a process of learning how to present it to an Israeli audience. In "Reconsidering the Negation of the Diaspora," the second half of this book, beginning with our study of Avner Holtzman's and Nurit Gertz's representations of their mothers' experiences in eastern Europe, we begin to see an articulation of the process of discovery. For S. Yizhar, it is the attempt to map his parents' eastern European background onto a musical landscape in early Israel. For Amos Oz, it is the discovery of his own literary ancestors in eastern Europe or in an eastern European-inflected idiom and influence.

S. Y. Agnon, the doyen of modern Hebrew fiction, eastern European born but inextricably identified with Israel and Israeli letters, takes something of a middle position within the discourse of Israeli salvage poetics, and that is why he was placed at the beginning of the second half of the book. Agnon, throughout his corpus, and particularly in *A Guest for the Night*, treated in chapter 5, seeks to reconcile his Israeli identity with his eastern European one. In many of his stories, he makes the journey back to Europe, either physically (as in *A Guest for the Night*) or metaphorically; for him, the journey between worlds is at the heart of his project. That journey, from Israel (or Palestine, in the case of *A Guest for the Night*) and back to eastern Europe, represents for Agnon a type of salvage poetics that cannot be reproduced in the works of those who follow him: He is going back to a place he came from, not a place he must imagine. He is going back to a place that still exists in time and in space. In *A Guest for the Night*, published in 1939 simultaneous with the outbreak of World War II, Agnon was the last of the writers explored here to actually be able to go back. After him, writers such as Yizhar, Oz, and most relevant to the current discussion, Grossman, must take that journey only in text. And that text, the Hebrew novel, serves as the site of exploration and reflection on what has been lost and forgotten and what can still be recuperated.

In *See Under: Love* we see the classic configuration of salvage poetics, one in which a Yiddish literary text serves as an artifact that, with some mediation and translation, can also serve as a bridge between the pre-Holocaust and the post-Holocaust, or the eastern European Jewish world and the Israeli one. In my earlier study of salvage poetics within an American context, Maurice Samuel does this with Sholem Aleichem's *Tevye the Milkman* stories (1894–1914), translating and glossing them for his American audience as an access point to the world of their ancestors. Momik, the nine-year-old protagonist of the first section of *See Under: Love*, looks for his parents' eastern European Jewish world in the stories of Sholem Aleichem as well. Interestingly, while Samuel designated the story of a hapless adult—Tevye—as the synecdoche for eastern European Jewish experience, it is the hapless child—Motl—whom Israelis consistently choose for that purpose. Grossman is, in fact, working from a long-standing Israeli identification with Motl in his selection of Sholem Aleichem's Motl as Momik's idol.

Motl, the endearing child protagonist from Sholem Aleichem's final novel, accompanies Momik on his fanciful journeys from Beit Mazmil, Jerusalem, to his parents' *shtetlakh* on almost a daily basis. While Motl traversed the old world in his journey to the new world, traveling across Europe to the United States during the great migration of eastern European Jews to the Lower East Side, Momik seeks to journey from 1950s Jerusalem back to the world from which his parents were exiled during the Holocaust. Motl, with his grace and good humor, his empathy for his mother, and his heartbreaking dependence on all the bumbling adults with whom he travels, models the kind of journey that Momik seeks.

Grossman sheds light on the importance of Sholem Aleichem for the novel when recounting his own first encounters with that author. When he was about nine years old, his father, a Jerusalem bus driver who immigrated to Palestine in 1936, handed him *Sipure Motl ben Peysie ha-ḥazan*, a Hebrew translation of Sholem Aleichem's Yiddish novel *Motl Peysie dem ḥazens*. The original Yiddish text was written from 1907 to 1916 and translated into Hebrew in 1929 by Sholem Aleichem's son-in-law Y. D. Berkowitz, a Hebrew writer in his own right. Grossman's father said, "Read this. This is what it was like over there," and Grossman describes having read the stories obsessively, looking for a window into the world his father had left behind.[7] Ultimately, though, what Grossman says he was seeking in the works of Sholem Aleichem was a way to understand the strange complexities of Israeli culture—a culture of fear and bravado, of Yiddish and the negation of Yiddish. Having grown up in Israel during the 1950s and 1960s, in a culture that vilified the cultures of the Jewish diaspora, most vehemently that of eastern Europe and especially Holocaust survivors who emblematized victimization, David Grossman struggled against his fascination with the world, quite literally, of his father. Sholem Aleichem's work, in Grossman's description, functions as far more than an engaging literary text. Indeed, it furnishes speech where otherwise there would be silence, images where otherwise there would be empty space.[8]

Interestingly, Sholem Aleichem's *Motl Peysie dem ḥazens* is, for Momik (as well as for Grossman), a Yiddish text in Hebrew translation. That fact further emphasizes the postvernacular nature of the Yiddish represented in *See Under: Love*. The main protagonist of *See Under: Love*, Momik, like Grossman, is exposed to *Motl Peysie dem ḥazens* in Hebrew translation, and he incorporates not only Motl's character but also his language (as derived from the 1929 Hebrew translation) into his psychic universe. For example, the very first chapter of *Motl Peysie dem ḥazens* in Hebrew is called "Has, yom tov hu mi-livkhot."[9] In Grossman's novel, this archaic formulation for "be quiet" (literally, "quiet, take a holiday from crying") is translated into a scene that Momik imagines between himself and his mother in which he attempts to keep her from mourning her lost past: "Cease your crying. Mister Doctor has forbidden you to strain your eyes with tears" (*has mi-livkot, ha'adon doktor 'amar she'asur leyag'ea bidma'ot et ha'ayin*).[10] This in turn alludes to a comic leitmotif throughout the novel by Sholem Aleichem in which Motl's mother, a compulsive weeper, is repeatedly told by Motl's brother, Eliyahu, not to cry because she may be turned back at immigration on suspicion that her weepy eyes have been infected with trachoma. Momik's fascination with Sholem Aleichem, along with the way this child character feels enthralled by Sholem Aleichem's prose, resembles Grossman's own relationship as a child with the works of Sholem Aleichem.

About his reading of these stories, Grossman notes in his essay "Books That Have Read Me":

> I did not know, I did not understand, but something inside me would not allow me to let go of the inscrutable stories written in a Hebrew I had never encountered before. . . . I belong to a generation that was accustomed to reading texts in which they did not understand every single word. In the early 1960s we read books in archaic and poetic Hebrew; we read translations from the 1920s and 30s that did not employ our daily language at all. . . . In hindsight I think that part of my reading experience in that period came from this very same incomprehensibility; the mystery and the exoticism of words with an odd ring, and the pleasure of inferring one thing from another.[11]

For Grossman, Sholem Aleichem in Hebrew was already so foreign it may as well have been in Yiddish. And that is what Yiddish became for him—an earlier Hebrew, a European Hebrew. In identifying a strategy for representing a Yiddish milieu in *See Under: Love*, Grossman turns to this earlier Hebrew literature as a stand-in for Yiddish.

Another text that plays a crucial role in *See Under: Love* is "The Children of the Heart," a story penned by Momik's great-uncle, Anshel Wasserman. Journalist George Packer, in a 2010 *New Yorker* essay on Grossman, mistakenly identifies Anshel Wasserman as a Yiddish writer, not a Hebrew one.[12] Grossman, in fact, explicitly casts Wasserman as a very particular type of Hebrew writer, a writer caught between the Hebrew of the Haskalah and the Hebrew of the period of the modern Hebrew renaissance. On reflection, however, Packer's gaffe forces a reconsideration of the different linguistic layers embedded in the novel. Momik, looking for his parent's eastern European Jewish world in the stories of his great-uncle, Anshel, whom he calls "grandfather" (as well as in the stories of Sholem Aleichem), finds a text written originally in a literary, eastern European Hebrew. It is a Hebrew text inflected by the Yiddish language and Yiddish culture, but only by geographic implication and inference. In Anshel's "The Children of the Heart," Yiddish functions, for Momik, as a spirit and a milieu but not as a language. While Momik can understand spoken Yiddish, his sense of the world "over there" is based on Hebrew texts that reverberate for him with Yiddish but are not actually written in that language.

"The Children of the Heart," Anshel's text, is presented in the novel as a material relic of the Haskalah. The story is crumbling and dog eared, printed on a leaf of aging newspaper, discovered by Momik in the journal pages of his late grandma Henny. He enshrines it, copying it word by word for posterity into his own "spy notebook" and sets himself the task of analyzing it and memorizing it, mastering it and emulating it, like a sacred text. This is clearly a Hebrew text, fetishized by the child. But it is a sort of Hebrew text that requires special consideration:

> He knew it was the most exciting story ever written, and the paper smelled about a thousand years old and seemed to come out of a Bible with all those biblical looking words Momik knew he would never understand no matter how many thousands of times he read the page over, because to get the meaning of a story like this you need a commentary by Rashi or somebody because people don't talk that way anymore except maybe Grandfather Anshel, though even without understanding every word in it you could tell this story was the origin of every book and work of literature ever written, and the books that came later were merely imitations of this page Momik had been lucky enough to find like a hidden treasure, and he felt that once he knew this he would know just about everything.[13]

Momik alludes here to Wasserman's text as a fascinating hybrid of traditional Jewish books (*sifrei kodesh*) and the literature of the modern Hebrew renaissance (*sifrei nusaḥ*). The former serves as the holy texts of the Jewish tradition (which require careful elucidation through commentary) and the latter represents the holy texts of modern Hebrew literature, with the *nusaḥ* being the vernacular Hebrew literary style developed by Mendele Mocher Sforim out of the many historical layers of the Hebrew language.[14] Wasserman's archaic Hebrew story serves as a key ingredient in the boy's quest to understand the world *be-'eretz sham* (in the land over there). Momik says that no one speaks the way this text reads anymore except Grandfather Anshel. And for Momik, Grandfather Anshel can provide the most direct, unmediated access he has to the world of the past, even though he is mad and virtually incoherent. Indeed, it may be Anshel's very madness that gives Momik confidence that whatever he can learn from his "grandfather" will be illuminating, because it hasn't been adapted for Momik's ears, as a way of protecting him. Momik trusts that Anshel's story, written "over there," is an artifact from "over there" and if carefully parsed could reveal the secrets about that world that are kept from him by his parents, by their friend Bella who takes care of Momik in the afternoon in her cafe down the block from his house, and by all the other survivors among whom Momik lives. Wasserman's text is more Yiddish than the Yiddish spoken by the adults in Momik's life, more "over there" than anything else he has ever encountered, even though it is actually written in Hebrew.

Yiddish for Grossman in *See Under: Love* is a language embedded in Hebrew; it is a language that can be mimetically presented in contemporary Hebrew through an imitation, in Anshel's stories, of the Hebrew of the Haskalah and the Hebrew renaissance. This is an ironic development in Hebrew literary history. In Mendele's Hebrew fiction, as students of his *nusaḥ* may recall, Yiddish is represented by Aramaic—the spoken vernacular is represented by the textualized vernacular of the Talmud.[15] In the case of Grossman's text, the entire Yiddish language is metonymically represented by the characters from Sholem Aleichem's work, and it is linguistically figured in parallel with archaic modern Hebrew stories written by the fictional Anshel Wasserman. The Yiddish postvernacular that Grossman forges in *See Under: Love* comprises, like Mendele's Hebrew *nusaḥ*, wholly literary elements. Grossman's Yiddish postvernacular, a new kind of Yiddish to be used in an Israeli culture highly conscious and self-conscious about its eastern European Jewish cultural and linguistic heritage, can be understood more as a gesture toward Yiddish than as an actual language.

Grossman affirms his complex relationship with Yiddish as the metonymy for eastern European Jewish life, which for him is mediated by Hebrew in an interview in *Modern Hebrew Literature*. In a 1995 issue titled "Looking Back: The Classics in the Eyes of Contemporary Writers," Grossman was asked to comment on Sholem Aleichem, and Yossl Birstein was asked to comment on Mendele.[16] In his presentation of Mendele's work, Birstein discusses it as having been read (and written) in Yiddish. Grossman's presentation of Sholem Aleichem's work, however, presumes his having read it in Hebrew. He discusses having read it in translation and remarks on it as having been particularly alien to him as a child because the Hebrew itself, into which it was translated, was archaic. That means the Yiddish language operated clandestinely here, rendering the Hebrew strange and unfamiliar. Yiddish in *See Under: Love* then becomes equated with the Hebrew of the Haskalah and the Hebrew renaissance. In Grossman's fiction, Yiddish and the world with which it has come to be associated is presented as a postvernacular in a certain type of Hebrew that was prevernacular: the Hebrew literary idiom that was born in literary circles in eastern Europe.

Grossman in *See Under: Love* gives new voice to Sholem Aleichem's texts, as well as to the literature of the Hebrew renaissance, effectively "salvaging" them; *See Under: Love*'s salvage poetics are expressed through patterns of intertextuality that posit the literary text as a locus for both preservation and presentation of prior literary texts. Momik, the character through whom these prior texts are focalized both thematically and narratively, has a foot in the vernacular Yiddish world as a native speaker of Yiddish and also one in a new Israeli postvernacular reality, where archaic Hebrew, composed in eastern Europe, and translations of Yiddish classics serve within the new Jewish state more as a stand-in for Yiddish and all its cultural associations than as a cipher for the language itself. Grossman, in his presentation of Yiddish through the medium of intertextual allusions to Sholem Aleichem and his thematization of the close proximity between the Hebrew of the modern Hebrew renaissance and Yiddish within the contemporary Israeli imagination, has done something that is neither translation nor adaptation. His is a psychological portrait of one child's reception and interpretation of earlier texts, largely inaccessible to him because he lives in a world where Yiddish is repressed and Hebrew is constantly shifting and changing, evolving from a wholly textual language into a vernacular one. The echoes of Yiddish that emerge from Momik's experience of Sholem Aleichem in Hebrew translation, alongside the fictional "The Children of the Heart" stories modeled on children's literature of the Hebrew renaissance, set the stage in the latter part of the twentieth century for a new postvernacular Yiddish reality, in both Hebrew literature and Israeli culture and, ultimately, as we have explored throughout this volume, for a movement toward a salvage poetics that acknowledges ever more urgently the need to do so much more than just capture a Yiddish spirit and move on.

Beginning with Iczkovits and ending with Grossman, this study of Israeli salvage poetics has documented how Israeli writers are tentatively exploring ways to do more beyond simply paying "homage" to Yiddish in a Knesset session. Both writers are caught within the Hebrew language, but from that vantage point they are taking serious steps toward engaging with the Yiddish literature that forged a modern Jewish literary consciousness and staked out Jewish modernity. The writers we considered between these two bookends—autobiographers, critics, and novelists—all articulate different approaches to salvaging the pre-Holocaust eastern European Jewish world in their Hebrew texts. Some—Gertz and Holtzman—were the children of pioneers and refugees seeking to find their own literary voices within the landscape of their parents' youth. Others—Shapiro, Kalish, and Guber—appointed themselves witnesses to a lost world; returning to their own eastern European youth in their autobiographical writings, they found ways, in their texts, to narrate their act of direct witnessing. Agnon—always an outlier—narrates a physical return and illuminates particular aspects of that world—the culture of Torah study and that of textual interpretation—that he seeks to salvage for his early Israeli readership. Finally, in the works of Yizhar and Oz, we see two major Hebrew writers, at the end of their careers, identifying and documenting the parts of their psyches and their literary output that are rooted in an earlier moment, an earlier place, and an earlier generation. As Israeli culture begins to come to terms with the "forgetting" it has enforced for over a century, it is exciting to see the way it articulates, through the emergence of a salvage poetics literature, what must *not* be forgotten.

Notes

Introduction

1 To avoid any confusion, when I use the phrase "turn of the twentieth century," I am referring roughly to the period between 1880 and 1920; "turn of the twenty-first century" refers approximately to the years 1990 to 2020.
2 Maurice Samuel, *The World of Sholem Aleichem* (New York: Atheneum, 1986).
3 Abraham Joshua Heschel, *The Earth Is the Lord's: The Inner World of the Jew in Eastern Europe* (Woodstock, VT: Jewish Lights, 1995).
4 Sheila E. Jelen, *Salvage Poetics: Post-Holocaust American Jewish Folk Ethnographies* (Detroit: Wayne State University Press, 2020).
5 Mark Zborowski and Elizabeth Herzog, *Life Is with People: The Culture of the Shtetl* (New York: Schocken, 1952).
6 Barbara Kirshenblatt-Gimblett, "Imagining Europe," in *Divergent Jewish Cultures*, ed. Deborah Dash Moore and S. Ilan Troen (New Haven, CT: Yale University Press, 2001), 169.
7 Jelen, *Salvage Poetics*, 24.
8 Jelen, 24.
9 See Jelen, chap. 3.
10 Jack Kugelmass, "Jewish Icons: Envisioning the Self in Images of the Other," in *Jews and Other Differences: The New Jewish Cultural Studies*, ed. Jonathan Boyarin and Daniel Boyarin (Minneapolis: University of Minnesota Press), 30–52, 42.
11 Jelen, *Salvage Poetics*, 27.
12 Naomi Brenner, *Lingering Bilingualism: Modern Hebrew and Yiddish Literatures in Contact* (Syracuse, NY: Syracuse University Press, 2016), 87.
13 Brenner, 93.

14 Rachel Rojanski, "Ben Gurion and Yiddish after the Holocaust," in *The Politics of Yiddish*, ed. Shlomo Berger (Amsterdam: Menasseh Ben Israel Institute, 2010), 37.
15 Jelen, *Salvage Poetics*, 307.
16 David Frischmann, "Mendele Mocher Sforim," *Kol kitvei David Frischmann* (Warsaw: Lilly Frischmann, 1931), 6:76. All translations are mine unless otherwise noted.
17 Dan Miron, "Folklore and Antifolklore in the Yiddish Fiction of the Haskalah," *The Image of the Shtetl and Other Studies of Modern Jewish Literary Imagination* (Syracuse, NY: Syracuse University Press, 2000), 49–80, 50–51.
18 Sheila E. Jelen, "Ethnopoetics in the Works of Malkah Shapiro and Ita Kalish: Gender, Popular Ethnography, and the Literary Face of Jewish Eastern Europe," in *Modern Jewish Literatures: Intersections and Boundaries*, ed. Sheila E. Jelen, Michael P. Kramer, and L. Scott Lerner (Philadelphia: University of Pennsylvania Press, 2011), 213–36.
19 Jeffrey Shandler, *Adventures in Yiddishland: Postvernacular Language and Culture* (Berkeley: University of California Press, 2006), 4.
20 Jelen, *Salvage Poetics*, 222.
21 Barbara Myerhoff, *Number Our Days: A Triumph of Continuity and Culture among Jewish Old People in an Urban Ghetto* (New York: Dutton, 1978), 30–31.
22 Yael Chaver, *What Must Be Forgotten: The Survival of Yiddish in Zionist Palestine* (Syracuse, NY: Syracuse University Press, 2004), 16.
23 Chaver, *What Must Be Forgotten*, 16.

Chapter 1

1 World Council for Yiddish and Jewish Culture, Association of Yiddish Writers and Journalists in Israel, "An Homage to Yiddish: Special Session of the Knesset Dedicated to the Yiddish Language and Yiddish Culture," Forty-Sixth Plenary Session of the 13th Knesset, 11 Tebeth 5753 (April 1, 1993).
2 Mordechai Tsanin (1906–2009) was the editor of the Tel Aviv–based *Letste Nayes* (Latest news), the last secular Yiddish newspaper to be established in the world. Founded in 1949, it was in high demand, but the Israeli government blocked its efforts to become a daily newspaper. At the same time, two daily newspapers in German were approved for publication, so clearly Yiddish was the specific target of prohibition. To bypass the Ministry of

the Interior, Tsanin decided to publish an additional newspaper, *Yidishe Tsaytung* (Yiddish newspaper), to fill in the missing days of the week and to function alongside *Letste Nayes* as a single paper. In 1959, *Letste Nayes* was finally permitted to publish daily, so this arrangement came to an end. The newspaper ceased publication in 2006. See Rachel Rojanski, "Keeper of the Flame," *Haaretz*, February 13, 2009. Also see Gali Drucker Bar-Am, "'Our Shtetl, Tel Aviv, Must and Will Become the Metropolis of Yiddish': Tel-Aviv a Center of Yiddish Culture?" *AJS Review* 41, no. 1 (April 2017): 111–32.

3 World Council, "Homage," 22.
4 Rachel Rojanski, "Ben Gurion and Yiddish after the Holocaust," in *The Politics of Yiddish*, ed. Shlomo Berger (Amsterdam: Menasseh Ben Israel, 2010), 36.
5 "Jewish & Non-Jewish Population of Israel/Palestine (1517–Present)," Jewish Virtual Library, accessed April 1, 2022, www.jewishvirtuallibrary.org/jewish-and-non-jewish-population-of-israel-palestine-1517-present.
6 World Council, "Homage," 9.
7 World Council, 15.
8 World Council, 16–17.
9 Jeffrey Shandler, *Adventures in Yiddishland: Postvernacular Language and Culture* (Berkeley: University of California Press, 2008).
10 Heidi J. Gleit, "Israel's Yiddish Romance," *Eretz* 106 (December 2006): n.p.
11 Benny [Beni] Mer, "Reimagining the Lively Character of Pre-War Smocza Street," *Forward*, May 2, 2017, forward.com/forverts-in-english/370230/reimagining-the-lively-character-of-pre-war-smocza-street/.
12 Beni Mer, *Smocze: The Biography of a Jewish Street in Warsaw* (Jerusalem: Magnes, 2018), 3.
13 Mer, *Smocze*, 6.
14 Mer, 6.
15 Mer, 6.
16 Sheila E. Jelen, "Auto-Ethnographic Salvage: Roman Vishniac's *A Vanished World*," in *Salvage Poetics: Post-Holocaust American Jewish Folk Ethnographies* (Detroit: Wayne State University Press, 2020), 217–52.
17 Mer, *Smocze*, 6.
18 Dan Miron, *A Traveler Disguised: The Rise of Modern Yiddish Fiction in the Nineteenth Century* (Syracuse, NY: Syracuse University Press, 1996).
19 Yaniv Iczkovits, *The Slaughterman's Daughter*, trans. Orr Scharf (New York: Schocken, 2020), 357–58.
20 Iczkovits, 121.

188 Notes to Chapter 2

21 Iczkovits, 203.
22 S. Y. Agnon, "Agunot," trans. Baruch Hochman, in *Twenty-One Stories*, ed. Nahum N. Glatzer (New York: Schocken, 1970), 30.
23 Iczkovits, *The Slaughterman's Daughter*, 411.
24 Iczkovits, 238.
25 Iczkovits, 374.
26 Yaniv Iczkovits, "Lo rak pogromim: Hasofer Yaniv Iczkovits rotse letaken 'et ha-sipur ha-histori shel yahadut ha-golah," *Haaretz*, September 22, 2015, www.haaretz.co.il/gallery/literature/.premium-MAGAZINE-1.2735957.

Chapter 2

1 Amos Oz, "Thank God for His Daily Blessings," in *Israel: A Traveler's Literary Companion*, ed. Michael Gluzman and Naomi Seidman (San Francisco: Whereabouts Press, 1996), 77.
2 Oz, 77.
3 In contemporary literary critical discourse, the term "ethnopoetics" was introduced by the poet, translator, and anthologist Jerome Rothenberg in a 1968 volume titled *Technicians of the Sacred*. There he called for recognition of "ethnic" poetics, particularly oral and visual ones, that pushed the boundaries of those poetics conventionally understood to be appropriate for inclusion in the Western canon. "Ethnocriticism," a related term, was introduced by the critic of Native American literature, Arnold Krupat, in the late 1980s, to gesture toward the frontier between literary studies and ethnography in work on Native American literature. Krupat, like Rothenberg, dwells on the need to expand the American literary canon and the notion of literary form to include alternative voices and genres, such as Native American oral storytelling, in the mainstream American literary canon. Krupat calls for literary recognition of ethnographically valuable texts. See Jerome Rothenberg, *Technicians of the Sacred: A Range of Poetry from Africa, America, Asia and Oceania* (New York: Doubleday-Anchor, 1968); Jerome Rothenberg and Diane Rothenberg, *Symposium of the Whole: A Range of Discourse toward an Ethnopoetics* (Berkeley: University of California Press, 1983); Arnold Krupat, *Ethnocriticism: Ethnography, History, Literature* (Berkeley: University of California Press, 1992); Arnold Krupat, "Native American Literature and the Canon," *Critical Inquiry* 10, no. 1 (September 1983): 145–71; and Arnold Krupat, "American Histories, Native American Narratives," *Early American Literature* 30 (1995): 165–74.

4 See S. Ansky, "Der kharakter un di eygnshaftn fun der yiddisher folks-poetisher shafung," in *Folklor un etnografye: Gezamelte shriftn* (Warsaw: Farlag An-Ski, 1925), 15:33–95. For a discussion of this programmatic essay, see David Roskies, *The Dybbuk and Other Writings*, Library of Yiddish Classics (New York: Schocken, 1992), xxii.

5 Interestingly, Ansky's ethnographic project is referred to as a new "oral" as well as "written" Torah. See Roskies, *Dybbuk*, xxii and xxiv.

6 Roskies, xxiii.

7 On Ansky's place within the field of modern Jewish ethnography, see Jack Kugelmass, "The Father of Jewish Ethnography?" in *The Worlds of S. Ansky: A Russian Jewish Intellectual at the Turn of the Century*, ed. Gabriella Safran and Steven J. Zipperstein (Stanford, CA: Stanford University Press, 2006), 346–59.

8 Autoethnography, the practice of performing ethnography on one's own culture and one's own self, has been linked to the practices of narrative, popular, and metaethnography. For a discussion of autoethnography within the context of narrative ethnography, see Barbara Tedlock, "From Participant Observation to the Observation of Participation: The Emergence of Narrative Ethnography," *Journal of Anthropological Research* 47, no. 1 (1991): 69–94. In this essay, Tedlock discusses the highly acclaimed 1945 ethnography *A Chinese Village* by Martin Yang, who did his field research in the village in which he grew up. On metaethnography and popular ethnography, see Yiorgos Anagnostou, "Metaethnography in the Age of Popular Folklore," *Journal of American Folklore* 119, no. 474 (2006): 381–412. In this essay Anagnostou points to the contemporary phenomenon of laypeople contributing to the professional folkloristic discourse. He argues that "the metaethnographic perspective calls on ethnographic practitioners to expand their reading repertoire beyond the literatures of academic ethnographies and to engage with the vast textual field of diverse genres of social representation" (382).

9 On the application of literary consciousness to ethnographic writings and on the identification of ethnographic terminology that can be useful to literary thought, see Clifford Geertz, *Works and Lives: The Anthropologist as Author* (Stanford, CA: Stanford University Press, 1988), 147–53. Also see his "Thick Description: Toward an Interpretive Theory of Culture," in *The Interpretation of Cultures* (New York: Basic Books, 1973), 3–32.

10 See Stephen Greenblatt and Catherine Gallagher, *Practicing New Historicism* (Chicago: University of Chicago Press, 2000).

11 For a discussion of this movement in modern Hebrew literature, see Sheila Jelen, "Things as They Are: The Mimetic Imperative," in *Intimations of*

Difference: Dvora Baron in the Modern Hebrew Renaissance (Syracuse, NY: Syracuse University Press, 2007), 51–78.

12 David Frischmann, "Mendele Mocher Sforim," in *Kol kitvei David Frischmann* (Warsaw: Lilly Frischmann, 1931), 76.

13 On Israel's attitude toward representations of eastern European Jewish culture from the 1950s to the present, see Mordechai Zalkin, "From the Armchair to the Archives: Transformations in the Image of the Shtetl during Fifty Years of Collective Memory in the State of Israel," *Studia Judaica* 8 (1999): 255–66. On the place of women in Israeli literary culture, see Amalya Kahana-Carmon, "The Song of the Bats in Flight," in *Gender and Text in Modern Hebrew and Yiddish Literature*, ed. Naomi Sokoloff, Anne Lapidus Lerner, and Anita Norich (New York: Jewish Theological Seminary, 1992), 235–45.

14 Judith Fetterley and Marjorie Pryse, *Writing Out of Place: Regionalism, Women, and American Literary Culture* (Urbana: University of Illinois Press, 2003).

15 S. Y. Pinless, "Mah shehayah," *Gilyonot* 1 (1939): 59.

16 For more on Baron's reception and its place within a discourse of ethnography, see Jelen, *Intimations of Difference*. In the preface to the book, I discuss "the tension that can be found throughout Baron's mature work between the author's impulse to represent a world that had, by the middle of the twentieth century, disappeared and her impulse to write fiction with no obligation toward historical ethnographic memory" (xix).

17 Karen Auerbach, "Bibliography: Jewish Women in Eastern Europe," in *Polin: Studies in Polish Jewry*, vol. 18, *Jewish Women in Eastern Europe*, ed. Chaeran Freeze et al. (Oxford: Littman Library of Jewish Civilization, 2005).

18 For a fuller discussion of "cross-disciplinary translation" in Polen's translation of Shapiro, see Sheila Jelen, "From an Old World to a New Language: Eastern European–born Israeli Women's Writing in Hebrew," *Jewish Quarterly Review* 96, no. 4 (2006): 591–602.

19 Malkah Shapiro, *Mi-tokh ha-se'arah* (Jerusalem: Hotsa'at R. Mas, 1943), *Belev ha-mistorin: Sipurim u-fo'emot* (Tel Aviv: Netsah, 1955); Malkah Shapiro, *Shnenu ba-meginim* (Tel Aviv: Hotsa'at Agudat ha-Sofrim ha-'Ivrim le-yad Dvir, 1952); Malkah Shapiro, *Mi-din le-raḥamim: Sipurim me-ḥatserot ha-'admorim* (Jerusalem: Mosad ha-Rav Kuk, 1969); and Malkah Shapiro, *Shiri li bat 'ami: Shirim, sonetot u-fo'emot* (Bene-Brak: Netsah, 1971).

20 Nehemia Polen, trans., introduction to *The Rebbe's Daughter: Memoir of a Hasidic Childhood* by Malkah Shapiro (Philadelphia: Jewish Publication Society, 2002).

21 Dan Miron, *A Traveler Disguised: The Rise of Modern Yiddish Fiction in the Nineteenth Century* (Syracuse, NY: Syracuse University Press, 1996); Benjamin Harshav, *Language in Time of Revolution* (Berkeley: University of California Press, 1993); and Robert Alter, *The Invention of Hebrew Prose: Modern Fiction and the Language of Realism* (Seattle: University of Washington Press, 1988).
22 Menachem Brinker, *'Ad ha-simtah ha-teveryianit: Ma'amar 'al sipur ve-maḥshavah be-yetsirat Brenner* (Tel Aviv: Am Oved, 1990).
23 Conceived in keeping with modernist trends that favored intimate glimpses into the consciousness of individual protagonists, Brenner was nodding, as well, to a tradition of Jewish fixation on identifying the origins of statements or narratives for purposes of legal reasoning. We see this in the Talmud where statements within a legal discussion are prefaced by chains of names of rabbis who are quoting one another until we get back to the name of the rabbi who originated the statement. This was essential to the creation of authority, wherein older generations would have precedence over younger generations, and laws evolved from seniority.
24 The rebbe's *tisch* is a gathering of Hasidim with their rebbe, usually on Sabbath or holidays, to partake of a meal and Torah study. It is generally accessible to the community at large, but men alone sit with the rebbe at his *tisch*, or table, while women look on from a distance.
25 Malkah Shapiro, *The Rebbe's Daughter: Memoir of a Hasidic Childhood*, trans. Nehemia Polen (Philadelphia: Jewish Publication Society, 2002), 108.
26 Shapiro, *The Rebbe's Daughter*, 115.
27 Shapiro, *The Rebbe's Daughter*, 97–98.
28 S. Avidor, "'Admorit hasoferet," *Panim 'el panim* (November 12, 1971): 13; and M. Ungerfeld, "Lezikhra shel meshoreret ha-ḥasidut," *Hado'ar* (March 17, 1972): 293.
29 Nehemia Polen, "Coming of Age in Kozienice: Malkah Shapiro's Memoir of Youth in the Sacred Space of a Hasidic Zaddik," in *Celebrating Elie Wiesel: Stories, Essays, Reflections*, ed. Alan Rosen (Notre Dame, IN: University of Notre Dame Press, 1998), 123–40.
30 Ita Kalish, "Life in a Hasidic Court in Russian Poland toward the End of the 19th and the Early 20th Centuries," *YIVO Annual of Jewish Social Science* 13 (1965): 264–78.
31 Kalish, "Hasidic Court," 278.
32 Ita Kalish, *'Etmoli* (Tel Aviv: ha-Kibuts ha-Me'uhad, 1970); and Kalish, *A rebishe heim in amolikn Poyln* (Tel Aviv: I. L. Peretz, 1963).

33 Gershon Bacon, "Ita Kalish (1903–1994)," in *Jewish Women: A Comprehensive Historical Encyclopedia*, ed. Paula Hyman and Dalia Ofer, accessed April 3, 2022, jwa.org/encyclopedia/article/kalish-ita.
34 Kalish, *'Etmoli*, 83–85.
35 Mary Antin, *The Promised Land* (New York: Houghton Mifflin, 1912), 122–25.
36 Kacyzne was S. Ansky's literary executor. He translated into Yiddish Ansky's originally Russian *The Dybbuk*, an ethnographic showpiece for some of the findings gleaned from his 1912–14 ethnographic expedition. In addition to his photography, Kacyzne aspired to become a well-known Yiddish author. Though Abraham Cahan of the *Forverts* chose Israel Joshua Singer as his Warsaw stringer instead of Kacyzne, and thus spoiled, in part, Kacyzne's ambitions for literary recognition in Yiddish communities across the Atlantic, Kacyzne was known in European Yiddishist circles as an accomplished writer. Through his affiliation with Ansky, as well as the juncture of his talents as a photographer and a literary writer, Kacyzne is brilliantly situated to illustrate, from another perspective, the nature of ethnopoetics in the post-Holocaust period. Kacyzne's photography and his writings have all been subsumed, in recent reception, by Kacyzne's relationship with Ansky as an ethnographer. His photographs have been published and republished in art volumes on the life of eastern European Jews and have been juxtaposed with the photographs, most notably, of his friend and colleague Menachem Kipnis, who was also a photographer but more importantly an ethnomusicologist. At the same time, Kacyzne's literary writings, with the exception of work he completed on behalf of Ansky, have fallen by the wayside. On Kacyzne's involvement with the *Jewish Daily Forward*, see Alter Kacyzne, *Poyln: Jewish Life in the Old Country*, ed. Marek Web (New York: Metropolitan Books, 1999), xix. On Kipnis, see Itzik Nakhmen Gottesman, *Defining the Yiddish Nation: The Jewish Folklorists of Poland* (Detroit: Wayne State University Press, 2003), 56–65.
37 Alan Mintz, *Banished from Their Father's Table: Loss of Faith and Hebrew Autobiography* (Bloomington: Indiana University Press, 1989).
38 Iris Parush, *Reading Jewish Women: Marginality and Modernization in Nineteenth-Century Eastern European Jewish Society* (Hanover, NH: University Press of New England, 2004), chap. 3.
39 Parush.

Chapter 3

1. Rivka Guber, *Village of the Brothers* (New York: Shengold, 1979), n.p.
2. Rivka Guber, *Only a Path* (Ramat Gan: Masada, 1972), 68.
3. Rivka Guber, *Sefer ha-'aḥim* (Tel Aviv: Masada, 1950), n.p.
4. See Yael Chaver, *What Must Be Forgotten: The Survival of Yiddish in Zionist Palestine* (Syracuse, NY: Syracuse University Press, 2004).
5. Guber, *Only a Path*, 61.
6. The root of *'emunah* is *'e-m-n*.
7. Rivka Guber, *The Signal Fires of Lachish* (Ramat Gan: Masada, 1964), 11–12.
8. Herzl coined this phrase in his novel *Altneuland*, first published in 1902.
9. Rivka Guber, *Morashah le-hanḥil* (Jerusalem: Kiryat Sefer, 1979), 148.
10. Guber, 149. Shlomo Tzemah (1974–1886) was an Israeli author and literary critic, a childhood friend of David Ben-Gurion's, also from Płońsk. He received the Bialik Prize in 1944 and the Israel Prize in 1965. See Nurit Govrin, "Shalvat ha-efes: Pariz ba-roman shel Shlomo Tzemah—Eliyahu Margalit," in *Kriyat ha-dorot: Sifrut 'Ivrit be-ma'agalehah*, vol. 7 (Tel Aviv: Tel Aviv University, 2019).
11. S. Y. Agnon, *Only Yesterday* (Princeton, NJ: Princeton University Press, 2018).
12. Y. H. Brenner, *Breakdown and Bereavement* (Jerusalem: Toby Press, 2003).
13. A. D. Gordon, *Selected Essays by Aaron David Gordon* (New York: Arno Press, 1973).
14. Saul Tschernikhovsky, "ha-'Adam 'eino 'ele," Project Ben Yehudah, accessed April 2, 2022, benyehuda.org/read/2722.
15. Guber, *Signal Fires*, 124.
16. Bialik's poem "ha-Matmid" (1894–95) addresses the years he spent in the Volozhin Yeshiva. Project Ben Yehudah, accessed April 2, 2022, benyehuda.org/read/6113.
17. Classic Yiddish and Hebrew autobiographies that address the culture of the heder include those of Mendele, Guenzberg, and Lilienblum, among many others.
18. Pierre Nora, "Between Memory and History: Les lieux de mémoire," *Representations* 26 (1989): 7.
19. Nora, 7.
20. Guber, *Village*, 162.
21. Guber, *Village*, 159.

22 Guber, *Signal Fires*, 43–45.
23 Guber, *Signal Fires*, 45.
24 There are two notable exceptions to this rule. Kibbutz Loḥame ha-Getaʾot (Ghetto Fighters Kibbutz) and Kibbutz Yad Mordechai were both founded by members of the ghetto uprisings who made it to Israel after the war. Thus, there are a few places in Israel that invoke the Holocaust in their names. But it is important to note that these two places invoke resistance, not victimization, and therefore were "acceptable" to the Israeli public in a way that naming a settlement after victims not necessarily involved in the resistance may not have been.
25 Guber, *Morashah le-hanḥil*, 68.
26 Guber, 54.
27 Eli Kavon, "When Zionism Feared Yiddish," *Jerusalem Post*, May 11, 2014, www.jpost.com/opinion/op-ed-contributors/when-zionism-feared-yiddish-351939.
28 Guber, *Only a Path*, 204.
29 Dorit Yosef, "Hakravah, meḥaʾah ve-mashmaʾut: ʿIyun ba-textim shel shte ʾimahot shkulot, Rivka Guber u-Manuela Deviri," *Masekhet* 9 (2009): 81–110.

Chapter 4

1 Marianne Hirsch, *The Generation of Postmemory: Writing and Visual Culture after the Holocaust* (New York: Columbia University Press, 2012).
2 As documented in Yael Chaver's important work on the subject of Yiddish poetry in early Israel and Palestine. See Yael Chaver, *What Must Be Forgotten: The Survival of Yiddish in Zionist Palestine* (Syracuse, NY: Syracuse University Press, 2004).
3 Barbara Kirshenblatt-Gimblett, "A Daughter's Afterword," in Mayer Kirshenblatt and Barbara Kirshenblatt-Gimblett, *They Called Me Mayer July: Painted Memories of a Jewish Childhood in Poland before the Holocaust* (Berkeley: University of California Press, 2007), 369.
4 Barbara Myerhoff, *Number Our Days: A Triumph of Continuity and Culture among Jewish Old People in an Urban Ghetto* (New York: Dutton, 1978), 30–31.
5 On that fall day, three thousand Jews from Święciany were murdered alongside five thousand others from nearby locales by the local Lithuanian militia under the supervision of the SS. Avner Holtzman, "The Birthday Party," *Commentary*, January 2000, 52.

6 See Sheila E. Jelen, "Images and Imaginings: Menachem Kipnis' Post-European Salvage Poetics" (paper, Association for Jewish Studies Conference, Chicago, December 2021).
7 Hanan Hever, "Mi-golah belo' moledet el moledet belo' golah: 'Al 'ikaron manḥe ba-siporet ha-'ivrit ben shete ha-milḥamot," in *Ben shete milḥamot 'olam*, ed. Chone Shmeruk and Samuel Werses (Jerusalem: Magnes, 1997), 45–72; Aaron Orinowsky (Aharon Ben-Or), *Toldot ha-sifrut ha-'ivrit ha-ḥadashah*, vol. 3 (Tel Aviv: Hotsaat Yizrael, 1954), 244–51; Gershon Shaked, *ha-Siporet ha-'ivrit, 1880–1970*, vol. 1 (Jerusalem: Keter, 1977); and Samuel Werses (Shemu'el Verses), "Kitve-'et 'ivriyim le-sifrut be-polin ben shete milḥamot 'olam," in *Ben shete milḥamot 'olam*, 96–127.
8 Nurit Gertz and Deborah Gertz, *'El mah she-namog* (Tel Aviv: Am Oved, 1997), 9.
9 Gertz and Gertz, 9.
10 Gertz and Gertz, 17. "Paiza" is derived from "paisan," which means "friend."
11 Gertz and Gertz, 18.
12 Gertz and Gertz, 84.
13 Gertz and Gertz, 80.
14 Gertz and Gertz, 73.
15 In another correlation between the limits of memory and the desire to erase, at the end of this chapter Nurit says that her father, Aharonchik, never once mentioned his family, never once discussed his siblings or his life in Poland. It is Dora who fleshes out that part of Nurit's own personal history for her. The assumption, of course, is that Aharonchik moved to Palestine against his family's wishes and in the heat of that decision left them behind forever. But, in fact, Aharonchik's family was fully in support of his Zionist aspirations. His wealthy industrialist father bought the plot of land outside Hadera that would become the kibbutz that his son and daughter-in-law would help to establish; he even purchased the kibbutz's first tractor. So what was Aharonchik doing? He was only doing what any good pioneer on the New Yishuv in the early years of the state was doing—he was erasing the past. This ability—to negate and erase—is echoed in his wife's experience of his relationship with her. He erased her name the way he erased the memory of his own family. And this erasure was the fate of eastern Europe within the Israeli imagination. Indeed, Nurit's own starting point for this book, in the original book she was planning to write, is about a different kind of erasure that was enforced in Israel—the erasure of its Palestinian history. But as a first-generation

Israeli, the child of pioneers, she is like the child who does not know how to ask, from the Passover seder. Gertz and Gertz, 74.
16 Gertz and Gertz, 149.
17 Gertz and Gertz, 151.
18 Gertz and Gertz, 151.
19 Gertz and Gertz, 156.
20 Gertz and Gertz, 103–27.
21 Gertz and Gertz, 157–58.
22 Gertz and Gertz, 159.
23 On Dror, see Dina Porat, "Zionist Pioneering Youth Movements in Poland and Their Attitude to Erets Israel during the Holocaust," in *Polin: Studies in Polish Jewry*, vol. 9, *Jews, Poles, Socialists: The Failure of an Ideal*, ed. Antony Polonsky et al. (Oxford: Littman Library of Jewish Civilization, 2007), 195–211.
24 On the Labor Party, see Tom Segev, *The Seventh Million: The Israelis and the Holocaust* (New York: Henry Holt, 1991), 285–86. On Yitzhak Tabenkin and his relationship with Holocaust survivors, see Israel Zertal, *From Catastrophe to Power: Holocaust Survivors and the Emergence of Israel* (Berkeley: University of California, 1998), 153–57.
25 For a full discussion of "hybrid" salvage poetic texts, see Sheila E. Jelen, *Salvage Poetics: Post-Holocaust American Jewish Folk Ethnographies* (Detroit: Wayne State University Press, 2020), xvii. There I write that hybrid texts are "texts that exist on the border between the literary and the ethnographic, whether re-workings and translations of fiction, works of nonfiction, or photo collections—in the reconstitution of an American Jewish ethnicity, or a sense of 'Jewishness,' during the postwar era from the mid-1940s through the turn of the twenty-first century."
26 Yizhar discusses Brenner's death in *Preliminaries*, which I explore briefly in chapter 6.
27 On Leah Goldberg, see Ruth Kartun-Blum and Anat Weisman, eds., *Pegishot ʿim meshoreret: Masot u-meḥkarim ʿal yetsiratah shel Leʾah Goldberg* (Tel Aviv: Sifriyat Poʾalim, 2000); on translation and Hebrew writers, see Adriana X. Jacobs, *Strange Cocktail: Translation and the Making of Modern Hebrew Poetry* (Ann Arbor: University of Michigan Press, 2018).
28 See Jelen, *Salvage Poetics*, 41–76.
29 Holtzman, "Birthday Party," 50.
30 Holtzman, 50.
31 Holtzman, 52–53.
32 Holtzman, 54.

33 Hanna Yablonka argues that the young survivor men who were drafted into the Israeli army were considered lesser soldiers because they were "damaged" through their association with those who were "led like sheep to the slaughter" in Europe; they were perceived as selfish, after years of deprivation, and not good members of a collective after having emerged from a system where only those who fended for themselves survived. Hanna Yablonka, *Survivors of the Holocaust: Israel after the War* (Palgrave: Macmillan, 1998), 139–51. Both men and women who survived were suspected of "collaborating" in some way, either as members of the ghetto *Judenrat*, or as part of the Jewish leadership in the camps. This assumption was fostered, to a large extent, by the 1950 Nazi and Nazi Collaborators Law passed in the Knesset, which, in the absence of access to most actual former Nazis outside of Israeli jurisdiction, focused its efforts on Jewish "collaborators" in Israel. High-profile trials, such as the Kastner trial (1954–55), demonstrated the dangers of such a law. While Kastner was exonerated of the charge of collaboration, he was subsequently murdered in the street. Segev, *Seventh Million*, 276–84.

34 Holtzman, "Birthday Party," 51.

35 Avner Holtzman, *Temunah le-neged 'einai* (Tel Aviv: Am Oved, 2002), 151.

36 On the Lovers of Zion, see Michael Stanislawsky, *For Whom Do I Toil? Judah Leib Gordon and the Crisis of Russian Jewry* (New York: Oxford University Press, 1988), 174–99.

37 Holtzman, *Temunah le-neged*, 152.

38 Holtzman, 152.

39 Holtzman, 157.

40 This narrative of shock at the Palestinian landscape and climate pervades the canonic literature of the modern Hebrew renaissance. See S. Y. Agnon, *Tmol shilshom* (Tel Aviv: Schocken, 1998); and Y. H. Brenner, *Shkhol ve-kishalon* (Bene Brak: Hakibbutz Hameuchad, 2006).

Chapter 5

1 On the publication and reception history of this essay, see Jeffrey Shandler, "Heschel and Yiddish: A Struggle with Signification," *Journal of Jewish Thought and Philosophy* 2, no. 2 (1993): 245–99.

2 Abraham Joshua Heschel, *The Earth Is the Lord's: The Inner World of the Jew in Eastern Europe* (Woodstock, VT: Jewish Lights, 2001), 92.

3 Heschel, *Earth Is the Lord's*, 42.

4 Dan Laor, *Ḥaye 'Agnon* (Tel Aviv: Schocken, 1998), 322–23.

5   S. Y. Agnon, *'Oreaḥ natah la-lun* (Tel Aviv: Schocken, 1976), 419.
6   Arnold Band, *Nostalgia and Nightmare: A Study in the Fiction of S. Y. Agnon* (Berkeley: University of California Press, 1968), 322; and Gershon Shaked, "Sofer be-divre torah: 'Al 'oreaḥ natah la-lun me-et s. y. agnon," *Meḥkere Yerushalayim be-sifrut 'ivrit* (2006): 237.
7   Agnon, *'Oreaḥ*, 23.
8   Agnon, *'Oreaḥ*, 109. Translation in S. Y. Agnon, *A Guest for the Night*, trans. Misha Louvish (New York: Schocken, 1968), 111.
9   See Sheila Jelen, "Things as They Are: The Mimetic Imperative," *Intimations of Difference: Dvora Baron in the Modern Hebrew Renaissance* (Syracuse, NY: Syracuse University Press, 2007), 51–78.
10 Agnon, *'Oreaḥ*, 109–10; and Agnon, *Guest*, 111–12.
11 Agnon, 419.
12 This is a common theme of Agnon's—the question of continuity between traditional authorship and modern authorship and the kinds of terms that can be used to unite the two. See his stories "Tehilah" and "Aggadat ha-sofer," for example.
13 While within the thematics of the story, one could argue that the key is the artifact, it is important to consider the way that the texts intertextually deployed by Agnon serve as überartifacts for him, the authorial equivalent to the "key" entrusted to the protagonist.
14 Agnon, *'Oreaḥ*, 128–29.
15 Agnon, 225.
16 Agnon, 226.
17 Agnon, 226.
18 Dan Laor, *Ḥaye 'Agnon*, 316.
19 Arnold Band, *Nostalgia*, 284.
20 Dvora Baron, *Parshiyot* (Jerusalem: Mosad Bialik, 1968).

Chapter 6

1   Guber also won the Israel Prize. See chap. 3.
2   Marianne Hirsch, *The Generation of Postmemory: Writing and Visual Culture after the Holocaust* (New York: Columbia University Press, 2012).
3   Zali Gurevitch and Gideon Aran, in an oft-cited meditation on the difference between "Place" and "place" within modern Zionism, write: "The return to the Land was intended to bring about a reintegrated Judaism—a reunification of Book, people and place. . . . The Zionist revolution was an attempt to reunite the place with the Place. The Zionist avant-garde, the pioneers

(*ḥaluzim*), who ascended to the Land of Israel, left not only one place to go to another but left one phase of Jewish history for another." Gurevitch and Aran, "The Land of Israel: Myth and Phenomenon," in *Reshaping the Past: Jewish History and the Historians*, ed. Jonathan Frankel, vol. 10, Studies in Contemporary Jewry (New York: Oxford University Press, 1994), 196.
4 Ariel Hirschfeld, "Mozart, S. Yizhar ve-kol ha-'einsof," in *Dvarim le-Yizhar*, ed. Nitsah Ben-Ari. (Tel Aviv: Zemorah Biton, 1996), 27–45.
5 S. Yizhar, *Preliminaries*, trans. Nicholas de Lange (New Milford: Toby Press, 2007), 193.
6 Dan Miron, introduction to Yizhar, *Preliminaries*, 23.
7 Yizhar, *Preliminaries*, 193.
8 Yizhar, 193.
9 Yizhar, 193.
10 Michael Wood, "Proust: The Music of Memory," in *Memory: Histories, Theories, Debates*, ed. Susannah Radstone and Bill Schwarz (New York: Fordham University Press, 2010), 109.
11 Sandra Garrido and Jane W. Davidson, *Music, Nostalgia and Memory: Historical and Psychological Perspectives* (Switzerland: Palgrave Macmillan, 2019), 8.
12 Garrido and Davidson, *Music*, 37.
13 Yizhar, *Preliminaries*, 196.
14 Yizhar, 107.
15 Yizhar, 111.
16 Yizhar, 186.
17 Yizhar, 49.
18 Yizhar, 215.
19 Yizhar, 193.
20 Yizhar, 90.
21 Yizhar, 115.
22 Yizhar, 50.
23 Yizhar, 62.
24 Yizhar, 69.
25 Moshe Shamir, *Bemo yadav: Pirke 'Elik* (Merḥavyah: Sifriyat Poalim, 1951), 11.

Chapter 7

1 Amos Oz, *A Tale of Love and Darkness*, trans. Nicholas de Lange (New York: Houghton Mifflin Harcourt, 2015), 130.

200   Notes to Chapter 7

2 There are two notable exceptions to this schema: Aharon Appelfeld and Yehudah Amichai are both considered "statehood" writers even though they were born in Europe and raised in the German language. Also, for the canonic generational schematics, see Gershon Shaked, *ha-Siporet ha-'ivrit, 1880–1970* (Yerushalayim: Keter, 1977).
3 A. B. Yehoshua, "The Literature of the Generation of the State," *Ariel: Israel Review of Arts and Letters* 107–8 (1998): 48–56.
4 Michael Gluzman, *The Politics of Canonicity: Lines of Resistance in Modernist Hebrew Poetry* (Palo Alto, CA: Stanford University Press, 2003). Viktor Shklovsky writes: "Art history has a very important feature: in it, it's not the eldest son who inherits seniority from his father, but the nephew who receives it from his uncle." See Viktor Shklovsky, "On Cinema," in *Viktor Shklovsky: A Reader*, ed. and trans. Alexandra Berlina (New York: Bloomsbury Academic, 2017), 352–53. In Russian, see V. B. Shklovskij, *Gamburgskij schyot: Stat'i—vospominaniya—esse (1914–1933)*, sost. A. Yu. Galushkin and A.P. Chudakov (Moscow: Sovetskij pisatel', 1990), 121. Thank you to my colleague Molly Blasing for helping me locate these texts.
5 "Leksikon ha-sifrut ha-'ivrit ha-hadashah," compiled by Joseph Galron-Goldschläger, accessed April 1, 2022, library.osu.edu/projects/hebrew-lexicon/02378.php.
6 Oz, *Tale*, 34–36.
7 Oz, 36.
8 Oz, 86.
9 Oz, 89.
10 Oz, 97.
11 Oz, 127.
12 For an archaeology of Oz's actual literary debt to the writers of the Hebrew renaissance, not just his own admitted debt, see Nurit Govrin, "ha-Mishpaḥah ha-sifrutit shel 'Amos' Oz," *Gag* 24 (2011): 151–66.
13 Oz, *Tale*, 68–69.
14 Oz, 471.
15 Sheila Jelen, "Israeli Children in a European Theater: Amos Oz's *A Tale of Love and Darkness* and S. Yizhar's *Preliminaries*," *Jewish Quarterly Review* 100, no. 3 (2010): 504–18.
16 Sheila Jelen, *Salvage Poetics: Post-Holocaust American Jewish Folk Ethnographies* (Detroit: Wayne State University Press, 2020), 198–99.
17 Eran Kaplan, "Amos Oz's *A Tale of Love and Darkness* and the Sabra Myth," *Jewish Social Studies* 14, no. 1 (Fall 2007): 130. Cited by Kaplan in this quotation is Yigal Schwartz, "Nikhnasta le-'armon mekhushaf

ve-shiḥrartah 'oto meha-kishuf: 'Al sipur 'al 'ahavah ve-ḥoshekh ke-sefer pulḥan," *Israel* 7 (Spring 2005): 188.
18 Iris Milner, "Sipur mishpaḥti: Mitos ha-mishpaḥah ba-sipur 'al 'ahavah ve-ḥoshekh uve-yetsirato ha-mukdemet shel 'Amos 'Oz," in *Yisrael: Ḥoveret myuḥedet ha-mukdeshet le sifro shel 'Amos 'Oz sipur 'al 'ahavah ve-ḥoshekh* (Spring 2005): 73–106.
19 Irving Howe, *World of Our Fathers* (New York: Harcourt Brace Jovanovich, 1976).
20 Oz, *Tale*, 138.
21 Oz, 252.
22 Oz, 270.
23 Oz, 271.
24 Art Spiegelman, *Maus: A Survivor's Tale* (London: Penguin, 2003).
25 Hana Wirth Nesher, "The Modern Jewish Novel and the City: Franz Kafka, Henry Roth, and Amos Oz," *Modern Fiction Studies* 24, no. 1 (Spring 1978): 91–109.
26 Oz, *Tale*, 248.
27 Oz, 538.
28 Oz, 284–85.
29 Oz, 286. Bialik's poem "Alone," translated by Ruth Nevo, opens in the following way: "Wind blew, light drew them all. / New songs revive their mornings. / Only I, small bird, am forsaken / under the Shekhina's wing." Poetry International Archives, accessed April 1, 2022, www.poetryinternational.org/pi/poem/3345/auto/0/0/Chaim-Nachman-Bialik/Alone/en/tile.
30 Oz, *Tale*, 289.
31 Oz, 290–91.
32 Oz, 294.
33 Gal Koplewitz, "Amos Oz and the Politics of the Hebrew Language," *New Yorker*, November 12, 2019, accessed April 2, 2022, www.newyorker.com/books/page-turner/amos-oz-and-the-politics-of-the-hebrew-language.
34 Shusha Guppy, "Amos Oz, The Art of Fiction No. 148," *Paris Review* 140 (Fall 1996), accessed April 2, 2022, www.theparisreview.org/interviews/1366/the-art-of-fiction-no-148-amos-oz.
35 On modern Hebrew as an echo chamber, see Robert Alter, *The Invention of Hebrew Prose: Modern Fiction and the Language of Realism* (Seattle: University of Washington Press, 1988).
36 Oz, *Tale*, 69.
37 Oz, 69.
38 Oz, 74–75.

39 One of only two books of literary criticism ever written by Oz is a study of Agnon, based on lectures Oz gave at Ben-Gurion University of the Negev where he was on the literature faculty: Amos Oz, *The Silence of Heaven: Agnon's Fear of God* (Princeton, NJ: Princeton University Press, 2012). His other work of nonfiction is *The Story Begins: Essays on Literature* (New York: Harcourt, 1999).
40 See Karen Grumberg, "Of Sons and Mothers: The Spectropoetics of Exile in Autobiographical Writing by Amos Oz and Albert Cohen," *Prooftexts* 3, no. 3 (Fall 2010): 373–401. Also see Natasha Wheatley, "'It Is the Hunter and You Are the Harpooned Dolphin': Memory, Writing, and Medusa—Amos Oz and His Women," *Jewish Quarterly Review* 100, no. 4 (Fall 2010): 631–48.
41 Oz, *Tale*, 245.
42 Oz, 331.

Postscript

1 See Heidi Gleit, "Israel's Yiddish Romance," *Eretz* 106 (December 2006): 44–51; Efrat Shalom, "The Great Yiddish Comeback," *Haaretz*, May 18, 2003; Avraham Noverstern, "Between Town and Gown: The Institutionalization of Yiddish at Israeli Universities," in *Yiddish in the Contemporary World: Papers of the First Mendel Friedman International Conference on Yiddish*, ed. Gennady Estraikh and Mikhael Krutikov (Oxford: Oxford University Press, 1999), 1–19; and Ruti Roso, "ha-'Ashkenazim ha-ḥadashim," *Maariv*, September 14, 2004.
2 In ultra-Orthodox circles in Israel Yiddish has long been the language of daily discourse and the frame language for Torah study. See Miriam Isaacs, "Haredi, Haymish and Frim: Yiddish Vitality and Language Choice in a Transnational, Multilingual Community," *International Journal of the Sociology of Language* 138 (1999): 9–30; and Miriam Isaacs, "Contentious Partners: Yiddish and Hebrew in Haredi Israel," *International Journal of the Sociology of Language* 138 (1999): 101–22.
3 Jeffrey Shandler, "Introduction: Postvernacularity, or Speaking of Yiddish," in *Adventures in Yiddishland: Postvernacular Language and Culture* (Berkeley: University of California Press, 2006), 1–30.
4 Shachar Pinsker, "'That Yiddish Has Spoken to Me': Yiddish in Israeli Literature," *Poetics Today* 35, no. 3 (Fall 2014): 325–56.
5 Sheila E. Jelen, *Salvage Poetics: Post-Holocaust American Jewish Folk Ethnographies* (Detroit: Wayne State University Press, 2020), 1.

6 Jelen, 1.
7 David Grossman, "Books That Have Read Me," in *Writing in the Dark: Essays on Literature and Politics*, trans. Jessica Cohen (New York: Farrar, Straus & Giroux, 2008), 3–28.
8 While Tevye has certainly had his share of the limelight in Israel, it is interesting that Motel is only popular in Israel and not at all in America. This could, of course, be a reflection of the popularity of the 1971 Hollywood production *Fiddler on the Roof* in which Tevye is centrally featured, but it could also have something to do with the role of the child between worlds, as opposed to the father, the keeper of traditions. Israelis may, indeed, identify more with the child than with the father, as a newly established country.
9 Sholem Aleichem, *Sipure Motl ben Peysie ha-ḥazan (bi-shnei sfarim)*, trans. Y. D. Berkovitz (Tel Aviv: Dvir, 1929).
10 David Grossman, *See Under: Love*, trans. Betsy Rosenberg (New York: Farrar, Straus & Giroux, 1989), 21; and the Hebrew original, *'Ayen 'erekh 'ahavah* (Tel Aviv: Keter, 1986), 24.
11 Grossman, "Books That Have Read Me," 7.
12 George Packer, "The Unconsoled: A Writer's Tragedy and a Nation's," *New Yorker*, September 27, 2010, 50–61.
13 David Grossman, *See Under: Love*, 10–11.
14 As Bialik articulates in his essay "Creator of the Nusaḥ," "the nusaḥ is not just a style. It is not just a rhythm, a literary effect alone. The nusaḥ is the foundation for them all, and perhaps even the origin of all of them." The text created by Wasserman becomes for Momik a kind of *nusaḥ*, both a foundational text of Hebrew literature, but also a holy text, as in the liturgical and oral meaning of *nusaḥ* from traditional synagogue culture. C. N. Bialik, "Mendele ba'al ha-nusaḥ," in *Kol kitvei Chaim Nachman Bialik* (Tel Aviv: Hotsa'at Va'ad ha-Yovel, 1932), 240.
15 Sheila Jelen, "Speakerly Texts and Historical Realities: Mendele's Relations to the Revival of Hebrew Speech," in *Jewish Literature and History*, ed. Eliyana Adler and Sheila Jelen (Bethesda: University of Maryland Press, 2008), 207–21.
16 David Grossman, "My Sholem Aleichem," *Modern Hebrew Literature* 14 (Spring/Summer 1995): 4–5; and Yossl Birstein, "A Little Story about Reading a Book," *Modern Hebrew Literature* 14 (Spring/Summer 1995): 7.

Selected Bibliography

Agnon, S. Y. "Agunot." Translated by Baruch Hochman. In *Twenty-One Stories*. Edited by Nahum N. Glatzer. New York: Schocken, 1970.
———. *A Guest for the Night*. Translated by Misha Louvish. New York: Schocken, 1968.
———. *Only Yesterday*. Princeton, NJ: Princeton University Press, 2018.
———. *'Oreaḥ natah la-lun*. Tel Aviv: Schocken, 1976.
———. *Tmol shilshom*. Tel Aviv: Schocken, 1998.
Alter, Robert. *The Invention of Hebrew Prose: Modern Fiction and the Language of Realism*. Seattle: University of Washington Press, 1988.
Anagnostou, Yiorgos. "Metaethnography in the Age of Popular Folklore." *Journal of American Folklore* 119, no. 474 (2006): 381–412.
Ansky, S. "Der kharakter un di eygnshaftn fun der yiddisher folks-poetisher shafung." *Folklor un etnografye: Gezamelte shriftn*. Warsaw: Farlag An-Ski, 1925.
———. *The Dybbuk*. New Haven, CT: Yale University Press, 2002.
Antin, Mary. *The Promised Land*. New York: Houghton Mifflin, 1912.
Auerbach, Karen. "Bibliography: Jewish Women in Eastern Europe." In *Polin: Studies in Polish Jewry*. Vol. 18, *Jewish Women in Eastern Europe*, edited by Chaeran Freeze, Paula Hyman, and Antony Polonsky, 273–303. Oxford: Littman Library of Jewish Civilization, 2005.
Avidor, S. "'Admorit hasoferet." *Panim 'el panim*. November 12, 1971.
Avrutin, Eugene M., Valerii Dymshits, Alexander Ivanov, Alexander Lvov, Harriet Murav, and Alla Sokolova, eds. *Photographing the Jewish Nation: Pictures from S. An-sky's Ethnographic Expeditions*. Hanover, NH: University Press of New England, 2009.
Bacon, Gershon. "Kalish, Ita (1903–1994)." In *Jewish Women: A Comprehensive Historical Encyclopedia*, edited by Paula Hyman and Dalia Ofer. Accessed April 3, 2022. jwa.org/encyclopedia/article/kalish-ita.

Selected Bibliography

Band, Arnold. *Nostalgia and Nightmare: A Study in the Fiction of S. Y. Agnon.* Berkeley: University of California Press, 1968.

Bar-Am, Gali Drucker. "Our Shtetl Tel Aviv." *AJS Review* 41, no. 1 (2017): 111–32.

Baron, Dvora. *Parshiyot.* Jerusalem: Mosad Bialik, 1968.

Bialik, C. N. "Alone." Translated by Ruth Nevo. Poetry International Archives. Accessed April 2, 2022. www.poetryinternational.org/pi/poem/3345/auto/0/0/Chaim-Nachman-Bialik/Alone/en/tile.

———. "Mendele ba'al ha-nusaḥ." *Kol kitvei Chaim Nachman Bialik.* Tel Aviv: Hotsa'at Va'ad ha-Yovel, 1932.

Birstein, Yossl. "A Little Story about Reading a Book." In *Modern Hebrew Literature* n.s., no. 14 (Spring/Summer 1995): n.p.

Brenner, Y. H. *Shkhol ve-kishalon: 'O sefer ha-hitlabtut.* Bene Brak: Hakibutz Hameyuhad, 2006.

Brenner, Naomi. *Lingering Bilingualism: Modern Hebrew and Yiddish Literatures in Contact.* Syracuse, NY: Syracuse University Press, 2016.

Brinker, Menachem. *'Ad ha-simtah ha-teveryianit: Ma'amar 'al sipur ve-maḥshavah be-yetsirat Brenner.* Tel Aviv: Am Oved, 1990.

Chaver, Yael. *What Must Be Forgotten: The Survival of Yiddish in Zionist Palestine.* Syracuse, NY: Syracuse University Press, 2004.

Fetterley, Judith, and Marjorie Pryse. *Writing Out of Place: Regionalism, Women, and American Literary Culture.* Urbana: University of Illinois Press, 2003.

Frischmann, David. "Mendele Mocher Sforim." In *Kol kitvei David Frischmann.* Warsaw: Lilly Frischmann, 1931.

Garrido, Sandra, and Jane W. Davidson. *Music, Nostalgia and Memory: Historical and Psychological Perspectives.* Switzerland: Palgrave Macmillan, 2019.

Geertz, Clifford. "Thick Description: Toward an Interpretive Theory of Culture." In *The Interpretation of Cultures,* 3–32. New York: Basic Books, 1973.

———. *Works and Lives: The Anthropologist as Author.* Stanford, CA: Stanford University Press, 1988.

Gertz, Nurit, and Deborah Gertz. *'El mah she-namog.* Tel Aviv: Am Oved, 1997.

Gleit, Heidi. "Israel's Yiddish Romance." *Eretz* 106 (December 2006): 44–51.

Gluzman, Michael. *The Politics of Canonicity: Lines of Resistance in Modernist Hebrew Poetry.* Palo Alto, CA: Stanford University Press, 2003.

Gottesman, Itzik Nakhmen. *Defining the Yiddish Nation: The Jewish Folklorists of Poland.* Detroit: Wayne State University Press, 2003.

Govrin, Nurit. "ha-Mishpaḥah ha-sifrutit shel 'Amos Oz." *Gag* 24 (2011): 151–66.

Greenblatt, Stephen, and Catherine Gallagher. *Practicing New Historicism*. Chicago: University of Chicago Press, 2000.
Greenspoon, Leonard J., Ronald A. Simkins, and Brian J. Horowitz. *Studies in Jewish Civilization: The Jews of Eastern Europe*. Omaha, NE: Creighton University Press, 2003.
Grossman, David. "Books That Have Read Me." In *Writing in the Dark: Essays on Literature and Politics*, translated by Jessica Cohen, 3–28. New York: Farrar, Straus & Giroux, 2008.
Grossman, David. "My Sholem Aleichem." *Modern Hebrew Literature* n.s., no. 14 (Spring/Summer 1995): n.p.
———. *See Under: Love*. Translated by Betsy Rosenberg. New York: Farrar, Straus & Giroux, 1989.
Grumberg, Karen. "Of Sons and Mothers: The Spectropoetics of Exile in Autobiographical Writing by Amos Oz and Albert Cohen." *Prooftexts* 3, no. 3 (2010): 373–401.
Guber, Rivka. *'Im ha-banim*. Tel Aviv: Masada, 1953.
———. *Morashah le-hanḥil*. Jerusalem: Kiryat Sefer, 1979.
———. *Only a Path*. Ramat Gan: Masada, 1972.
———. *Sefer ha-'aḥim*. Tel Aviv: Masada, 1950.
———. *The Signal Fires of Lachish*. Ramat Gan: Masada, 1964.
———. *Village of the Brothers*. New York: Shengold, 1979.
Guppy, Shusha. "Amos Oz: The Art of Fiction No. 148." *Paris Review* 140 (Fall 1996). www.theparisreview.org/interviews/1366/the-art-of-fiction-no-148-amos-oz.
Gurevitch, Zali, and Gideon Aran. "The Land of Israel: Myth and Phenomenon." In *Reshaping the Past: Jewish History and the Historians*, edited by Jonathan Frankel, 195–210. Studies in Contemporary Jewry, vol. 10. New York: Oxford University Press, 1994.
Hacohen, Dvora. "Rivka Guber." *The Shalvi/Hyman Encyclopedia of Jewish Women*. Jewish Women's Archive. Accessed April 2, 2022. jwa.org/encyclopedia/article/guber-rivka.
Handelman, Susan A. *The Slayers of Moses: The Emergence of Rabbinic Interpretation in Modern Literary Theory*. Albany: State University of New York Press, 1982.
Handlin, Oscar. Foreword to *The Promised Land*, by Mary Antin, v–xv. North Stratford, NH: Ayer, 1969.
Harshav, Benjamin. *Language in Time of Revolution*. Berkeley: University of California Press, 1993.

Heschel, Abraham Joshua. *The Earth Is the Lord's: The Inner World of the Jew in Eastern Europe*. Woodstock, VT: Jewish Lights, 2001.

Ḥever, Hanan. "Mi-golah belo' moledet 'el moledet belo' golah: 'Al 'ikaron manhe ba-siporet ha-'ivrit ben shete ha-milḥamot." In *Ben shete milḥamot 'olam*, edited by Chone Shmeruk and Samuel Werses, 45–72. Jerusalem: Magnes, 1997.

Hirsch, Marianne. *The Generation of Postmemory: Writing and Visual Culture after the Holocaust*. New York: Columbia University Press, 2012.

Hirschfeld, Ariel. "Mozart, S. Yizhar ve-kol ha-'einsof." In *Dvarim le-Yizhar*, edited by Nitsah Ben-Ari, 25–45. Tel Aviv: Zemorah Biton, 1996.

Holtzman, Avner. "The Birthday Party." *Commentary*, January 2000. www.commentary.org/articles/avner-holtzman/the-birthday-party/.

———. *Temunah le-neged 'einai*. Tel Aviv: Am Oved, 2002.

Howe, Irving. *World of Our Fathers*. New York: Harcourt Brace Jovanovich, 1976.

Iczkovits, Yaniv. "Lo rak pogromim: Hasofer Yaniv Iczkovits rotse letaken et ha-sipur ha-histori shel yahadut ha-golah." *Haaretz*, September 22, 2015. Accessed April 2, 2022. www.haaretz.co.il/gallery/literature/.premium-MAGAZINE-1.2735957.

———. *The Slaughterman's Daughter*. Translated by Orr Scharf. New York: Schocken, 2020.

Isaacs, Miriam. "Haredi, Haymish and Frim: Yiddish Vitality and Language Choice in a Transnational, Multilingual Community." *International Journal of the Sociology of Language* 138 (1999): 9–30.

Jacobs, Adriana X. *Strange Cocktail: Translation and the Making of Modern Hebrew Poetry*. Ann Arbor: University of Michigan Press, 2018.

Jelen, Sheila E. "The Cracow Ghetto Resistance and Its Testimonies." In *Testimonial Montage: A "Family" of Testimonies about the Cracow Ghetto Resistance*. Lanham, MD: Lexington Press, forthcoming.

———. "Ethnopoetics in the Works of Malkah Shapiro and Ita Kalish." In *Modern Jewish Literatures*, edited by Sheila E. Jelen, Michael P. Kramer, and L. Scott Lerner, 213–36. Philadelphia: University of Pennsylvania Press, 2011.

———. "From an Old World to a New Language: Eastern European–born Israeli Women's Writing in Hebrew." *Jewish Quarterly Review* 96, no. 4 (2006): 591–602.

———. "Images and Imaginings: Menachem Kipnes' Post-European Salvage Poetics." Paper presented at Association for Jewish Studies Conference, Chicago, December 2021.

———. *Intimations of Difference: Dvora Baron in the Modern Hebrew Renaissance.* Syracuse, NY: Syracuse University Press, 2007.

———. "Israeli Children in a European Theater: Amos Oz's *A Tale of Love and Darkness* and S. Yizhar's *Preliminaries.*" *Jewish Quarterly Review* 100, no. 3 (2010): 504–18.

———. *Salvage Poetics: Post-Holocaust American Jewish Folk Ethnographies.* Detroit: Wayne State University Press, 2020.

———. "Speakerly Texts and Historical Realities: Mendele's Relations to the Revival of Hebrew Speech." In *Jewish Literature and History*, edited by Eliyana Adler and Sheila Jelen, 207–21. Bethesda: University of Maryland Press, 2008.

———. "Things as They Are: The Mimetic Imperative." Chap. 3 in *Intimations of Difference.*

"Jewish & Non-Jewish Population of Israel/Palestine (1517–Present)." Jewish Virtual Library. Last modified January 1, 2022. www.jewishvirtuallibrary.org/jewish-and-non-jewish-population-of-israel-palestine-1517-present.

Kacyzne, Alter. *Poyln: Jewish Life in the Old Country.* Edited by Marek Web. New York: Metropolitan Books, 1999.

Kahana-Carmon, Amalya. "The Song of the Bats in Flight." In *Gender and Text in Modern Hebrew and Yiddish Literature*, edited by Naomi Sokoloff, Anne Lapidus Lerner, and Anita Norich, 235–45. New York: Jewish Theological Seminary, 1992.

Kalish, Ita. *'Etmoli.* Tel Aviv: Hakibbutz Hameuchad, 1970.

———. "Life in a Hasidic Court in Russian Poland toward the End of the 19th and the Early 20th Centuries." *YIVO Annual of Jewish Social Science* 13 (1965): 264–78.

———. *A rebishe heim in amolikn Poyln.* Tel Aviv: I. L. Peretz, 1963.

Kaplan, Eran. "Amos Oz's *A Tale of Love and Darkness* and the Sabra Myth." *Jewish Social Studies* 14, no. 1 (2007): 119–43.

Kartun-Blum, Ruth, and Anat Weisman, eds. *Pegishot 'im meshoreret: Masot u-meḥkarim 'al yetsiratah shel Le'ah Goldberg.* Tel Aviv: Sifriyat Po'alim, 2000.

Kavon, Eli. "When Zionism Feared Yiddish." *Jerusalem Post*, May 11, 2014. www.jpost.com/opinion/op-ed-contributors/when-zionism-feared-yiddish-351939.

Kirshenblatt-Gimblett, Barbara. "A Daughter's Afterword." In Mayer Kirshenblatt and Barbara Kirshenblatt-Gimblett, *They Called Me Mayer July: Painted Memories of a Jewish Childhood in Poland before the Holocaust.* Berkeley: University of California Press, 2007.

Kirshenblatt, Mayer, and Barbara Kirshenblatt-Gimblett. *They Called Me Mayer July: Painted Memories of a Jewish Childhood in Poland before the Holocaust.* Berkeley: University of California Press, 2007.

Koplewitz, Gal. "Amos Oz and the Politics of the Hebrew Language." *New Yorker*, November 12, 2019. www.newyorker.com/books/page-turner/amos-oz-and-the-politics-of-the-hebrew-language.

Krupat, Arnold. "American Histories, Native American Narratives." *Early American Literature* 30 (1995): 165–74.

———. *Ethnocriticism: Ethnography, History, Literature.* Berkeley: University of California Press, 1992.

———. "Native American Literature and the Canon." *Critical Inquiry* 10, no. 1 (September 1983): 145–71.

Kugelmass, Jack. "The Father of Jewish Ethnography?" In *The Worlds of S. An-sky: A Russian Jewish Intellectual at the Turn of the Century*, edited by Gabriella Safran and Steven J. Zipperstein, 346–59. Stanford, CA: Stanford University Press, 2006.

Laor, Dan. *Ḥaye 'Agnon.* Tel Aviv: Schocken, 1998.

Mer, Beni. *Biografiyah shel reḥov yehudi ve-Varshe.* Jerusalem: Magnes, 2018.

Milner, Iris. "Sipur mishpaḥti: Mitos ha-mishpaḥah ba-sipur 'al 'ahavah ve-ḥoshekh uve-yetsirato ha-mukdemet shel 'Amos 'Oz." *Yisrael: Ḥoveret myuḥedet ha-mukdeshet le sifro shel 'Amos 'Oz sipur 'al 'ahavah ve-ḥoshekh.* Ktav 'et le-heker ha-ziyonut u-medinat yisrael—historiyah, tarbut, hevrah 7 (5765).

Mintz, Alan. *Banished from Their Father's Table: Loss of Faith and Hebrew Autobiography.* Bloomington: Indiana University Press, 1989.

Miron, Dan. "A Late New Beginning." Introduction to *Preliminaries*, by S. Yizhar, 1–28. Translated by Nicholas de Lange. New Milford, CT: Toby Press, 2007.

———. *A Traveler Disguised: The Rise of Modern Yiddish Fiction in the Nineteenth Century.* Syracuse, NY: Syracuse University Press, 1996.

Myerhoff, Barbara. *Number Our Days: A Triumph of Continuity and Culture among Jewish Old People in an Urban Ghetto.* New York: Dutton, 1978.

Nesher, Hana Wirth. "The Modern Jewish Novel and the City: Franz Kafka, Henry Roth, and Amos Oz." *Modern Fiction Studies* 24, no. 1 (Spring 1978): 91–109.

Nora, Pierre. "Between Memory and History: Les lieux de mémoire." *Representations* 26 (1989): 7–24.

Noverstern, Avraham. "Between Town and Gown: The Institutionalization of Yiddish at Israeli Universities." In *Yiddish in the Contemporary World: Papers of the First Mendel Friedman International Conference on Yiddish*, edited by

Gennady Estraikh and Mikhael Krutikov, 1–19. Oxford: Oxford University Press, 1999.

Orinowsky, Aaron [Aharon Ben-Or]. *Toldot ha-sifrut ha-'ivrit ha-ḥadashah*. Vol. 3. Tel Aviv: Hotsaat Yizrael, 1954.

Oz, Amos. *A Tale of Love and Darkness*. Translated by Nicholas de Lange. New York: Houghton Mifflin Harcourt, 2015.

———. "Thank God for His Daily Blessings." In *Israel: A Traveler's Literary Companion*, edited by Michael Gluzman and Naomi Seidman, 74–94. San Francisco: Whereabouts Press, 1996.

Packer, George. "The Unconsoled: A Writer's Tragedy and a Nation's." *New Yorker*, September 27, 2010.

Pinless, S. Y. "Mah she-hayah." *Gilyonot* 1 (1939): 59–61.

Pinsker, Shachar. "'That Yiddish Has Spoken to Me': Yiddish in Israeli Literature." *Poetics Today* 35, no. 3 (Fall 2014): 325–56.

Polen, Nehemia. "Coming of Age in Kozienice: Malkah Shapiro's Memoir of Youth in the Sacred Space of a Hasidic Zaddik." In *Celebrating Elie Wiesel: Stories, Essays, Reflections*, edited by Alan Rosen, 123–40. Notre Dame, IN: University of Notre Dame Press, 1998.

Porat, Dina. "Zionist Pioneering Youth Movements in Poland and Their Attitude to Erets Israel during the Holocaust." In *Polin: Studies in Polish Jewry*. Vol. 9, *Jews, Poles, Socialists: The Failure of an Ideal*, edited by Antony Polonsky, Israel Bartal, Gershon Hundert, Magdalena Opalski, and Jerzy Tomaszewski, 195–211. Oxford: Littman Library of Jewish Civilization, 2007.

Rojanski, Rachel. "Ben Gurion and Yiddish after the Holocaust." In *The Politics of Yiddish*, edited by Shlomo Berger, 31–49. Amsterdam: Menasseh Ben Israel Institute, 2010.

Roskies, David. *The Dybbuk and Other Writings*. Library of Yiddish Classics. New York: Schocken, 1992.

Roso, Ruti. "ha-'Ashkenazim ha-ḥadashim." *Maariv*, September 14, 2004.

Rothenberg, Jerome. *Technicians of the Sacred: A Range of Poetry from Africa, America, Asia and Oceania*. New York: Doubleday-Anchor, 1968.

———, and Diane Rothenberg. *Symposium of the Whole: A Range of Discourse toward an Ethnopoetics* (Berkeley: University of California Press, 1983).

Safran, Gabriella, and Steven J. Zipperstein, eds. *The Worlds of S. An-sky: A Russian Jewish Intellectual at the Turn of the Century*. Stanford, CA: Stanford University Press, 2006.

Schwartz, Yigal. "Nikhnasta le-'armon mekhushaf ve-shiḥrarta 'oto mehakishuf: 'Al sipur 'al 'ahavah ve-ḥoshekh ke-sefer pulḥan." *Israel* 7 (Spring 2005): n.p.

Segev, Tom. *The Seventh Million: The Israelis and the Holocaust*. New York: Henry Holt, 1991.
Shaked, Gershon. *Modern Hebrew Fiction*. Bloomington: University of Indiana, 2000.
———. "Sofer be-divre torah: 'Al 'oreaḥ natah la-lun me-et S. Y. 'Agnon." *Meḥkere Yerushalayim be-sifrut 'ivrit* (2006): 237–52.
Shalom, Efrat. "The Great Yiddish Comeback." *Haaretz*, May 18, 2003.
Shamir, Moshe. *Bemo yadav: Pirke 'Elik* (Merḥavyah: Sifriyat Poalim, 1951).
Shandler, Jeffrey. *Adventures in Yiddishland: Postvernacular Language and Culture*. Berkeley: University of California Press, 2008.
———. "Heschel and Yiddish: A Struggle with Signification." *Journal of Jewish Thought and Philosophy* 2, no. 2 (1993): 245–99.
Shapiro, Malkah. *Belev ha-mistorin: Sipurim u-fo'emot*. Tel Aviv: Netsah, 1955.
———. *Mi-din le-raḥamim: Sipurim me-ḥatserot ha-'admorim*. Jerusalem: Mosad ha-Rav Kuk, 1969.
———. *Mi-tokh ha-se'arah*. Jerusalem: Hotsa'at R. Mas, 1943.
———. *The Rebbe's Daughter: Memoir of a Hasidic Childhood*. Translated by Nehemia Polen. Philadelphia: Jewish Publication Society, 2002.
———. *Shiri li bat 'ami: Shirim, sonetot u-fo'emot*. Bene-Brak: Netsah, 1971.
———. *Shnenu ba-meginim*, Tel Aviv: Hotsa'at Agudat ha-Sofrim ha-'Ivrim le-yad Dvir, 1952.
Shklovsky, Viktor. "On Cinema." In *Viktor Shklovsky: A Reader*. Edited and translated by Alexandra Berlina. New York: Bloomsbury Academic, 2017.
"Shlomo Breiman." Lexicon of Modern Hebrew Literature. Accessed April 2, 2022. library.osu.edu/projects/hebrew-lexicon/02378.php.
Sholem Aleichem [Shalom Rabinowitz]. *Sipure Motl ben Peysie ha-ḥazan (bishnei sfarim)*. Tel Aviv: Dvir, 1929.
Spiegelman, Art. *Maus: A Survivor's Tale*. London: Penguin, 2003.
Stanislawsky, Michael. *For Whom Do I Toil? Judah Leib Gordon and the Crisis of Russian Jewry*. New York: Oxford University Press, 1988.
Tedlock, Barbara. "From Participant Observation to the Observation of Participation: The Emergence of Narrative Ethnography." *Journal of Anthropological Research* 47, no. 1 (1991): 69–94.
Tschernikhovsky, Saul. "he-'Adam 'eino 'ele," Project Ben Yehudah. Accessed April 2, 2022. benyehuda.org/read/2722.
Ungerfeld, M. "Lezikhra shel meshoreret ha-ḥasidut." *Hado'ar*, March 17, 1972.
Werses, Samuel [Shemu'el Verses]. "Kitve-'et 'ivriyim le-sifrut be-polin ben shete milḥamot 'olam." In *Ben shete milḥamot 'olam*, edited by Chone Shmeruk and

Samuel Werses, 96–127. Jerusalem, Hotsa'at sefarim 'al shem Y. L. Magnes, 1997.

Wheatley, Natasha. "'It Is the Hunter and You Are the Harpooned Dolphin': Memory, Writing, and Medusa—Amos Oz and His Women." *Jewish Quarterly Review* 100, no. 4 (Fall 2010): 631–48.

Wood, Michael. "Proust: The Music of Memory." In *Memory: Histories, Theories, Debates*, edited by Susannah Radstone and Bill Schwarz, 109–22. New York: Fordham University Press, 2010.

World Council for Yiddish and Jewish Culture, Association of Yiddish Writers and Journalists in Israel. "An Homage to Yiddish: Special Session of the Knesset Dedicated to the Yiddish Language and Yiddish Culture." The Forty-Sixth Plenary Session of the 13th Knesset, 11 Tebeth 5753 (April 1, 1993).

Yablonka, Hanna. *Survivors of the Holocaust: Israel after the War*. London: Macmillan, 1999.

Yehoshua, A. B. "The Literature of the Generation of the State." *Ariel: Israel Review of Arts and Letters* 107–8 (1998): 48–56.

Yizhar, S. *Mikdamot*. Tel Aviv: Zmora Bitan, 1992.

———. *Preliminaries*. Translated by Nicholas de Lange. New Milford, CT: Toby Press, 2007.

Yosef, Dorit. "Hakravah, meha'ah ve-mashmaut: 'Iyun ba-textim shel shte 'imahot shkulot, Rivka Guber u-Manuela Deviri." *Masekhet* 9 (2009): 81–110.

Zalkin, Mordechai. "From the Armchair to the Archives: Transformations in the Image of the Shtetl during Fifty Years of Collective Memory in the State of Israel." *Studia Judaica* 8 (1999): 255–66.

Zertal, Israel. *From Catastrophe to Power: Holocaust Survivors and the Emergence of Israel*. Berkeley: University of California, 1998.

Index

Note: Page numbers in italics indicate figures.

Abramovitsh, Sholem Yankev (Mendele Mocher Sforim). *See* Mendele Mocher Sforim (Sholem Yankev Abramovitsh); Mendele Mocher Sforim (Sholem Yankev Abramovitsh), and narrator/s

Agnon, S. Y.: about, 131, 149, 151, 184; "Agunot" and third-person narrative, 35–36; Buczacz and, *119*, 120, *123*, 127; canonic male Hebrew writers, 9, 11–12, 16, 151; *A City and the Fullness Thereof* (*'Ir u-melo'ah*), 158–59; classic/archaic Hebrew, 34, 36–37, 40; *In the Prime of Her Life* (*Bidmi yameha*), 168; literary genealogy and, 16–17, 128–29, 158–59, 167–69, 202n39; *Only Yesterday* (Tmol Shilshom), 76; return to / exile from eastern Europe, 13, 177–78; Yiddish-inflected Hebrew, 36–37, 40. See also *Guest for the Night, A* (*Oreaḥ natah la-lun*; Agnon)

"Agunot" (Agnon), 35–36

Ahad Ha'am (Asher Zvi Hirsch Ginsberg), 155, 166

Aloni, Shulamit, 23–24

Alter, Robert, 51, 164–65

America/Americans, and Yiddish culture, 10–11, 203n8

America / American writers: artifacts, 2–3, 4, 36–37, 103, 145; "back to the roots" movement, 162; bridge between past/present/future, 2, 12, 39–40; hybrid texts, 16, 102, 196n25; nostalgic memory and Yiddish literature, 137; postvernacular Yiddish, 10–11, 24, 25; pre-Holocaust eastern European Jewry and, 90

Amichai, Yehudah, 200n2

Amiel, Rabbi Moshe Avigdor, 106

Anagnostou, Yiorgos, 189n8

Ansky, S. (Solomon Rappoport), 8, 44–45, 53, 121, 160, 189n5, 192n36

Antin, Mary, 59

Appelfeld, Aharon, 200n2

Aran, Gideon, 198n3

archaic/classic Hebrew. *See* classic/archaic Hebrew

artifacts: about, 1–3, 14; America / American writers, 2–3, 4, 36–37, 103, 145; bridge between past/present/future and, 27, 28–29, 30, 178; canonic male Hebrew writers, 121, 198n13; eastern European Jewry and, 4, 15, 31, 36–37, 145–46; ethnography/ies and, 45, 60, 61, 91–92, 101, *101*; Hasidic tales, 145–46; insider/outsider mediators, 39–40; memory/ies, 91, 95, 99–100; music, 135–39; words, 135–36, 138–39, 140–41; Yiddish literature, 178, 179, 181–82. *See also* photographs/photographers, and artifacts

Asch, Sholem, 23, 24

Ashkenazi-centric approach, 12, 79–80. *See also* eastern European Jewry
authenticity: male writers as eastern European–born Israelis, 51, 53, 54; women writers as eastern European–born Israelis, 45, 52–54, 56–57
author/narrator, 34, 40, 114–26, 127–28, 198n12
autobiographical literary trope, 16–17, 49–50, 61–62, 150, 159–60. *See also* biographical writings
autoethnographies: about, 12, 16, 44, 127–28, 189n8; auto-ethnographic salvage, 12, 30, 31, 137. *See also* ethnography/ies

"back to the roots" movement, 17, 162
Band, Arnold, 114, 127
Baron, Dvora, 36, 47–48, 49–50, 127, 151, 190n16
Ben-Gurion, David, 22, 65, 68, 69–70, 85, 86, 87
Ber, Rabbi Wolf, 100
Berdyczewski, M. J.: autobiographical literary trope, 49–50; ethnography/ies, 46–47; Hebrew literature, 43, 151; Holtzman, Avner and, 93, 101, 103, 107
Berdyczewski, Rachel, 101
Bergelson, Dovid, 57
Berman, Reyla, 86
Bhabha, Homi K., 16
Bialik, Chaim Nachman: about, 43, 71, 151; education and eastern European Jewry, 79, 193n16; ethnography/ies, 46–47; familial genealogy and, 152–53, 155, 156, 157, 158, 166, 201n29; *nusaḥ*, 203n14; Weinberg, Tzvi-Zevulin and, 99
biographical writings: about, 15–16, 89–92; eastern European landscape, 107, 197n40; forgetting / not forgotten past, 12, 16, 69, 90, 94, 113, 128, 129; Hebrew language/literature in eastern Europe, 101, 102–3, 105, 106–8; Holocaust, 102, 106, 194n5; hybrid texts, 16, 102, 196n25; Israel/Israelis, 95, 103–4, 107, 197n40; literary history, 92–93, 99, 102–3, 104; memory/ies, 91, 95, 99–100; photographs, 91–92, 101, *101*, 102, 104–6; pre-Holocaust eastern European Jewry, 91–92, 96–102, *101*, 104–6; Russian culture and eastern Europe, 102–4, 106; salvage poetics, 90, 91–92, 101, 102, 103; third voice, 91, 100–101, 102, 104, 106, 107–9; translations, 102–3, 104–6; women's histories and, 94–96, 98, 99–100; Zionism in eastern Europe, 101, 102, 104, 106–8. *See also* autobiographical literary trope; image before my eyes, An (*Temunah le-neged 'einai*; Avner Holtzman); Not from here (*'El mah she-namog*; Gertz and Gertz)
Birstein, Yossl, 182
Boas, Franz, 9
Book of the Brothers, The (*Sefer ha-'aḥim*; Rivka Guber), 68, 69–70
"Books That Have Read Me" (Grossman), 180
Breiman, Shlomo, 149, 152
Brenner, Naomi, 5
Brenner, Y. H.: about, 36, 43, 196n26; authenticity, 51, 53; autobiographical literary trope, 49–50; *Breakdown and Bereavement*, 76; characters-narrator relationship, 50, 191n23; ethnography/ies, 46–47, 62; Holtzman, Avner and, 101, 103, 107; *In Winter* (*Ba-ḥoref*), 62
bridge between past/present/future: about, 17–18, 22, 30; America / American writers, 2, 12, 39–40; artifacts, 27, 28–29, 30, 178; canonic male writers, 13, 16, 36–37, 91; native-born (*dor ha-medina*) male Hebrew writers, 13, 91, 134, 146–47; women writers, 69–70, 74–75, 76–77, 193n10
Brinker, Menachem, 51
Burg, Avraham, 23

Cahan, Abraham, 192n36
Cahan, Mendy, 25, 173
canonic male Hebrew writers: artifacts, 121, 135–39, 198n13; author/narrator,

Index 217

34, 40, 114–26, 127–28, 198n12; bridge between past/present/future, 13, 16, 36–37, 91; classic/archaic Hebrew, 34, 36–37, 40; diaspora, 9, 11–13, 16, 46, 158–59, 167, 197n40; eastern European Jewry, 151, 200n2; farming, 75–76, 139, 143–45; house of study (*bet midrash*), 114, 115, 119–20, 121–25; insider/outsider mediators, 116; intertextuality, 113, 114–15, 128, 198n13. *See also* biographical writings; male writers, and eastern European–born Israelis; postvernacular Yiddish; *and specific male writers and writings*

characters-narrator relationship, and Hebrew literature, 49–52, 191nn23–24. *See also* narrator/s

Chaver, Yael, 16, 194n2

childhood memories: about, 77, 147; eastern European Jewry, 120, 121–22; Israel/Israelis, 134, 145–46, 154–55, 162–63

City and the Fullness Thereof, A ('*Ir u-melo'ah*; Agnon), 158–59

classical music, and postmemory, 133, 140–41, 142–43

classic/archaic Hebrew: about, 14, 175, 180; canonic male Hebrew writers, 34, 36–37, 40; postvernacular Yiddish and, 36, 37, 181, 182, 183. *See also* Hebrew language; Hebrew literature

classic Yiddish literature, 14, 32, 34, 38, 40, 183. *See also* Yiddish literature

Clifford, James, 7

culture / cultural models / cultural salvage, 44, 45, 46, 80–81, 113

Davidson, Jane W., 136–37

Days of Ziklag (S. Yizhar), 131, 146

diaspora: Israeli environment versus, 11, 14, 40; male writers, 9, 11–13, 16, 46, 158–59, 197n40; negation of diaspora (*shlilat ha-galut*), 12, 13, 132, 134, 149, 159; women writers, 11, 65, 67, 69–70. *See also* biographical writings; *and specific writers*

Dinur, Bilhah, 48

dor ha-medina (native-born) Hebrew writers. *See* native-born (*dor ha-medina*) male Hebrew writers

eastern Europe: eastern European–born Israelis, 45–46, 47–48, 49, 55–57, 150; landscape, 107, 197n40; return to / exile from, 12, 13, 113, 128–29, 177–78

eastern European Jewry: Aliyah and immigrant statistics, 22; artifacts, 2–3, 15, 31, 36–37, 145–46; childhood memories, 77, 120, 121–22; cultural memory, 48; demonization of, 4, 12, 22, 25, 38; education of, 77–79, 80, 193n16; Jewish Enlightenment, 37, 46, 56, 62, 175; literature, 4, 9; negative image of, 1, 38–39; Orthodox community, 43, 47; post-Holocaust and, 1, 179; postvernacular Yiddish border, 10, 11, 13, 36–37; return to / exile from eastern Europe, 12, 13, 113, 128–29, 177–78; smells/tastes/sounds of eastern Europe, 155, 158, 160, 165; writers, 80–81, 151, 200n2; Yiddish language and, 5–6. *See also* America / American writers; Holocaust/post-Holocaust, and women writers as eastern European–born Israelis; male writers, and eastern European–born Israelis; memoirists, and eastern European–born Israelis; women's histories, and eastern European–born Israelis; women writers, and eastern European–born Israelis; women writers, and Hasidim; women writers, and valorization of eastern European Jewry; *and specific women writers and writings*

eastern European literature: classic Yiddish literature and, 14, 32, 34, 38, 40, 175, 183; Hebrew literature and, 151–52, 200n4; literary history, 151–52, 200n4

Edelstein, Zelda, 48

education: eastern European Jewry, 77–79, 80, 193n16; Middle Eastern Jewry, 78, 79, 80

"Efraim Goes Back to Alfalfa" (S. Yizhar), 131
Eli, Ovadiah, 21
English translations: biographical writings, 102, 104–6; women writers and, 8, 48–49, 56–57, 62
ethnography/ies: artifacts, 45, 60, 61, 91–92, 101, *101*; autoethnography, 16, 44, 60–61, 127–28, 189n8; biographical writings, 90, 91, 92; eastern European–born Israelis, 45–46, 47–48, 49, 55–57; folk ethnography, 2–4; hybrid texts, 16, 102, 196n25; literary memoirists, 44, 48; male writers as eastern European–born Israelis, 46–48; pre-Holocaust eastern European Jewry and, 4, 44–45, 46, 90; salvage ethnography, 9, 12, 30, 31, 44, 137, 189n8; salvage poetics, 2, 3–4, 6–7; third voice, 90–91. *See also* autoethnographies
ethnopoetics: described, 8–9, 44–45, 188n3; eastern European Jewish writers, 53, 121, 160; women writers and Hasidim, 8, 14. *See also* salvage poetics

familial genealogy, 149–50, 158–60, 163, 164, 200n4. See also *Tale of Love and Darkness, A* (*Sipur 'al 'ahavah ve-ḥoshekh*; Oz)
farming: canonic male writers and, 75–76, 139, 143–45; writers as eastern European–born Israelis, 74, 75–76, 77, 82, 84
Feierberg, M. Z., 151
Foer, Jonathan Safran, 45
Fogel, David, 57
Fogelman, Bella, 48
folk ethnography, 2–4. *See also* ethnography/ies
folktales, 149, 150, 162–63, 164, 166–67
forgetting / not forgotten past: biographical writings, 12, 16, 69, 90, 94, 113, 128, 129; music, 133, 134, 136, 145; native-born (*dor ha-medina*) male Hebrew writers, 134, 146–47, 173; return to / exile from eastern Europe, 12, 13, 113, 128–29, 177–78, 184. *See also* salvage memory

Frischmann, David, 6, 7, 15, 46, 47, 49, 51, 53

Garrido, Sandra, 136–37
Gdud Megine ha-Safah ("Brigade for the Protection of the Language"), 4–5
Geertz, Clifford, 7
Gertz, Aharonchik, 96–97, 195n15
Gertz, Dalit, 95
Gertz, Dora (Deborah; née Dora Weinberg): Europe (Italy) and histories, 94–96, 98; Gertz, Aharonchik as husband, 96–97; Gertz, Nurit as daughter/co-author, 93, 94–97, 100, 195n15; memory/ies as artifacts, 91, 99; Weinberg, Motel as grandmother, 95, 98, 99; Weinberg, Ruchele as sister, 99; Weinberg, Tzvi-Zevulin as grandfather, 93, 99; women's histories and eastern European–born Israelis, 94–95, 99–100. *See also* Not from here (*'El mah she-namog*; Gertz and Gertz)
Gertz, Nurit, 93, 94–97, 100, 183, 195n15. *See also* Gertz, Dora (Deborah; née Dora Weinberg); Not from here (*'El mah she-namog*; Gertz and Gertz)
Ginsberg, Asher Zvi Hirsch (Ahad Ha'am), 155, 166
Gluzman, Michael, 152
Gnessin, U. N., 101, 103, 107, 151, 163
Goldberg, Leah, 102–3, 104, 106
Gordon, A. D., 76
Greenberg, Uri Zvi, 36
Grossman, David, 11–12, 13, 178–79, 180, 182. See also *See Under: Love* (Grossman)
Grumberg, Karen, 169
Guber, Ephraim: about, 65; commemoration of, 66, 84–85; War of Independence, 67, 68–69, 72, 73, 74
Guber, Mordecai, 66, 74, 76, 81, 82, *83*, 85, 86
Guber, Rivka: about, 10, 14, 65, *72*, *83*, 183–84, 198n1; Ashkenazi-centric approach, 79–80; *The Book of the Brothers*

(*Sefer ha-'aḥim*), 68, 69–70; bridge between past/present/future, 69–70, 74–75, 76–77, 193n10; diaspora, 11, 65, 67, 69–70; Guber, Mordecai as husband, 66, 74, 76, 81, 82, *83*, 85, 86; Hebrew language, 74, 87; legacy, 67, *69*; literary legacy, 11, 17, 63, 65, 66–67, 73, 88; memoirists, 48; Middle Eastern Jewry, 78, 79, 80; *Only a Path*, 87; Sachs and, 70–73, 85, 87; salvage poetics, 10, 65–66, 67, 69–70, 81–82; *The Signal Fires of Lachish* ('*El mas'uot Lachish*), 73–74, 77–78, 82–83; *Village of the Brothers* ('*Eleh toldot kfar 'aḥim*), 66, 81–82; War of Independence, 65, 66, 74, 85; Yiddish language, 86–87; Zionism, 11, 14, 66, 67–68, 69, 73–74. *See also* Guber, Ephraim; Guber, Tzvi; Mother of Sons ("'Em ha-Banim") appellation

Guber, Rivka, and eastern European Jewry valorization: about, 10, 14, 65; bridge between past/present/future, 69, 76–77; cultural models, 80–81; education, 77–79, 80; farming, 74, 75, 76, 77, 82, 84; *A Legacy to Impart*, 74–77, 86–87; literary legacy, 67, 74–77, 86–87; memory/ies, 66–67, 74–75, 76, 80, 81–82. *See also* Guber, Rivka

Guber, Rivka, and Holocaust: bridge between past/present/future, 69; commemoration of dead, 85; literary legacy, 63, 65, 66–67; Mother of the Holocaust appellation for Sachs, 71–73; survivors of, 73, 74, 81–82, 85; Zionism, 73–74. *See also* Guber, Rivka; Guber, Rivka, and eastern European Jewry valorization

Guber, Tzvi: about, 65; commemoration of, 66, 84–85; War of Independence, 67, 68–69, 72, 73, 74

Guest for the Night, A (*Oreaḥ natah la-lun*; Agnon): about, 11–12, 16, 36–37, 178; artifacts, 121, 198n13; autoethnography, 127–28; bridge between past/present/future, 13, 36–37; childhood memories, 120, 121–22; forgetting / not forgotten past, 113, 128–29; Hebrew literature, 34, 43, 118, 121; house of study (*bet midrash*), 114, 115, 119–20, 121–25; intertextuality, 113, 114, 115, 128, 198n13; Jewish texts/liturgy, 113, 114–15; World War I, 121, 124, 128. *See also* Agnon, S. Y.

Guest for the Night, A (*Oreaḥ natah la-lun*; Agnon), and narrator: author/narrator, 114–15, 121, 127–28, 198n12; author/s (*sofer/sofrim*), 114, 120–21; homodiegetic narrator, 34, 127–28; house of study (*bet midrash*), 115, 120, 121–24, 125; imaginary real, 115–20, 121; insider/outsider mediators, 40, 116; preacher-narrator and sermons, 122–26, 127; word/s of Torah (*dvar/divre Torah*), 114–15, 120, 121, 122, 125–26. *See also* Agnon, S. Y.; *Guest for the Night, A* (*Oreaḥ natah la-lun*; Agnon)

Gurevitch, Zali, 198n3

Harshav, Benjamin, 51
Hasidim: about, 2, 24, 26; literary figures, 39, 166–67, 168–69; melodies, 141–43; tales, 145–46. *See also* women writers, and Hasidim
Hazaz, Haim, 36
Hebrew language: biographical writings, 101, 102–3, 105, 106–8; ethnography/ies, 6, 7; Jewish Enlightenment, 37, 46, 62; male writers as eastern European–born Israelis, 50–52, 62–63, 151, 191n23; native-born (*dor ha-medina*) male Hebrew writers, 9, 16, 146, 150–51, 200n2; protection of, 4–5, 22; salvage poetics, 1, 4–5, 6, 7, 46; women writers as eastern European–born Israelis, 49–51, 52, 62–63, 74, 87, 191n24; Yiddish-inflected Hebrew, 36–38, 40, 175, 180–82; Yiddish literature, 36–37, 40; Zionism and, 22, 86. *See also* classic/archaic Hebrew

Hebrew literature: about, 9, 17, 33; autobiographies, 61–62; biographical writings, 101, 102–3, 105, 106–8; characters-narrator relationship, 49–52, 191nn23–24; ethnography/ies, 6, 7, 15; familial genealogy, 200n4; folklore, 6–7; imaginary real, 115–16; literary history, 92–93, 99, 102–3, 151–52; male writers and eastern European–born Israelis, 33, 34, 43, 50–52, 191n23; native-born (*dor ha-medina*) male Hebrew writers, 9, 16, 146–47, 150–51; statehood generation and, 146, 150, 151, 160, 200n2; translations, 14, 29–30; women writers as eastern European–born Israelis, 49–51, 52, 62–63, 103, 191n24; Yiddish-inflected Hebrew, 36–38, 40, 175, 180–82; Yiddish language, 86–87, 174, 175; Zionism, 15, 134, 143, 145, 159–60, 198n3. *See also* biographical writings; canonic male Hebrew writers; classic/archaic Hebrew; Hebrew language; *Tale of Love and Darkness, A* (*Sipur 'al 'ahavah ve-ḥoshekh*; Oz); *and specific Hebrew writers*

Hebrew literature, and eastern European Jewry: about, 15, 37, 99; demonization and loss of culture and language, 4, 5–6, 12, 38; eastern European literature and, 151–52, 200n4; pre-Holocaust depictions, 4, 44–45, 46, 174. *See also* Hebrew literature

Hebrew renaissance. *See* Hebrew language; Hebrew literature

Heineman, Malkah, 48

Herzl, Theodor, 73–74, 193n8

Herzog, Elizabeth, 2–3, 14

Heschel, Abraham Joshua, 2–3, 4, 113–14, 137, 145

Hirbet Hizeh (S. Yizhar), 132, 146

Hirsch, Marianne, 89–90, 133

Hoffman, Allen, 45

Holocaust/post-Holocaust: biographical writings and, 102, 106, 194n5; eastern European legacy, 1, 2, 47, 85, 179, 194n24; Israel/Israelis, 1, 9, 26, 85, 175, 176, 179, 194n24. *See also* Holocaust survivors; World War II

Holocaust/post-Holocaust, and women writers as eastern European–born Israelis: bridge between past/present/future, 69; commemoration of dead, 85; literary legacy, 63, 65, 66–67; Mother of the Holocaust appellation for Sachs, 71–73; survivors of, 73, 74, 81–82, 85; Zionism, 73–74. *See also* Holocaust/post-Holocaust; women writers, and eastern European–born Israelis

Holocaust survivors: children of, 17, 26, 106, 133, 176–77; demonization of, 38, 106, 197n33; grief, 66, 67; support for, 85, 86. *See also* Holocaust/post-Holocaust; Holocaust/post-Holocaust, and women writers as eastern European–born Israelis

Holtzman, Avner, 15, 17, 93, 101, 102, 104, 108, 183. *See also* Holtzman, Leah Svirsky; image before my eyes, An (*Temunah le-neged 'einai*; Avner Holtzman)

Holtzman, Haim, 101, 102

Holtzman, Leah Svirsky, 91–92, *101*, 101–2, 104

"Homage to Yiddish, An": about, 13, 21, 173; postvernacular Yiddish literature, 30–31, 36; salvage poetics, 22–23, 25; Yiddish-inflected Hebrew, 36; Yiddish literature, 22–24, 25, 31, 175

homodiegetic narrator/s, 33–35, 51, 127–28, 175

house of study (*bet midrash*), 114, 115, 119–20, 121–25

Howe, Irving, 137, 162

hybrid texts, 16, 40, 102, 196n25

Iczkovits, Yaniv. See *Slaughterman's Daughter, The* (*Tikun 'aḥar ḥatsot*; Iczkovits); *Slaughterman's Daughter, The* (*Tikun 'aḥar ḥatsot*; Iczkovits), and Yiddish

image before my eyes, An (*Temunah le-neged 'einai*; Avner Holtzman):

Index 221

about, 15, 17, 89; artifacts, 91–92, 101, 103; Berdyczewski, M. J. and, 101, 103; Brenner, Y. H. and, 101, 103, 107; English translations, 102, 104–6; forgetting / not forgotten past, 16, 90; Gnessin and, 101, 103, 107; Goldberg and translations, 102–3, 104, 106; Hebrew language/literature in eastern Europe, 101, 102–3, 105, 106–8; Holocaust, 102, 106, 194n5; Holtzman, Haim and, 101, 102; Holtzman, Leah Svirsky, 101–2, 104; hybrid texts (literary/ethnographic texts), 102, 196n25; Israel/Israelis' link with eastern Europe, 103–4; landscapes, 107, 197n40; literary history, 92–93, 102–3, 104; Russian culture and eastern Europe, 102–4, 106; salvage poetics, 90, 91, 102; Svirsky, Hanale and birthday party photograph, 91–92, 101, *101*, 102, 104–6; Svirsky, Rachel, 104, 108; third voice, 101, 102, 104, 106, 107–8; Zionism in eastern Europe, 101, 102, 104, 106–8

insider/outsider mediators: about, 30; artifacts and, 39–40; male writers and eastern European–born Israelis, 32, 33, 38, 40, 116; women writers as eastern European–born Israelis, 49, 50, 52, 54–55, 60–61, 191n24

intertextuality, 113, 114, 115, 128, 175, 182–83, 198n13

"In the Prime of Her Life" (*Bidmi yameha*; Agnon), 168

In Winter (*Ba-ḥoref*; Y. H. Brenner), 62

Israel/Israelis: aliyot, 14, 22, 85, 94, 106–7, 128; Ashkenazi-centric approach, 12, 79–80; "back to the roots" movement, 17, 162; biographical writings and, 94–95, *95*, 103–4, 107, 197n40; childhood memories, 134, 145–46, 154–55, 162–63; eastern European Jewry and demonization, 4, 25, 38; eastern European link, 103–4; forgetting / not forgotten past, 16, 194n2; Goldberg and literature, 103; Holocaust and, 38, 85, 106, 176, 194n24, 197n33; hybrid texts, 102, 196n25; kibbutz life, 94–95, *95*; landscape, 107, 131–32, 160, 197n40; literary legacies, 11, 17, 63, 65, 66–67, 73, 88; masculine quality, 11; Orthodox eastern European Jewry, 43; postage stamp, *69*; postvernacular Yiddish culture, 24, 26–27, 31; pre-Holocaust eastern European Jewry memory/ies, 90, 195n15; salvage poetics continuum, 10, 11, 13, 36–37; translations and, 103–4; ultra-Orthodox Jews, 43, 202n2; War of Independence, 65, 66, 74, 84, 85, 131–32, 146; Yiddish culture and, 179, 203n8; Yiddish language and, 22, 26, 134, 159, 173, 179. *See also* Holocaust/post-Holocaust, and women writers as eastern European–born Israelis; male writers, and eastern European–born Israelis; memoirists, and eastern European–born Israelis; native-born (*dor ha-medina*) male Hebrew writers; native-born (*dor ha-medina*) women Hebrew writers; women's histories, and eastern European–born Israelis; women writers, and eastern European–born Israelis; women writers, and Hasidim; women writers, and valorization of eastern European Jewry; Zionism

Jewish Enlightenment (Haskalah, Maskilic), 37, 46, 56, 62, 175

Jewish texts/liturgy: canonic male Hebrew writers, 113, 114–15; culture and, 113–14; music, 132, 141, 142, 143; native-born (*dor ha-medina*) male Hebrew writers, 134, 149, 150

Kacyzne, Alter, 58, 59–60, 61, 192n36
Kacyzne, Hannah, 58, 59
Kalish, Ita: about, 8, 44, 56, 57, 59, 60–61, 183–84; apostasy narratives, 57, 59, 60–61; authenticity and Hasidim and narratives from women's point of view, 45, 56–57; ethnography/ies, 45, 46, 47, 49;

Kalish, Ita (*continued*)
insider/outsider mediators, 60–61; "Life in a Hasidic Court in Russian Poland [. . .]," 56–57; literary artistry, 48, 57, 60; marginality of women writers, 47, 49, 57, 62; memoirists, 44, 45, 48–49, 56; *My yesterday* (*'Etmoli*), 56–58, 59–61, 62; narrator/s, 58, 59–60; photographs of, 58, 60, 61; *A rebishe heim in amolikn Poyln*, 56–57; secular world versus Hasidim, 57–58, 59; translation narratives into English, 8, 48–49, 56–57; witnesses as women, 45, 48
Kaniuk, Yoram, 150–51
Kaplan, Eran, 160–62
Kenaz, Yehoshua, 150–51
Kfar 'Ahim, Israel, 66, 81–82, 84, 85
Kipnis, Levin, 150, 153
Kirshenblatt-Gimblett, Barbara, 3
Klausner, Alexander, 150, 152–53, 155–56, 158
Klausner, Aryeh Leib, 157, 158–59, 168
Klausner, Fania Mussman. *See* Oz, Fania Mussman Klausner
Klausner, Joseph, 12, 153, 157, 158, 159, 168
Klausner, Joseph Gedalya, 5, 157
Klausner, Shlomit, 156–57, 158
Klausner, Sonia, 163, 164
Knesset, and Yiddish culture, 25, 173. *See also* "Homage to Yiddish, An"
Korngold, Sheyna, 48
Korszak, Rozka, 87
Krupat, Arnold, 188n3
Kugelmass, Jack, 3–4

Laor, Dan, 127
Legacy to Impart, A (Rivka Guber), 74–77, 86–87
"Life in a Hasidic Court in Russian Poland [. . .]" (Kalish), 56–57
Life Is with People (Zborowski and Herzog), 2–3, 14
Lilienblum, Moshe Leib, 155
literary genealogy: about, 151; literary influences and, 16–17, 128–29, 158–59, 167–69, 202n39; Oz, Fania and, 150, 160, 162–63, 164–65, 167. *See also Tale of Love and Darkness, A* (*Sipur 'al 'ahavah ve-ḥoshekh*; Oz)
literary history: biographical writings, 92–93, 102–3, 104; eastern European literature and, 151–52, 200n4; Hebrew literature and, 92–93, 99, 102–3, 151–52
literary legacies, and women writers as eastern European–born Israelis, 11, 17, 63, 65, 66–67, 73, 88. *See also* women writers, and valorization of eastern European Jewry

male writers, and eastern European–born Israelis: about, 11–12; authenticity, 51, 53, 54; autobiographical literary trope, 49–50; characters-narrator relationship, 50–52, 191n23; ethnography/ies, 46–48, 57, 62; farming, 75–76; Hebrew language, 50–52, 62–63, 151, 191n23; Hebrew literature, 34, 43; insider/outsider mediators, 32, 33, 38, 40, 116; memoirists, 17, 31; valorization of eastern European Jewry, 77, 146. *See also* biographical writings; native-born (*dor ha-medina*) male Hebrew writers; *and specific male writers and writings*
Mead, Margaret, 3
Medem, Vladimir, 160
memoirists, and eastern European–born Israelis: literary memoirists, 44, 48; male writers, 17, 31; women writers, 14, 15, 44, 45, 48–49, 56
memory/ies: as artifacts, 91, 95, 99–100; ethnography/ies and, 45; music, 136–37, 141–42; valorization of eastern European Jewry, 66–67, 74–75, 76, 80, 81–82
Mendele Mocher Sforim (Sholem Yankev Abramovitsh): artifacts, 4, 15, 40; authenticity, 53, 54; autobiographical literary trope, 49–50; culture at a distance studies (eastern European Jewry), 3; ethnography/ies, 6, 46–47; familial genealogy, 151, 155, 166; Hebrew

literature, 33, 43, 49, 50–51, 52, 151, 182; insider/outsider mediators, 33, 40; literary genealogy, 151, 166; *nusaḥ*, 181; Yiddish culture identification with Yiddish literature, 23; Yiddish literature, 33, 67

Mendele Mocher Sforim (Sholem Yankev Abramovitsh), and narrator/s: apostrophic narrator, 33; characters-narrator relationship, 50–51, 52; homodiegetic narrator, 33–35, 175; Iczkovits's intimations, 36; insider/outsider mediators, 40. See also Mendele Mocher Sforim (Sholem Yankev Abramovitsh)

Mer, Beni, 26, 27, 29–30, 31, 38. See also *Smocze: The Biography of a Jewish Street in Warsaw* (Mer)

Middle Eastern Jewry, 13, 78, 79–81

Milner, Iris, 162

Mintz, Alan, 61

Miron, Dan, 6–7, 33, 51, 135

Mishkovsky, Zelda Schneurson, 149, 150, 165–67, 169

Modan, Rutu, 25

Mother of Sons ("'Em ha-Banim") appellation: Ben-Gurion, 65, 68, 69–70, 86; inscription and signature, 72; memory/ies, 81–82; speech, 69–73, 193n6; sublimation of grief by mothers, 66, 67; War of Independence, 65, 66, 67, 68–69, 74; Zionism, 11, 14. See also Guber, Rivka

Motl, Peysie the cantor's son (*Motl Peysie dem ḥazens*; Sholem Aleichem), 24, 175, 179

music. See *Preliminaries* (*Mikdamot*; S. Yizhar), and music

Myerhoff, Barbara, 15, 90–91

My Michael (Oz), 162

My yesterday ('*Etmoli*; Kalish), 56–58, 59–61, 62

narrator/s: apostrophic narrator, 33, 51, 60–61; author/narrator, 34, 40, 114–26, 127–28, 198n12; author/s (*sofer/sofrim*), 114, 120–21; characters-narrator relationship and Hebrew literature, 49–52, 191nn23–24; first-person narrator/s, 59–60; homodiegetic narrator, 33–35, 51, 127–28, 175; house of study (*bet midrash*), 115, 120, 121–24, 125; imaginary real, 115–20, 121; insider/outsider mediators, 40, 116; preacher-narrator and sermons, 122–26, 127; third-person narrative, 34–36, 58, 59, 60; women writers as eastern European–born Israelis, 58, 59; word/s of Torah (*dvar/divre Torah*), 114–15, 120, 121, 122, 125–26

National Authority for Yiddish Culture, 25, 173

nationalism. See Zionism

native-born (*dor ha-medina*) male Hebrew writers: author/narrator, 34, 40; bridge between past/present/future, 13, 91, 134, 146–47; forgetting / not forgotten past, 134, 146–47, 178; Hebrew language/literature, 9, 16, 146–47, 150–51, 167, 200n2; Jewish texts/liturgy, 134, 149, 150; lived experience, 139–40; statehood generation and, 146, 150, 151, 160, 200n2; Yiddish language, 134, 143–44, 159, 167, 168–69; Zionism, 134, 143, 145, 159–62, 198n3

native-born (*dor ha-medina*) women Hebrew writers, 169–71. See also women writers, and eastern European–born Israelis; women writers, and Hasidim; women writers, and memories; women writers, and valorization of eastern European Jewry

Navon, Yitzhak, 66, 67

negation of diaspora (*shlilat ha-galut*), 12, 13, 132, 134, 149, 159

Nora, Pierre, 80

nostalgic memory: eastern Europeans as Israeli and, 77, 136–37; music, 136–37

Not from here ('*El mah she-namog*; Gertz and Gertz): about, 15, 16, 17,

224 Index

Not from here (*'El mah she-namog*; Gertz and Gertz) (*continued*)
89, 90, 93–94; Europe (Italy) and women's histories, 94–96, 98; kibbutz life and women's histories, 94–95, *95*; literary history, 92–93, 99; memories as artifacts, 91, 94, 95, 99–100; pre-Holocaust eastern European Jewry, 96–102, *101*, 104; salvage poetics, 90, 91; third voice, 100–101, 108–9
nusaḥ, 181, 182, 203n14

"On Account of a Hat" (Sholem Aleichem), 39–40
Only a Path (Rivka Guber), 87
Only Yesterday (*Tmol shilshom*; Agnon), 76
Opatoshu, Joseph, 23, 24
Orthodox eastern European Jewry, 43, 47
Oz, Amos: eastern European Jewry and, 4, 43, 160; forgetting / not forgotten past, 9, 150, 178; literary history, 151–52; *My Michael*, 162; native-born (*dor ha-medina*) male Hebrew writers, 9, 150–51, 167; nonfiction writings, 202n39; return to / exile from eastern Europe, 178, 184; "Thank God for His Daily Blessings," 43; "The Hill of Evil Counsel," 162. See also *Tale of Love and Darkness, A* (*Sipur 'al 'ahavah ve-ḥoshekh*; Oz)
Oz, Fania Mussman Klausner: about, 77, 170–71; folktales, 149, 150, 162–63, 164, 166–67; literary genealogy, 150, 160, 162–63, 164–65, 167; suicide, 160, 165, 168, 169

Packer, George, 180
Papish, Tova Berlin, 48
Parush, Iris, 62–63
Peretz, I. L., 23, 24, 103, 159
photographs/photographers: auto-ethnographic salvage, 12, 30, 31, 137; insider/outsider mediators, 30
photographs/photographers, and artifacts: about, 2, 22; birthday party photograph, 91–92, 101, *101*, 102, 104–6;

ethnography/ies, 60, 61. See also artifacts; photographs/photographers
Pinkus, Yirmi, 25
Pinless, S. Y., 47–48, 49, 53
Place/place, and Zionism, 134, 198n3
Polen, Nehemia, 49, 50, 56
postmemory, 89–90, 133, 137, 142–43
postvernacular Yiddish: about, 10–11, 13–14, 17, 18, 24, 40–41, 173–74; America / American writers, 10–11, 24, 25; classic/archaic Hebrew, 36, 37, 181, 182, 183; "An Homage to Yiddish," 13, 30–31, 36; Israel/Israelis, 11, 13, 26, 31, 36–37; Yiddishland, 31, 40, 41; Yiddish literature, 30–31, 36. See also *Slaughterman's Daughter, The* (*Tikun 'aḥar ḥatsot*; Iczkovits); Yiddishland; Yiddish language; Yiddish literature; *and specific Israeli Hebrew writers*
postvernacular Yiddish, and salvage poetics: about, 17–18, 174; border and, 11, 13, 26–27, 36–37; continuum and, 11–12, 13, 18, 36–37, 38. See also postvernacular Yiddish
pre-Holocaust eastern European Jewry: America / American writers and, 90; biographical writings and, 91–92, 96–102; ethnography/ies, 4, 44–45, 46, 90; Israel/Israelis and memory/ies of, 90, 195n15; photographs as artifacts, 91–92, *101*, 101–2, 104–6; salvage poetics and, 183
Preliminaries (*Mikdamot*; S. Yizhar): about, 4, 9, 132–33, 146, 152, 196n26; artifacts and Hasidic tales, 145–46; autobiographical literary trope, 159–60; bridge between past/present/future, 13, 91; eastern European Jewry and culture as missing/loss, 131, 134, 137, 138, 147, 160; farming as failure, 75–76, 139, 143–45; postmemory, 137, 141–43; salvage memory, 137; Yiddish phrases, 143–44; Zionism, 143, 159–60. See also S. Yizhar (Yizhar Smolenski)
Preliminaries (*Mikdamot*; S. Yizhar), and music: about, 131, 146, 147, 177; artifacts,

Index 225

135–39; forgetting / not forgotten past, 133, 134, 136, 145, 178; Hasidic melodies, 141–43; Jewish texts/liturgy, 132, 141, 142, 143; loss, 137–38; memory, 136–37, 141–42; nostalgic memory, 136–37; postmemory and classical music, 133, 140–41, 142–43; salvage memory, 135, 136, 142–43, 145; words, 135–36, 138–39, 140–41. See also *Preliminaries* (*Mikdamot*; S. Yizhar); S. Yizhar (Yizhar Smolenski)

"Prisoner, The" (S. Yizhar), 132

Proust, Marcel, 93, 99, 108, 136

Rachel (biblical figure), 70, 71

Rappoport, Solomon (S. Ansky), 8, 44–45, 53, 121, 160, 189n5, 192n36

Rebbe's Daughter, The (*Mi-din le-raḥamim: Sipurim me-ḥatserot ha-'admorim*; Shapiro): authenticity, 52–54; autobiographical literary trope, 49–50; characters-narrator relationship, 50–51, 52, 191n24; Hebrew literature, 50–51, 52, 191n24; insider/outsider mediators, 49, 50, 52, 54–55, 191n24; marginality of women writers, 62; translation narratives into English, 48–49; witnesses as women, 45, 48, 50, 52, 53–54, 140. See also Shapiro, Malkah

rebishe heim in amolikn Poyln, A (Kalish), 56–57

Renan, Ernest, 16

return to / exile from eastern Europe, 12, 13, 113, 128–29, 177–78, 184

Rojanski, Rachel, 5

Roskies, David, 44

Roth, Philip, 39

Russian culture: biographical writings and, 102–4, 106; language, 86, 87; literature, 99, 102–4, 106, 155, 192n36

Sachs, Esther, 70–73, 85, 87

salvage ethnography, 9, 12, 30, 31, 44, 137, 189n8

salvage memory: about, 133, 134, 137; music, 135, 136, 142–43, 145.

See also forgetting / not forgotten past

salvage poetics, 1–5, 6–7, 9–10, 13, 183–84, 185n1

Samuel, Maurice: artifacts of eastern European Jewry, 2–3, 4, 36–37, 145, 178; nostalgic memory, 137; translations and salvage poetics, 103; *The World of Sholem Aleichem*, 2, 36–37

Schneerson, Rebbe Menachem Mendel, 167

Schwartz, Yigal, 160, 161

See Under: Love (Grossman): about, 17, 25–26, 176; artifacts, 178, 181–82; bridge between past/present/future, 13, 178; canonic male Hebrew writers and, 11–12; classic/archaic Hebrew, 37, 181, 182, 183; forgetting / not forgotten past, 176, 178; Holocaust/post-Holocaust, 9, 26, 175, 176–77; intertextuality, 175, 182–83; Jewish Enlightenment, 175; negation of diaspora, 12, 13; *nusaḥ*, 181, 182, 203n14; postvernacular Yiddish, 37, 174, 179, 182; salvage poetics and, 9, 182–83; Sholem Aleichem's texts, 175, 179, 180, 182–83; Yiddish-inflected Hebrew, 175, 180–82. See also Grossman, David

Segev, Tom, 176

Shabtai, Yaakov, 150–51, 174

Shaked, Gershon, 114

Shamir, Moshe, 146–47

Shandler, Jeffrey, 10–11, 24, 173–74

Shapiro, Malkah: about, 8, 11, 17, 44, 49, 177, 183–84; authenticity, 45, 52–54; characters-narrator relationship, 50–51, 52, 191n24; ethnography/ies, 45, 46, 47, 48, 49, 55–56; Hasidim and narratives from women's point of view, 45, 49, 50; Hebrew literature, 50–51, 52, 191n24; insider/outsider mediators, 49, 50, 52, 54–55, 191n24; literary artistry, 48, 55–56; marginality of women writers, 47, 49, 62; memoirists, 44, 45, 47, 48–49; salvage poetics, 9, 48; translation narratives into English, 8, 48–49.

Shapiro, Malkah (*continued*)
  See also *Rebbe's Daughter, The* (*Mi-din le-rahamim: Sipurim me-hatserot ha-'admorim*; Shapiro)
Sheinfeld, Ilan, 26
Shilansky, Dov, 23, 24
Shklovsky, Viktor, 152, 200n4
Shlonsky, Avraham, 36
Shneour, Zalman, 159
Sholem Aleichem (Sholem Rabinovitch): about, 4, 54, 103; autobiographical literary trope, 49–50; bridge between past/present/future, 39–40; characters-narrator relationship, 50, 51; culture studies, 3, 4; Grossman on, 178–79, 182; Motl, Peysie the cantor's son (*Motl Peysie dem hazens*), 24, 175, 179; "On Account of a Hat," 39–40; salvage poetics, 22–23, 103; Samuel and, 2, 36–37; *Sipure Motl ben Peysie ha-hazan* (trans. Berkowitz), 179; *Tevye the Milkman* (*Tevye der milkhiker*), 51, 178; Yiddish culture, 22–23, 179, 203n8; Yiddish literature, 22–23, 37. See also "Homage to Yiddish, An"
Singer, Israel Joshua, 192n36
Sipure Motl ben Peysie ha-hazan (Sholem Aleichem, trans. Berkowitz), 179
Slaughterman's Daughter, The (*Tikun 'ahar hatsot*; Iczkovits): about, 13, 14, 31–33, 174; artifacts, 39–40; classic/archaic Hebrew, 36–37, 40; eastern European Jewry, 13–14, 38; Hebrew literature, 14, 33, 34, 37, 40; insider/outsider mediators, 32, 38–39, 40; Israeli environment versus diaspora, 11, 14, 40; Israel/Israelis and, 14, 38; narrator/s, 32, 33–35, 36, 38, 40, 175; salvage poetics, 18, 31, 174
Slaughterman's Daughter, The (*Tikun 'ahar hatsot*; Iczkovits), and Yiddish: classic Yiddish, 14, 34, 40; postvernacular Yiddish, 13, 18, 36, 37, 38, 40–41; salvage poetics border, 13, 18; Yiddish-inflected Hebrew, 37–38; Yiddishland, 40, 41. See also *Slaughterman's Daughter, The* (*Tikun 'ahar hatsot*; Iczkovits); Yiddish culture

Smocze: The Biography of a Jewish Street in Warsaw (Mer): about, 26, 27, 31; bridge between past/present/future, 27, 28–29; eastern European Jewry world and negative image, 38–39; photographs, 27, 28, 29; postvernacular Yiddish, 26–27; Yiddish language and Israel/Israelis, 26. See also Mer, Beni
Smolenski, Miriam, 131, 147
Smolenski, Yizhar (S. Yizhar). See *Preliminaries* (*Mikdamot*; S. Yizhar); *Preliminaries* (*Mikdamot*; S. Yizhar), and music; S. Yizhar (Yizhar Smolenski)
Smolenski, Ze'ev, 131, 134, 145, 147
Solomiak, Abraham, 106–7
Spiegelman, Art, 164
statehood generation, and Hebrew writers, 146, 150, 151, 160, 200n2. See also native-born (*dor ha-medina*) male Hebrew writers; native-born (*dor ha-medina*) women Hebrew writers
Steinberg, Yaakov, 36
Svirsky, Hanale, 91–92, 101, *101*, 102, 104–6
Svirsky, Leah. See Holtzman, Leah Svirsky
Svirsky, Rachel, 104, 108
S. Yizhar (Yizhar Smolenski): about, 16, 131, 149, 184; *Days of Ziklag*, 131, 146; "Efraim Goes Back to Alfalfa," 131; forgetting / not forgotten past, 9, 16, 134, 146, 178; *Hirbet Hizeh*, 132, 146; Israeli landscape, 131–32; native-born (*dor ha-medina*) male Hebrew writers, 9, 16, 146; negation of diaspora (*shlilat ha-galut*), 12, 132; "The Prisoner," 132; return to / exile from eastern Europe, 178; Smolenski, Miriam as mother, 131, 147; Smolenski, Ze'ev as father, 131, 134, 145, 147; writings described, 11–12, 13, 16; Zionism, 134, 145, 198n3. See also *Preliminaries* (*Mikdamot*; S. Yizhar); *Preliminaries* (*Mikdamot*; S. Yizhar), and music

Tabenkin, Yitzhak, 101
Tale of Love and Darkness, A (*Sipur 'al 'ahavah ve-hoshekh*; Oz)

—autobiographical literary trope, 16–17, 150, 159–60
—bridge between past/present/future, 13, 91
—eastern European Jewry and, 4, 43, 46, 160
—familial genealogy, 149–50, 158–60, 163, 164
—familial genealogy and literary figures: Ahad Ha'am, 155, 166; Bialik, 152–53, 155, 156, 157, 158, 166, 201n29; Hasidim, 166–67, 169; Mendele, 151, 155, 166; Mishkovsky, Zelda Schneurson, 149, 150, 165–67, 169; Tschernikhovsky, 146, 150, 151, 153–54, 156–57, 160, 166
—Hebrew literature, 11–12, 158–59, 167
—Jewish texts/liturgy, 149, 150
—literary genealogy and family figures: about, 150; Klausner, Alexander as Oz's grandfather, 150, 152–53, 155–56, 158; Klausner, Aryeh Leib as Oz's father, 157, 158–59, 168; Klausner, Joseph as Oz's uncle, 12, 153, 157, 158, 159, 168; Klausner, Shlomit as Oz's grandmother, 156–57, 158
—literary genealogy and literary influences: Agnon, 16–17, 128–29, 158–59, 167–69, 202n39; Brenner, 158; valorization of eastern European Jewry, 146
—negation of diaspora, 12, 149
—salvage poetics, 9, 160–62
—smells/tastes/sounds of eastern Europe, 150, 153, 154, 155, 158, 160, 165
—women and writings, 169–71
—Yiddish language/literature, 134, 159, 167, 168–69
—Zionism, 159–62
—*See also* Oz, Amos; Oz, Fania Mussman Klausner
Tedlock, Barbara, 189n8
Tevye the Milkman (*Tevye der milkhiker*; Sholem Aleichem), 51, 178
"Thank God for His Daily Blessings" (Oz), 43
"The Hill of Evil Counsel" (Oz), 162

third voice: biographical writings, 100–101, 102, 104, 106, 107–9; ethnography/ies, 90–91
Tolstoy, Leo, 93, 102–3, 104, 143
translations: biographical writings and, 102–3, 104–6; salvage poetics and, 103; translation narratives into English, and women writers, 8, 48–49, 56–57
Trunk, Yehiel Yishayahu, 57
Tsanin, Mordechai, 21, 24, 25, 186n2
Tschernikhovsky, Saul: childhood memories, 77, 147; familial genealogy and literary figures, 146, 150, 151, 153–54, 156–57, 160, 166
Tzemah, Shlomo, 75, 193n10

United States. *See* America / American writers
Ushensky, Shoshana, 48
Ussishkin, Menachem, 155

valorization of eastern European Jewry, and male writers, 77, 146. *See also* women writers, and valorization of eastern European Jewry
Village of the Brothers (*'Eleh toldot kfar 'aḥim*; Rivka Guber), 66, 81–82
Vishniac, Roman, 12–13, 30, 31, 137

War of Independence (1948), 65, 66, 74, 84, 85, 131, 146
Weinberg, Dora. *See* Gertz, Dora (Deborah; née Dora Weinberg); Not from here (*'El mah she-namog*; Gertz and Gertz)
Weinberg, Motel, 95, 98, 99
Weinberg, Ruchele, 99
Weinberg, Tzvi-Zevulin, 93, 99
Weiss, Shevah, 21
Werses, Shmuel, 149, 152
Wheatley, Natasha, 169
witnesses as women, 45, 48, 50, 52, 53–54, 140
women's histories, and eastern European–born Israelis: kibbutz life, 94–95, *95*; memory/ies as artifacts, 91,

women's histories, and eastern European–born Israelis (*continued*) 95; pre-Holocaust eastern European Jewry, 96–102, *101*, 104–6; salvage poetics, 90, 91; third voice, 91, 100–101, 108–9

women writers, and eastern European–born Israelis: about, 11, 14, 17, 62–63; Ashkenazi-centric approach, 12, 79–80; autobiographies, 49–50; bridge between past/present/future, 69–70, 74–75, 76–77, 193n10; characters-narrator relationship, 50–51, 52, 191n24; diaspora, 11, 65, 67, 69–70; ethnography/ies, 45–46, 47–48, 49, 55–57; ethnopoetics described, 8–9, 44–45, 188n3; Hebrew language, 74, 87; Hebrew literature, 49–51, 52, 62–63, 191n24; insider/outsider mediators, 49, 50, 52, 54–55, 60–61, 191n24; literary artistry, 47, 48, 55–56, 57, 60; literary legacies, 63, 65, 66–67, 73; marginality of women writers, 47–48, 49, 62, 190n16; memoirists, 14, 15, 44, 45, 48–49, 56; narrator/s, 50–51, 52, 58, 59–60, 191n24; salvage poetics, 80–81; translations into English, 8, 48–49, 56–57, 62; Yiddish language, 86–87; Zionism, 11, 14, 66, 67–68, 69, 73–74. *See also* biographical writings; Mother of Sons ("'Em ha-Banim") appellation; native-born (*dor ha-medina*) women Hebrew writers; women writers, and memories; *and specific women writers and writings*

women writers, and Hasidim: authenticity, 45, 52–54, 56–57; ethnopoetics and, 8, 14; memoirists, 44; secular world versus, 57–58, 59; women's point of view, 45, 49, 50, 52–54, 56–57. *See also* Hasidim; women writers, and eastern European–born Israelis; women writers, and valorization of eastern European Jewry

women writers, and memories: pride for eastern European Jewry, 66–67, 69, 74–75, 76, 80, 81–82. *See also* women writers, and eastern European–born Israelis

women writers, and valorization of eastern European Jewry: about, 10, 14, 65, 67; bridge between past/present/future, 69, 76–77; cultural models and, 80–81; education, 77–79, 80; farming, 74, 75, 76, 77, 82, 84; literary legacy, 67, 74–77, 86–87; memory/ies, 66–67, 69, 74–75, 76, 80, 81–82; salvage poetics, 80–81. *See also* women writers, and eastern European–born Israelis; women writers, and Hasidim

words as artifacts, and music, 135–36, 138–39, 140–41

World of Sholem Aleichem, The (Samuel), 2, 36–37

World War I, 21, 46, 52, 58, 121, 124, 128

World War II, 27, 57, 60, 72–73. *See also* Holocaust/post-Holocaust; Holocaust/post-Holocaust, and women writers as eastern European–born Israelis; Holocaust survivors

Yablonka, Hanna, 197n33

Yang, Martin, 189n8

Yehoshua, A. B., 150–51

Yiddish and Ladino Heritage Law in 1990, 25, 173

Yiddish culture: activism, laws and programs, 25, 173; America/Americans and, 10–11, 203n8; Yiddishland, 24, 31, 41; Yiddish literature identification with, 22–24, 25, 31. *See also* "Homage to Yiddish, An"; *Slaughterman's Daughter, The* (*Tikun 'aḥar ḥatsot*; Iczkovits), and Yiddish

Yiddish-inflected Hebrew, 36–38, 40, 175, 180–82

Yiddishland, 24, 31, 41. *See also* postvernacular Yiddish; Yiddish literature

Yiddish language: about, 1, 5–6; Hebrew language, 4–5; Hebrew literature, 37–38, 86–87, 174, 175; Israel/Israelis and, 22,

173–74, 179; native-born (*dor ha-medina*) male Hebrew writers, 134, 143–44, 159, 167, 168–69; ultra-Orthodox Jews, 43, 202n2; women writers, 86–87, 194n2; Yiddish-inflected Hebrew, 36–38, 40, 175, 180–82; Yiddishland, 24, 31, 41. *See also* "Homage to Yiddish, An"; postvernacular Yiddish; Yiddish literature

Yiddish literature: about, 3, 6–7, 33, 194n2; artifacts and, 178, 179, 181–82; classic Yiddish literature, 14, 32, 34, 38, 40, 183; forgetting / not forgotten past, 16, 194n2; nostalgic memory, 137; salvage poetics, 10–11, 46; translations, 29–30; Yiddish-inflected Hebrew, 36–38, 40, 175, 180–82; Yiddishland, 24, 31, 41.

See also postvernacular Yiddish; Yiddish culture; Yiddish language

Yizhar. *See* S. Yizhar (Yizhar Smolenski)

YUNG YiDiSH, 25, 173

Zborowski, Mark, 2–3, 14

Zionism: biographical writings and eastern Europe, 101, 102, 104, 106–8; farming, 76; feminine quality, 11; Hebrew language, 22, 86; Hebrew literature, 15, 134, 143, 145, 159–60, 198n3; male leaders of movement, 22, 73–74, 193n8; Place/place within, 134, 198n3; women writers as eastern European–born Israelis, 11, 14, 66, 67–68, 69, 73–74; Yiddishland, 41. *See also* Israel/Israelis

Printed in the USA
CPSIA information can be obtained
at www.ICGtesting.com
CBHW031755200624
10314CB00001B/1